M.ʳ Galley and M.ʳ Chater put by y.ᵉ Smugglers on one Horse near Rowland Castle.
A. Steele who was Admitted a Kings Evidence. B Little Harry. C Jackson D Carter.
E. Downer. F. Richards.   1 M.ʳ Galley.   2. M.ʳ Chater.

Smuggling & Smugglers in Sussex.

THE GENUINE HISTORY

OF THE INHUMAN AND

UNPARALLELED MURDERS

OF

Mr. WILLIAM GALLEY,

A CUSTOM-HOUSE OFFICER, AND

Mr. DANIEL CHATER,

A SHOEMAKER,

BY FOURTEEN NOTORIOUS SMUGGLERS,

WITH THE

TRIALS AND EXECUTION OF

SEVEN OF THE CRIMINALS AT CHICHESTER,

1748-9.

Illustrated with Seven Plates, Descriptive of the Barbarous Cruelties.

ALSO THE

Trials of John Mills and Henry Sheerman; with an account of the wicked lives of the said Henry Sheerman, Lawrence and Thomas Kemp, Robert Fuller and Jockey Brown; and the Trials at large of Thomas Kingsmill and other Smugglers for Breaking open the Custom House at Poole; with the Sermon preached in the Cathedral Church of Chichester, at a Special Assize held there, by Bp. Ashburnham; also an Article on "Smuggling in Sussex," by William Durrant Cooper, Esq., F.S.A. (Reprinted from Vol. X. of the "Sussex Archæological Collections"), and other Papers.

W. J. SMITH, 41-43 NORTH STREET, BRIGHTON.

This edition published by:
Country Books
Courtyard Cottage, Little Longstone, Derbyshire DE45 1NN

ISBN 1 898941 61 0

*A full catalogue of titles in print
is available from the publisher on request.*

TO THE PUBLIC.

THIS History was first published in 1749, soon after the execution of Jackson, Carter, and other Smugglers, upon the Broyle, near Chichester. The writer in his Preface, says: " I do assure the Public that I took down the facts in writing from the mouths of the witnesses, that I frequently conversed with the prisoners, both before and after condemnation; by which I had an opportunity of procuring those letters which are hereinafter inserted, and other intelligence of some secret transactions among them, which were never communicated to any other person." Its authenticity thus shewn, he further says: " Of all the monstrous wickedness with which the age abounds, nothing, I will be bound to say, can parallel the scenes of villainy that are here laid open. In all the Histories I have ever read, of all the barbarous stories I have heard related, never did I meet with an instance where cruelty was carried to such an excess as here. We have an instance of two men suffering the most cruel torments that malice itself could invent, without any provocation given, and for no other crime but a duty to serve their king and country.

He also says: " When the facts were proved by undeniable evidence in the face of the Court, what horror and detestation appeared in the countenance of everyone present ! Everyone shuddered when they heard the aggravating circumstances of the murders related, and how barbarously the villains handled their two wretched victims. The judges themselves declared on the bench, that in all their reading they never met with such a continued scene of barbarity, so deliberately carried on and so cruelly executed. The Council, Jury, and all present, were astonished and shocked, to hear proved beyond contradiction, facts of so monstrous a nature as the sufferings were of Mr. Galley and Mr. Chater."

"But how monstrous and unnatural soever the facts here related appear, yet they are certainly true : everything is related just in the manner it was acted, without the least aggravation to set it off. I have set down nothing but what the witnesses themselves declared upon their oaths, except in some few circumstances which Steele declared on his first examination, but was not examined upon his trial. And therefore, upon the whole, I affirm that the following account is genuine and authentic."

A reverend writer says : "In order to deter mankind from the perpetration of notorious crimes, nothing can be so effectual as to represent, in the most striking colours, the punishments that naturally attend them. The fear of shame as often preserves a person from the commission of a crime, as the expectation of a reward for his continuing in the paths of virtue." Mr. Pope also says,

> " Vice is a *Monster* of such frightful mien,
> As, to be hated, needs but to be seen."

These authorities, it is hoped, will be a sufficient apology for reprinting the said History ; and as the chief motive thereto is that of serving the community, the editor humbly hopes it will meet with due encouragement, more especially as such republication may justly be considered as one means (among many others) of checking that audacious spirit which now daily gains ground, by reminding those violators of the laws, that, like Jackson and the other miscreants mentioned in this work, they will most assuredly receive that just punishment their crimes merit, if they continue their unlawful and wicked practices. On the other hand, did they seriously consider the dreadful consequences which frequently follow, they would shudder to think of them ; they would at once see and confess their own unworthiness ; they would be thoroughly sensible, that to answer the purposes of their Great Creator, they should use their utmost endeavours to get an honest livelihood in the stations to which they may respectively be called ; they would then be useful members of the community ; and by such conduct would avoid those dreadful horrors and most bitter pangs which for ever haunt guilty minds.

The better to attain these most desirable and salutary ends, parents, guardians, and others who have the tuition of youth (we mean here the youth of the poor and the illiterate in general) should now and then take occasion to read, or cause to be read, to their servants, etc., divers passages of this true history ; at the same time make such remarks and draw such inferences from

them, as their own natural good sense and experience
might point out; and more especially they should put
them in mind that God, by the mouth of His servant
Moses, expressly declares, " He who sheddeth man's
blood, by man shall his blood be shed."

" I have drawn it up in the way of a Narrative, as
the best method of giving a full view of the whole
affair.   When that is over, I proceed to give an account
of their Trials ; after which I conclude with their lives,
confessions, behaviour, and last dying words at the place
of execution.

" I cannot omit to mention here, that Mr. Banks
made a speech, exceedingly eloquent and judicious,
which drew the attention of the whole court; and
which he concluded with that wise saying of the wisest
of men, ' That the mercies of the wicked are cruelties ';
the truth of which will evidently appear in the following pages.

HISTORY OF THE SMUGGLERS.

IN SEPTEMBER, 1747, one John Diamond, otherwise
Dymar, agreed with a number of smugglers to go over
to the Island of Guernsey, to smuggle tea, where, having
purchased a considerable quantity, on their return in a
cutter, were taken by one Capt. Johnson, who carried
the vessel and tea to the port of Poole, and lodged the
tea in the Custom-house there.

The smugglers being very much incensed at this fatal
miscarriage of their purchase, resolved not to sit down
contented with the loss; but, on a consultation held
among them, they agreed to go and take away the tea
from the warehouse where it was lodged. Accordingly,
a body of them, to the number of sixty, well-armed,
assembled in Charlton Forest, and from thence proceeded on their enterprise; to accomplish which, they
agreed, that only thirty of them should go upon the
attack, and that the remaining thirty should be placed as
scouts upon the different roads, to watch the motions of
the officers and soldiers, and to be ready to assist or
alarm the main body, in case any opposition should be
made.

In the night-time, between the 6th and 7th of October,
they went to Poole, about thirty only present, broke
open the Custom-house, and took away all the said tea,
except one bag about five pounds.

The next morning they returned with their booty
through Fordingbridge, in Hampshire, where some
hundreds of people were assembled to view the caval-
cade. Among the spectators was Daniel Chater, a

shoemaker (one of the unhappy persons murdered)
known to Diamond, one of the gang then passing, as
having formerly worked together in harvest time.
Diamond shook hands with him as he passed along, and
threw him a bag of tea.

His Majesty's proclamation coming out with a
promise of a reward for apprehending those persons
who were concerned in breaking open the Custom-house
at Poole, and Diamond being taken into custody at
Chichester, on a suspicion of being one of them, and
Chater saying in conversation with his neighbours, that
he knew Diamond, and saw him go by with the gang,
the day after the Custom-house at Poole was broken
open, it came to the knowledge of Mr. Shearer, collector
of the Customs at the port of Southampton, when, after
some things had passed by letter, between him and
Chater, he was ordered to send Mr. William Galley
(the other unfortunate person murdered) with Chater,
with a letter to Major Battin, a Justice of Peace for the
county of Sussex, the purport of which was, to desire
the justice to take an examination of Chater, in relation
to what he knew of that affair ; and whether he could
prove the identity of Diamond's person.

On Sunday, the 14th of February, they set out, and
going for Chichester, they called at Mr. Holton's, at
Havant, who was an acquaintance of Chater's ; Holton
asked Chater where they were going, and Chater told
him they were going to Chichester, to carry a letter to
Major Battin ; when Mr. Holton told him the Major
was at East Murden, near Chichester, and directed him
and Galley to go by Stanstead, near Rowland's Castle.
Galley and Chater, pursuing their journey, and going
through Leigh, in the parish of Havant, in their way to
Rowland's Castle, they called at the New Inn, and

asking the nearest way, they saw Mr. George Austin, and Mr. Thomas Austin, two brothers, and their brother-in-law, Mr. Jenkes ; when the elder brother, G. Austin, said they were going the same way, and would shew them ; and they all set out together (Galley, Chater, and the rest being all on horseback) ; and about 12 at noon came to the White Hart at Rowland's Castle, a house kept by one Elizabeth Payne, widow, who had two sons, both men grown, and black-smiths, and reputed smugglers, in the same village. After calling for some rum, Mrs. Payne took Mr. George Austin aside, and told him she was afraid these two strangers were come with intent to do some injury to the smugglers. He replied he believed she need be under no such apprehension on that account, for they were only carrying a letter to Major Battin ; and as he did not know the purport of it, he imagined it was only about some common business. The circumstance, how-ever, of their having a letter for the Major, increased her suspicion ; upon which she sent one of her sons who was then in the house, for William Jackson and William Carter, two of the murderers (as will appear hereafter), who lived within a small distance of her house. While her son was gone, Chater and Galley wanted to be going, and asked for their horses ; but Mrs. Payne told them, that the man was gone out with the key of the stables, and would be at home presently, which words she said in order to keep them till Jackson and Carter came, who lived very near. As soon as Jackson came, who was there first, he ordered a pot of hot to be made, and while that was getting ready Carter came in ; Mrs. Payne immediately took them aside, and told them her suspicions concerning Chater and Galley, and likewise the circumstance of a letter which they were carrying to

Major Battin ; and soon after advised George Austin to go away about his business, telling him, as she respected him, he had better go and not stay, lest he should come to some harm ; upon which he went away, and left his brother Thomas and brother-in-law Mr. Jenkes there.

During this time, Mrs. Payne's other son came in, and finding there were grounds to suspect that the two strangers were going to make information against the smugglers, he went out and fetched in William Steel (who was one of the King's witnesses upon trial), and Samuel Downer, otherwise Samuel Howard, otherwise Little Sam, Edmund Richards, Henry Sheerman, otherwise Little Harry, all smugglers, and all belonging to the same gang, and were indicted for the murder of Mr. Galley, but not then taken.

After they had drank a little while, Jackson took Chater into the yard, and asked him how he did, and where Diamond was ; Chater said he believed he was in custody, but how he did he did not know ; but that he was going to appear against him, which he was sorry for, but he could not help it.   Galley soon after came into the yard to them, to get Chater in again, suspecting that Jackson was persuading Chater not to persist in giving information against the smugglers, and upon Galley's desiring Chater to come in, Jackson said, "G...d d......n your b......d, what is that to you ?" strikes him a blow in the face and knocks him down, and set his nose and mouth a-bleeding ; after which they all came into the house, Jackson abusing Galley ; when Galley said he was the King's officer, and could not put up with such usage ; then Jackson replied, "You a King's officer ! I'll make a King's officer of you ; and for a quartern of gin I'll serve you so again ;" and some time after offering to strike him again, one of the

Paynes interposed, and said, " Don't be such a fool, do you know what you are doing ?"

Galley and Chater began to be very uneasy, and wanted to be going ; upon which Jackson, Carter, and the rest of them persuaded them to stay and drink more rum, and make it up, for they were sorry for what had happened ; when they all sat down together, Mr. Austin and Mr. Jenkes being present. After they had sat a little while, Jackson and Carter wanted to see the letter which Galley and Chater were carrying to Major Battin ; but they refused to show it ; upon which they both made a resolution they would see it. They then drank about pretty plentifully, and made Galley, Chater, and Thomas Austin fuddled ; when they persuaded Galley and Chater to go into another room where there was a bed, and lie down ; which they did, and fell asleep ; and then the letter was taken out of one of their pockets, and brought into the kitchen, where Carter or Kelly read it ; and the contents of it being plainly a design to promote an information against some of their gang, they immediately entered into consultation what course to take on this occasion. Some proposed one thing, some another ; but all agreed in this, that the letter should be first destroyed, and then they would consider what to do with the men, in order to prevent their giving the intended information.

Before this, one John Race (who was also one of the King's witnesses) and Richard Kelly came in, when Jackson and Carter told them that they had got the old rogue the shoemaker of Fordingbridge, who was going to give an information against John Diamond, the shepherd, who was then in custody at Chichester. Then they all consulted what was best to be done with him and Galley, when William Steel proposed to take them both to a well, a little way from the house, and to murder them and throw them in.

At this consultation were present only these seven smugglers; namely, William Jackson, William Carter, William Steel, John Race, Samuel Downer, Edmund Richards, and Henry Sheerman, and this proposal was disagreed to, as they had been seen in their company by the Austins, Mr. Jenkes, Mr. Garrat, Mr. Poate, and others who came into Payne's house to drink. This being disagreed to, another proposal was made, which was, to take them away, and send them over to France; but that was objected against, as there was a possibility of their coming over again, and then they should be all known. At these consultations Jackson and Carter's wives were both present, and who both cried out "Hang the dogs, for they came here to hang us." Then another proposition was made, which was that they should take them and carry them to some place where they should be confined, till it was known what would be the fate of Diamond, and in the mean time each of them to allow three-pence a week to subsist Galley and Chater; and that whatever Diamond's fate was, they determined that theirs should be the same.

Galley and Chater continued all this while asleep upon the bed; then Jackson went in and began the first scene of their cruelty; for having first put on his spurs, he got upon the bed and spurred their foreheads to awake them, and afterwards whipped them with a horsewhip, so that when they came out into the kitchen, Chater was as bloody as Galley. This done, all the abovesaid smugglers being present, they took them out of the house, when Richards with a pistol cocked in his hand, swore he would shoot any person through the

Galley & Chater falling off their Horse at Woodash, draggs thier Heads on the Ground, while the Horse kicks them as he goes; the Smugglers still continuing thier brutish Usage.

head that should mention anything of what was done, or what they had heard.

When they were all come out of the house, Jackson returned with a pistol in his hand, and asked for a belt, a strap, or string: but none of the people in the house presumed to give him either; upon which he returned to the rest of the gang, who were lifting Galley on a horse, whose legs they tied under the horse's belly; then they lifted Chater on the same horse, and tied his legs under the horse's belly, and then tied their four legs together.

All this time John Race was with them; but when they began to set forward, Race said, "I cannot go with you for I have never a horse," and so stayed behind.

They had not gone above a hundred yards, before Jackson called out "Whip them, cut them, slash them, damn them"; and then all fell upon them except the person who was leading the horse, which was Steel; for the roads were so bad that they were forced to go very slow.

They whipped them till they came to Wood's Ashes, some with long whips and some with short, lashing and cutting them over the head, face, eyes and shoulders, till the poor men, unable any longer to bear the anguish of their repeated blows, rolled from side to side, and at last fell together with their heads under the horse's belly; in which posture every step the horse made, he struck one or the other of their heads with his feet. This happened at Wood's Ashes, which was more than half a mile from the place where they began their whipping, and had continued it all the way thither. When their cruel tormentors saw the dismal effects of their barbarity, and that the poor creatures had fallen

under it, they sat them upright again in the same
position as they were before, and continued whipping
them in the most cruel manner over the head, face,
shoulders, and everywhere, till they came beyond
Goodthorpe Dean, upwards of half a mile farther, the
horse still going a very slow pace ; where they both fell
again as before, with their heads under the horse's belly,
and their heels up in the air.

Now they found them so weak that they could not
sit upon the horse at all, upon which they separated
them, and put Galley behind Steel, and Chater behind
Little Sam, and then whipped Galley so severely, that
the lashes coming upon Steel, he desired them to desist,
crying out himself that he could not bear it, upon which
they desisted accordingly. All the time they so continued to whip them, Jackson rode with a pistol cocked,
and swore as they went along through Dean, if they
made any noise he would blow their brains out. They
then agreed to go up with them to Harris's Well near
Lady Holt Park, where they swore they would murder
Galley ; accordingly they took him off the horse and
threatened to throw him into the well. Upon which
the poor unhappy man desired them to dispatch him at
once, or even throw him down the well, to put an end
to his misery. "No, G...d d...n your blood," says
Jackson, " if that's the case, we must have something
more to say to you " ; and then put him on a horse again,
and whipped him over the Downs till he was so weak
that he fell.

Was ever cruelty like this ! To deny a miserable
wretch, who was half dead with their blows and bruises,
the wretched favour of a quick dispatch out of his
tortures ! Could the devil himself have furnished a more
execrable invention to punish the wretched victims of

his malice, than to grant them life only to prolong their torments!

Poor Galley not being able to sit on horseback any longer, Carter and Jackson took him up and laid him across the saddle, with his breast over the pommel, as a butcher does a calf, and Richards got up behind him to hold him, and after carrying him in this manner above a mile, Richards was tired of holding him, so let him down by the side of the horse; and then Carter and Jackson put him upon the grey horse that Steel had before rode upon; they set him up with his legs across the saddle, and his body over the horse's mane; and in this posture Jackson held him on for half a mile, most of the way the poor man cried out "Barbarous usage! barbarous usage! for God's sake shoot me through the head"; Jackson all the time squeezing his private parts.

After going on in this manner upwards of a mile, Little Harry tied Galley with a cord, and got up behind him, to hold him from falling off; and when they had gone a little way in that manner, the poor man, Galley, cried out "I fall, I fall, I fall"; and Little Harry, giving him a shove as he was falling, said, "Fall and be d......d"; upon which he fell down, and Steel said that they all thought he had broke his neck, and was dead; but it must be presumed he was buried alive, because when he was found, his hands covered his face, as if to keep the dirt out of his eyes.

Poor unhappy Galley! who can read the melancholy story of thy tragical catastrophe without shedding tears at the sorrowful relation? What variety of pains did thy body feel in every member of it, especially by thy privy parts being so used? What extremity of anguish didst thou groan under, so long as the small remains of life permitted thee to be sensible of it! And after all, to be buried while life was yet in thee, and to struggle with death even in thy wretched grave, what imagination can form to itself a scene of greater horror, or more detestable villainy? Sure thy murderers must be devils incarnate! for none but the fiends of Hell could take pleasure in the torments of two unhappy men, who had given them no offence, unless their endeavouring to serve their king and country may be deemed such. This indeed was the plea of these vile miscreants; but a very bad plea it was to support as bad a cause. But such is the depravity of human nature, that when a man once abandons himself to all manner of wickedness, he sets no bounds to his passions, his conscience is seared, every tender sentiment is lost, reason is no more, and he has nothing left him of the man but the form.

We forgot to mention in its proper place that in order to make their whipping the more severely felt, they pulled off Galley's great coat, which was found in the road next morning all bloody.

They, supposing Galley was dead, laid him across a horse, two of the smugglers, one on each side, holding him to prevent his falling, while the third led the horse, and as they were going up a dirty lane, Jackson said, "Stop at the swing gate beyond the water till we return, and we will go and seek for a place to carry them both to; when he and Carter went to the house of one Pescod, who had been a reputed smuggler, and knocked at the door. The daughter came down, when they said they had got two men whom they wanted to bring to the house. The girl told them her father was ill, and had been so for some time, and that there was no conveniency for them, nor any body to look after them ; and they insisting that she should go up and ask him, she did, and brought down word that her father would suffer nobody to be brought there, be they who they would ; upon which they returned to the rest.

Though this Pescod was (as I have observed) a reputed smuggler, and therefore these fellows supposed he would give them harbour upon this occasion, yet it does not appear that he had gone such lengths as the rest of them had done ; for if he had, he would not have refused admitting them at any hour of the night, notwithstanding his illness ; but he imagining they were upon some villainous expedition, resolved to have no hand in it, or have his name brought in question on that account. But to proceed.

By this time it was between one and two in the morning, when they agreed to go to one Scardefield's at the Red Lion at Rake, which was not far from them. When they came there, they knocked at the door, but the family being all in bed, Scardefield looked out of the window, and asked who was there. Carter and Jackson told him who they were, and desired him to get up, for they wanted something to drink, and there were more company coming ; Scardefield refused several times, but they pressing him very hard, he put on his clothes and came down, and let them in after many times refusing.

As soon as he was down, and had let Steel, Jackson, Carter and Richards in, he made a fire in the parlour, and then went to draw some liquor, while he was doing which he heard more company come in ; and he going into the brewhouse saw something lie upon the ground like a dead man. They then sent him to fetch them some rum and some gin, and while he was gone for the same, they had got poor Chater into the parlour, and on his bringing the liquor, they refused to let him in ;

but he saw a man, he says, stand up very bloody, whom he supposed to be Chater. They told him, Scardefield, that they had an engagement with some officers, and had lost their tea, and were afraid that several of their people were killed; which they probably said, as well to conceal their murder of Galley, as to account for Chater's being bloody.

All this time poor Mr. Chater was in expectation every moment of being killed, and indeed, when I am speaking of it, my heart bleeds for his sufferings; but they sent him now out of the way, for Jackson and Little Harry carried him down to Old Mills's, which was not far off, and then returned again to the company.

After they had drank pretty plentifully, they all went out, taking Galley, or his corpse, if he was quite dead, with them; when Carter and Richards returned to Scardefield's, and asked him if he could find the place out where they had some time before lodged some goods; and he said he believed he could, but could not go then. But Richards and Carter insisted he should; and then Carter took a candle and lantern, and borrowed a spade, and they went together, and had not gone far when they came to the rest, who were waiting; and then Scardefield saw something lie across a horse, which he thought looked like the dead body of a man; and then Little Sam having a spade, began to dig a hole, and it being a very cold morning, he helped, but did not know what it was for; and in this hole they buried poor Mr. Galley.

They then returned to Scardefield's, and sat carousing the best part of Monday, having, as Jackson told them, secured Chater.

This Scardefield was formerly thought to have

William Galley, brought cross a Horse to a Sand Pit where a deep Hole is Dug to Bury him in.

The unfortunate William Galley put by the Smugglers into the Ground & as is generally believed before he was quite DEAD.

been concerned with the smugglers; and as he kept a public house, they thought they might take any liberties with him. And it seems evident, by what they did after they had gained admission, that they only wanted a convenient place to consult at leisure what course to pursue on this occasion. They had two prisoners, one of whom they supposed they had already murdered, whose body they must dispose of in some manner or other. The other, though yet living, they resolved should undergo the same fate, but by what means it does not appear they had yet agreed. The better to blind Scardefield, whom they did not care to let into the secret of their bloody scheme, and likewise to give some colourable pretence for what his own eyes had been witness to (a dead corpse in his brewhouse, and a man all over blood standing in his parlour), they tell him a plausible story of an engagement they had with the king's officers. Now whether Scardefield gave entire credit to what they told him, or whether he really suspected what they were upon, did not appear from the evidence. This, however, is certain, that he went with them to the place, and assisted them in burying the body of Galley; and therefore one would imagine he could not be entirely ignorant of what they were doing. But as he was one of the witnesses by which this iniquity was brought to light, and as he was likewise a person of fair character, we shall forbear saying any thing that may seem to throw a slur on his reputation.

But now we must return to the melancholy story of the unfortunate man, unhappy in the hands of the most cruel wretches surely ever breathing.

While they were sitting at Scardefield's, consulting together what they were to do next, Richard Mills came by ; this Richard was the son of old Richard Mills, to whose house they had conveyed Chater for his better security, till they had resolved what to do with him. When they saw young Mills they called him in, and related to him in what manner they had treated Chater, who was going to make information against their friend Diamond, the shepherd, and that in their way they came by a precipice thirty feet deep. To this Mills made answer, that if he had been there he would have called a council of war, and thrown him down headlong. So it seems as if cruelty was the ruling principle among the whole body of smugglers, and that nothing less than death or destruction of all those they deemed their adversaries—that is, all such as endeavoured to prevent or interrupt them in the pernicious trade of smuggling—would content them.

They continued drinking at Scardefield's all that day, which was Monday, Chater being chained all the while by the leg, with an iron chain about three yards long, in a place belonging to old Mills, called a skilling, which is what they lay turf up in, and looked after by little Harry and old Mills ; and in the dead of that night they agreed to go home separately, and to rally up some more of their gang, and to meet at Scardefield's on Wednesday.

Their design in this was, that they might appear at their own homes on Tuesday morning early, so that their neighbours might have no suspicion of what they had been about, or of what they had in hand still to do, and likewise to consult with the rest of the gang what was best to be done.

They all met at Scardefield's on Wednesday evening according to appointment ; that is, William Jackson, William Carter, William Steel (one of the king's witnesses),

Edmund Richards, of Long Coppice, in the parish of Walderton, in the County of Sussex, and Samuel Howard, otherwise Little Sam, of Rowland's Castle, in the county of Hants, who were five of the six concerned in the murder of Galley, as has been before related. Also John Cobby, William Hammond, Benjamin Tapner, Thomas Stringer, of the city of Chichester, cordwainer, Daniel Perryer, otherwise Little Daniel, of Norton, and John Mills, of Trotton, both in the county of Sussex, and Thomas Willis, commonly called the Coachman, of Selbourne, near Liphook, in the county of Hants, Richard Mills, jun., and John Race (another King's witness), being fourteen in number; Richard Mills, sen., and Henry Sheerman, alias Little Harry, stayed at home to take care of Chater, in whose custody they had left him. They dropped in one after another, as if by accident, so that it was late in the night before they were all got together. Being all of them at last come in, they entered upon the business for which they were then met, namely, to consult coolly and sedately what was to be done with Chater, that is, how to dispatch him in such a manner as would be least liable to discovery; for that he must be destroyed, had been already unanimously determined, as the only method they could think of to prevent his telling tales about Galley. Thus, when a course of villainy is once begun, it is impossible to say where it will end; one crime brings on another, and that treads on the heels of a third, till at length both the innocent and the guilty are swept away into the gulf of destruction.

I cannot pass in silence, without making mention of the readiness old Mills shewed when they brought poor Chater first down to his house; for he fetched them victuals and drink, and they all eat and drank, except Chater, who could not eat, but vomited very much.

After they had debated the matter some time among them, Richard Mills, jun., proposed this method: "As Chater is already chained to a post, let us," said he, "load a gun with two or three bullets, lay it upon a a stand, with the muzzle of the piece levelled at his head, and, after having tied a long string to the trigger, we will all go to the butt end, and, each of us taking hold of the string, pull it together; thus we shall be all equally guilty of his death, and it will be impossible for any one of us to charge the rest with his murder, without accusing himself of the same crime ; and none can pretend to lessen or mitigate their guilt by saying they were only accessaries, since all will be principals." But some, more infernally barbarous than the rest (but who, the witness Steel could not recollect), objected to this proposal as too expeditious a method of dispatching him, and that it would put him out of his misery too soon ; for they were resolved that he should suffer as much and as long as they could make his life last, as a terror to all such informing rogues (as they termed it) for the future.

This proposal being rejected, another was offered and agreed to, and that was—to go to old Major Mills, and fetch him away from thence, and carry him up to Harris's Well, near Lady Holt Park, and throw him in there, as they intended to have done with Galley, as the most effectual method to secrete the murder from the knowledge of the world ; forgetting that the eye of Providence was constantly upon them, watched all their motions, and would certainly, one day or other, bring to light their deeds of darkness ; and that Divine Justice never forgets the cries of the oppressed, but will, in due time, retaliate the cruelties exercised on the innocent, on the heads of their inexorable tormentors.

All this while the unhappy Chater remained in the most deplorable situation that ever miserable wretch was confined to; his mind full of horror, and his body all over pain and anguish with the blows and scourges they had given him, and every moment in expectation of worse treatment than he had yet met with, without any sustenance to support his wretched life, than now and then a little bread and water, and once some pease porridge. Besides all this, he was continually visited by one or other of them, not to comfort or relieve him with words of kindness, or promises of better usage; not to refresh him with cordials or agreeable nourishment, but to renew their cruel exercise of beating and abusing him, and to swear and upbraid him in the vilest terms and the most scurrilous language that their tongues could utter.

Having at length concluded what to do with their poor unhappy prisoner, they all went down to Old Mills's, where they immediately opened a fresh scene of barbarity. For as soon as they came in, Tapner, Cobby, and some others of them, went directly into the turf-house, where they found Chater in the most piteous condition, enough to melt a heart not made of stone into compassion; but was so far from moving the pity of these merciless bloodhounds, that it only served them as a fresh motive to renew their cruelties, and aggravate his afflictions. Tapner, in particular, immediately pulled out a large clasp knife, and expressed himself in this horrible manner: " G...d d......n your b......d, down on your knees and go to prayers, for with this knife I will be your butcher." The poor man being terrified at this dreadful menace, and expecting that

every moment would be his last, knelt down upon a
turf, as he was ordered, and lifted up his heart and
hands to Heaven, in the best manner that his pains and
anguish would suffer him; and while he was thus
piously offering up his prayers to God, Cobby got
behind him, and kicked him, and with the most bitter
taunts, upbraided him for being an informing villain.
Chater suffered all his torments with great patience and
resignation ; and though there was scarce a limb or a
joint of him free from the most excruciating pains, yet
in the midst of all he did not forget his friend Galley,
and believing that he was either dead or very near it, he
begged they would tell him what they had done with
him. Tapner replied, "D......n you, we have killed
him, and we will do so by you"; and then, without
more ado, or any other provocation, drew his knife
aslant over his eyes and nose, with such violence, that
he almost cut both his eyes out, and the gristle of his
nose quite through. Poor Chater was absolutely at his
mercy, for it was not in his power to make any resistance ; his great and only comfort was that he suffered in
a righteous cause, and supported with this consideration,
he resigned himself to the will of heaven, which he was
persuaded took cognizance of his sufferings, and would
reward his tormentors according to their demerits.

Tapner, however, not satisfied with this wanton act
of cruelty, in another fit of frenzy, aimed another stroke
at his face, designing to cut him again in the same
wound ; but happening to strike a little higher, made a
terrible gash across his forehead, from which the blood
flowed in abundance. What a lamentable figure must
the poor creature make ! His face deeply furrowed
with the most ghastly wounds, his eyes cut almost out
of his head, and the blood running down in torrents

Chater, Chained in y.ͤ Turff House at Old Mills's.
Cobby, kicking him. & Tapner, cutting him Cross y.ͤ
Eyes & Nose, while he is saying the Lords Prayer.
Several of y.ͤ other Smugglers standing by.

upon the rest of his body. What a spectacle was here! yet not miserable enough to move the compassion of these bloodthirsty tigers! Old Mills, however, not from any pity, or that his heart relented at the terrible condition of this deplorable object, but apprehending bad consequences to himself, in case he should die under their hands, and under his roof, said to them, "Take him away, and do not murder him here, but murder him somewhere else."

It is surprising that this poor miserable man, who was far advanced in years, had strength and vigour enough to sustain such a variety of torments, which were inflicted upon him, almost without intermission, for several days successively; yet even after this last act of barbarity, he had more severe trials to come before he was suffered to part with his wearisome life. And as the last scene of this woful tragedy appears more astonishing and more monstrous than anything they had hitherto transacted, we shall give a very particular and circumstantial account of everything that was done on this sad occasion. Being all agreed in the measures they were about to take, they mounted Chater on a horse, and set out together for Harris's Well. Mills, however, and his two sons, stayed behind, desiring to be excused, because their horses were not in the way; or they would readily have borne them company on the occasion if they could, for they were as hearty in the same cause as the best of them. Besides, there was no great necessity for their assistance, since there were enough of them, as the Mills's said, to kill one man; and as Harris's Well lay just in their way homewards, the execution would be little or no hindrance to them in their journey.

Everything being now settled, they proceeded

towards the well. Tapner, however, more cruel, if possible than the rest, fell to whipping poor Chater again over his face and eyes, and made his wounds, which he had before given him with his murdering knife, bleed afresh; and, what was still more amazing, swore, "That if he blooded his saddle" (for it seems Chater was set upon his horse) "he would destroy him that moment and send his soul to Hell:" which is such an unparalleled instance of barbarity, that one would think it impossible that there should be a creature living, that pretends to reason, and would be ranked among men, could be guilty of. What! to threaten to murder a man for a thing which was not in his power to avoid, and which the villain himself was the sole occasion of! Horrible, shocking wickedness! but let us proceed in our melancholy story.

At last poor Chater, in this disfigured lamentable condition, is brought to the well. By the time they got there, it was the very dead of night, and so near the middle of it, that it was uncertain whether it was Wednesday night or Thursday morning. The well was between twenty and thirty feet deep, without water, and paled round at a small distance to keep the cattle from falling in. Being come up to the pales, they dismounted Chater, and Tapner, taking a cord out of his pocket which he had brought for that purpose, made a noose in it and then fastened it round his neck. This being done, they bade him get over the pales to the well. The poor man observing a small opening, where a pale or two had been broken away, made an attempt to go through; but that was a favour too great to be allowed to so heinous an offender, as it seems poor Chater was in their opinion; and therefore one of them swore he should get over in the condition he was and

Chater hanging at the Well in LADY HOLT Park.
the Bloody Villains standing by

The Bloody Smugglers flinging down Stones after
they had flung his Dead Body into the Well.

with the rope about his neck, all over blood, his wounds gaping and himself extremely weak and ready to faint through loss of blood; yet in this miserable plight these cruel executioners obliged him to get over the pales as well as he could.

With a great deal of difficulty he got over the pales, when he found himself just upon the brink of the well, the pales standing very near to it. Being over, Tapner took hold of the rope which was fastened to Chater's neck, and tied it to the rail of the pales where the opening was, for the well had neither kerb, lid nor roller. When the rope was thus fixed to the rail, they all got over to him and pushed him into the well; but the rope being of no great length, would not suffer his body to hang lower than knee-deep in it; so that the rest of his body, from his knees upwards, appeared above the well, bending towards the pales, being held in that position by the rope that was tied to the rail. But as in this posture he hung leaning against the side of the well, the weight of his body was not of sufficient force to strangle him presently. For his inhuman executioners, whether wearied with tormenting him so long or whether they wanted to get home to their several places we cannot say, but they seemed now resolved to dispatch him as soon as they could.

After they had waited about a quarter of an hour, and perceiving by the struggles he made that he would be a considerable time in dying, they altered the method of his execution. Thomas Stringer therefore, with the assistance of Cobby and Hammond, pulled his legs out of the well, and Tapner untying the cord that was fastened to the rail, his head fell down upon the ground, and then, bringing it round to the well, put it in. Then Stringer, who had hold of his legs, assisted by Cobby and Hammond, let them go, and the body fell head foremost into the well.

Now one would think they had entirely finished this tragedy and that this miserable creature was quite out of his misery, and beyond the reach of any further injury. No, he had yet some further remains of life in him, and while he had any sense left, he must feel the exercise of their cruelty.

After they had thrown the body into the well, they stood by it some time; and it being the dead of night and every thing still, they heard him breathe or groan, and from thence being assured that he was still alive, and that if they should leave him in that condition somebody accidentally passing that way might possibly hear him; and in that case if the man should be relieved and brought to life again, the consciousness of their own horrid crimes and the enormous barbarities they had exercised upon him and Galley, told them that they would certainly be discovered, and then they knew they were dead men.

Upon which they immediately came to a resolution to procure a ladder that should reach to the bottom of the well, and one of them would go down by it and dispatch him at once. Accordingly they went to William Combleach, a gardener, who lived but a little way off, and knocked him up, telling him that one of their companions was fallen into Harris's Well and begged the favour he would lend them a ladder and a rope to get him out again. Combleach knowing nothing more of the matter but what they had told him, lent them the ladder, and they carried it to the well. Having brought it to the pales, whether through the surprise and confusion they were in or the dread and horror that might have seized their minds from the consideration of the dreadful work they were about, or from what other cause is uncertain, they had not all of them power sufficient to raise the ladder high enough to get it over the pales, it being a very long one, though there were six of them employed in doing it, namely, Stringer, Steel, Perryer, Hammond, Cobby and Tapner.

When they had tried some time, and found all their efforts ineffectual to raise the ladder, they left it upon the ground, and went again to the well side to listen, and hearing the poor man still groaning, they were at a stand what they should do to put a quick end to the life of the miserable creature. But recollecting themselves, they hunted about for something heavy to throw in upon him, and found two logs of wood that had been gate-posts, which they threw into the well; and being resolved to do the business effectually, got together as many great stones as they could find, and threw them in likewise. And now they thought they had done his business, and they were undoubtedly right in their guess, for on listening again they could hear nothing of him; and therefore, concluding he was dead, as most certainly he was, they mounted their horses and went to their respective homes.

Thus are we brought to the fatal and final catastrophe of the unhappy Chater, and whoever seriously reflect on the cause for which he suffered, the torments he underwent, the variety of punishments with which he was continually exercised, from the time he set out from Rowland's Castle till he finished his miseries in Harris's Well, which was from Sunday afternoon to the dead of the night between the Wednesday and Thursday following, must feel their hearts melt with compassion, and in some measure be sensible of the variegated pains and tortures with which the poor creature was

constantly racked and torn during this time.   But who
can think on his tormentors without horror and
detestation ?   Bloody villains ! had you thought that
his death was absolutely necessary to secure your own
lives, could you not have dispatched him at once,
without exercising such a variety of merciless cruelties
upon him ?   It is true, even in this case you would not
have been excused, because you would have slain him
while he was actually discharging his duty to his
country, that is, endeavouring to detect and to bring to
punishment wretches that live only by rapine and the
plunder of the public.   I say, had this been the case,
and upon meeting him on the road you had shot him
through the head, merely to prevent his bringing you
to that righteous judgment which your country has
since passed upon you, it might have been some
mitigation of your crime ; but to torture and to destroy
a man by inches, to be constantly afflicting and
lacerating his body for so many days together with
every cruelty that malice itself could suggest ; this
surely must convince mankind that some malicious
demon had taken possession of your souls, and banished
every sentiment of humanity from your hardened
hearts.

But let us now proceed to those other matters which
we promised to give an account of.   The first thing we
shall mention ought indeed to have been taken notice
of before, but we were not willing to interrupt the story
of Chater till we had brought him to the last stage of
his sufferings, and his final destruction in this world.

When these miscreants had brought their unhappy
victim within about two hundred yards of the well,
Jackson and Carter stayed behind and bid Tapner,
Cobby, Stringer, Steel, Perryer and Hammond go

forward and do their business. "You," says Jackson, "go and do your duty and kill Chater, as we have done ours in killing Galley, and then there will be a final end of the two informing rogues"; for Hammond, Stringer, Cobby, Tapner and Perryer were neither of them concerned in the murder of Galley, who was killed on Sunday night, or early on Monday morning, as before mentioned, of which they were entirely ignorant, till informed by Jackson, Carter, Little Harry, Richards, Steel and Little Sam.

But though these wretches had perpetrated the murders of these two unhappy men with such secrecy (notwithstanding they had them so long in hold) that they thought it next to impossible that they should ever be discovered, unless they had traitors among themselves; yet they were sensible that there were two witnesses still living, which, though dumb, would certainly render them suspected, if suffered to survive their masters; and these were the two horses that belonged to Galley and Chater; and therefore a consultation was held what was best to be done with them. Some were for turning them adrift in a large wood, where they might range about a long while before they could be owned. But others alleged that whenever they were found, they would undoubtedly soon be known to belong to the rightful owners, and as Galley and Chater might possibly have been seen riding upon them in their company but a very little before these men were missing, some curious people might imagine they were, some way or other, concerned in conveying them away; to prevent which, let us, said they, put them on board the first French vessel that shall bring goods on the coast and send them to France. This however, was objected to, as liable to some miscarriage ; and therefore, after much debate, it was unanimously agreed to knock them on the head at once, and then take their skins off. Accordingly they killed the horse which Galley rode on, which was a grey, and having flayed him, cut his hide into small bits, which they disposed of in such a manner, that it was impossible for any discovery to be made from thence. As to the horse which Chater rode on, which was a bay, when they came to look for him they could not find him, for he had got away, and not long after was delivered to his owner ; but the grey, which Mr. Shearer, of Southampton, had hired for Mr. Galley, and which they had now killed, he was obliged to pay for.

Thus we have given a full and circumstantial account of all the particulars relating to the murders of these two unhappy men, whose misfortune it was to fall into the hands of these savage brutes. But as Providence seldom suffers such atrocious crimes to go undiscovered or unpunished even in this world, so in this case, though the Divine justice seemed dormant for a while, yet the eye of Providence was not asleep, but was still watching their motions and taking the necessary steps to bring to light these horrible deeds of darkness, and to punish the perpetrators of such abominable wickedness in the most exemplary manner.

The first thing that gave occasion to suspect that some such misfortune as above related had befallen these men was that they did not return in the time which it was reasonable to suppose they might have done, from Major Battin's, to whom Mr. Shearer had sent them with a letter, as before related. Another circumstance that served to strengthen the suspicion that they had fallen into the hands of the smugglers, who had privately made away with or destroyed them, was that exactly at the time when they were sent on the abovesaid message, the great coat of Mr. Galley was found on the road very bloody. This circumstance the reader will remember we mentioned when we gave an account of their first setting out from Rowland's Castle, when these tormenters began their cruel discipline of whipping, and that they pulled off Galley's great coat, that he might the more sensibly feel their lashes.

The long absence of these men from their homes, and the reasons there were to conclude that the smugglers had either murdered them or sent them to France, being laid before the commissioners of the customs, a proclamation was immediately ordered, offering a reward to anyone who should discover what was become of them, with his Majesty's pardon to such discoverer. However, six or seven months passed before the Government could get the least light into the affair ; and then a full discovery was gradually made by the following means.

One of the persons who had been a witness to some of the transactions of this bloody tragedy, and knew of the death of either Galley or Chater, and where one was buried, though he was no way concerned in the murder, sent an anonymous letter to a person of distinction, wherein he intimated that he thought the body of one of the unfortunate men mentioned in his Majesty's proclamation was buried in the sands in a certain place near Rake (but for some particular reason did not think it prudent to make himself known) ; whereupon some people went in search, where they found the corpse of Galley buried; and the reason why it is supposed he was buried alive, they found him standing almost upright, with his hands covering his eyes.

The discovery being made by this letter, another letter was sent, wherein an account was given that one William Steel, otherwise Hardware, was one concerned in the murder of the man that was found buried in the sands, and mention was made therein where they might find him, and he was accordingly taken into custody; when he offered himself to be an evidence for the King, and to make a full discovery and disclosure of the whole wicked transaction, and of all the persons concerned therein.

Steel being now in custody, he gave an account of the murder of Galley, and further informed in what manner Chater was murdered and thrown into Harris's Well; whither messengers being likewise sent, and one of them let down into the well, the body was found with a rope about his neck, his eyes appeared to have been cut or picked out of his head, and his boots and spurs on. They got his body out of the well with only one leg on; the other was brought up by itself, with the boot and spur on it, which, it is supposed, was occasioned by his fall down the well, or else by throwing the logs of wood and stones upon him.

But Steel did not only give information of all the particulars of this transcendent wickedness, but likewise acquainted the justice with the names of the principal actors in it; pursuant to which, warrants were immediately issued, and several of them taken in a short time, and committed to gaol.

John Race, who was another of the King's witnesses, and concerned with them at the beginning of the affair at Rowland's Castle, came in and voluntarily surrendered himself, and was admitted an evidence, as Steel had been.

Hammond was taken the beginning of October, and

being carried before two magistrates, and it appearing that he was privy to, and concerned in, the murder of Chater, and throwing him into a well near Harting, in the County of Sussex, was committed to Horsham gaol.

John Cobby, being likewise apprehended, was committed to Horsham gaol the 18th of the same month, and for the same crime of murdering Chater.

Benjamin Tapner was also committed to the same gaol the 16th of November following, and on his own confession, of murdering Chater in the manner above stated. He was betrayed by his master, one T—ff, a shoemaker in Chichester, of whom we shall have occasion to speak more at large when we come to give an account of the life of Tapner.

Richard Mills, jun., was apprehended in Sussex, with George Spencer, Richard Payne and Thomas Reoff, about the 16th of August, 1748 ; and being all brought together under a strong guard to Southwark, were carried before Justice Hammond, who committed them all to the county gaol of Surrey, for being concerned with divers other persons armed with fire-arms, in running uncustomed goods, and for not surrendering themselves after publication in the *London Gazette.*

And on the 5th day of October, Richard Mills was detained in the said gaol, by virtue of a warrant under the hand and seal of Justice Hammond, for being concerned in the murder of William Galley and Daniel Chater, whose bodies had a little before been found, as has been related.

William Jackson and William Chater were taken November the 14th, near Godalming in Surrey, and brought up to London under a strong guard the 17th November ; and being carried before Justice Poulson in Covent Garden, were, after examination, committed to

Newgate, for being concerned with divers other persons
in running uncustomed goods, and for not surrendering
after publication in the *London Gazette*.

Old Richard Mills, notwithstanding he knew that all
these were taken, and that warrants were out against
Henry Sheerman, otherwise Little Harry, of Leigh, near
Warblington, labourer; Edmund Richards, of Long
Coppice, in the Parish of Walderton, labourer; Thomas
Stringer, of Chichester, cordwainer; Daniel Perryer,
otherwise Little Daniel, of Norton, labourer; and John
Mills (his other son), of Trotton, labourer; all which
places are in the county of Sussex; as also against
Thomas Willis, commonly called the Coachman, of Selbourne, near Liphook; and Samuel Howard, otherwise
Little Sam, of Rowland's Castle, labourer; both in the
county of Hants; for being concerned with the others
before-mentioned, in the murders of Galley and Chater,
yet he continued at home, never absconding, thinking
himself quite safe, as he knew nothing of the murder of
Galley, and as to that of Chater, he was seemingly very
easy, as he was not murdered in his house, nor he
present when the wicked deed was done: but Steel
having given an account in his information of the whole
affair, which was laid before the Attorney General, that
old Major Mills was concerned, as has been before
related, by keeping the poor man chained in his skilling
or turf-house; and that he was present when they all
came down from Scardefield's, and told him they were
come to take Chater up to Harris's Well, where they
intended to murder him, and fling him into it; as likewise that he was present in the turf-house when Tapner
cut Chater across his eyes, nose and forehead; and that
he did express these words, " Don't murder him here;
take him somewhere else and do it," it was thought

necessary to apprehend him, and accordingly on the 16th of December he was taken, committed to Horsham gaol as being accessary to the murder of Daniel Chater, before the same was committed, and concealing the same ; which offence subjects the person so guilty to be hanged.

Combleach, the gardener, who lent them the ladder and rope to get Chater out of the well, when they found that he was not quite dead, having been heard to say, that some of the persons in custody had told him they had murdered two informers against the smugglers, it was thought proper to take him up and examine him, in expectation of some further discoveries ; but when Combleach was brought before the magistrates, he refused to give satisfactory answers to the questions asked him, and idly and obstinately denied all that was sworn against him, whereupon he was committed to Horsham gaol on suspicion of being concerned in the murder of Chater.

The smugglers had reigned a long time uncontrolled ; the officers of the customs were too few to encounter them ; they rode in troops to fetch their goods, and carried them off in triumph by day-light; nay, so audacious were they grown, that they were not afraid of regular troops, that were sent into the country to keep them in awe; of which we had several instances. If any one of them happened to be taken, and the proof ever so clear against him, no magistrate in the county durst commit him to gaol ; if he did, he was sure to have his house or barns set on fire, or some other mischief done him, if he was so happy to escape with his life, which has been the occasion of their being brought to London to be committed. But for a man to inform against them, the most cruel death was his undoubted portion; of which we already have given two melancholy instances, and could produce more; one especially is so very notorious, that we shall make a little digression, and relate a few particulars of it, and reserve a more circumstantial account till the trials of these cruel villains are over, who were the horrid perpetrators of it.

Richard Hawkins, of Yapton, in the county of Sussex, labourer, being at work in a barn, two of their gang, in January 1747-8, came to the barn in the said Parish of Yapton, where the poor man was threshing corn.

The names of the two men who came to him were Jeremiah Curtis, of Hawkhurst, in Kent, butcher, and John Mills, of Trotton, in Sussex, labourer (this last one of those who were concerned in the murder of Chater, and who is not yet taken), and having found Hawkins at work, as before mentioned, they told him that he must go along with them; and on his showing some reluctance to comply with their commands, they swore they would shoot him through the head that instant if he did not come away without any more words. Poor Hawkins being terrified at their threats, put on his clothes, and went along with them to the sign of the Dog and Partridge, an alehouse, on Slindon Common, and going into a back room, he saw Thomas Winter, of Poling, near Arundel, and one called Rob, or Little Fat Back, servant to Jeremiah Curtis, who lived in or near East Grinstead. In the back room these two were waiting for them. This was in the afternoon, and having kept Hawkins there till about twelve o'clock at night, took him away; but whither they carried, or what they did with him, was not known for a long time; for the man was not seen, nor heard of, till the body was found in a pond in Parham Park, belonging to Sir Cecil Bishop, in Sussex, upwards of nine months afterwards ; and the coroner's inquest, having sat on the body, they brought in their verdict of wilful murder by persons unknown.

The only reason these villains had to commit this murder on the poor wretch, who left behind a wife and many children, was, on a supposition only, that he had concealed a small bag of tea from them ; for they had lodged a quantity of run tea near the barn where the man worked, and when they came to look for it, missed one bag, and imagined he had taken it away ; though the villains, on a second search, after they had murdered the man, found the bag of tea where they had hid it, and had overlooked it before.

This murder in itself was as barbarous as that of Mr. Galley ; for they made him go with them upwards of ten miles, all the way whipping him, and beating him with the handles of their whips till they had killed him, and then tied stones to his legs and arms and flung him into the pond, which kept the body under water.

These terrible executions, committed by the smugglers on these poor men, and the dreadful menaces which they uttered against any person that should presume to interrupt them, so terrified the people everywhere, that scarce anybody durst look at them as they passed in large bodies in open day-light. And the custom officers were so intimidated, that hardly any of them had courage enough to go on their duty. Some of them they knew they had already sent to France, others had been killed or wounded in opposing them, and Galley, in particular, had been inhumanly murdered by them : so that not only the honest trader suffered by the running of prodigious quantities of goods, which were sold again at a rate that he could not buy them at, unless he traded with them; but the King's revenue was considerably lessened by this smuggling traffic.

It is no wonder, indeed, that when once a set of men commenced as smugglers, that they should go on to commit the vilest excesses; for when a man has wrought himself into a firm persuasion that it is no crime to rob his King or his country, the transition is easy to the belief, that it is no sin to plunder or destroy his neighbour; and therefore we need not be much surprised that so many of the smugglers have turned highwaymen, housebreakers, and incendiaries, of which we have had but too many instances of late.

The body of the smugglers was now increased to a prodigious number, and the mischiefs they did wherever they came, at least wherever they met with opposition, were so enormous, that the whole country was afraid of them; and even the government itself began to be alarmed, and to apprehend consequences that might be fatal to the public peace, in case a speedy check was not put to their audacious proceedings. His Majesty, therefore, being perfectly informed of their notorious villainies, and informations being given of many of the names of the most desperate of their gangs, particularly those who broke open the custom house at Poole, issued a proclamation, with lists of their several names, declaring, that unless they surrendered themselves to justice at a day appointed, they should be outlawed, and out of the protection of the laws of their country; promising a reward of £500, to be paid by the commissioners of the customs, for the apprehension of every one who should be taken, and convicted in pursuance thereof. This, in great measure, has had the desired effect, and several of them have been apprehended, tried, convicted and executed, which was the only satisfaction they could make to public justice. But to return from this digression.

Seven of the notorious villains, who had confederated in the murder of Galley and Chater, being apprehended by the diligence of Government, the noblemen and gentlemen of Sussex, being desirous of making public examples of such horrible offenders, and to terrify others from committing the same crimes, requested his Majesty to grant a special commission to hold an assize on purpose to try them; and represented that as Chichester was a city sufficiently large to entertain the judges and all their train, and as it was contiguous to the place where the murders were committed, they thought it the most proper place for the assizes to be held. Accordingly a commission passed the seals to hold a special assize there the 16th day of January, 1748-9.

On Monday, January 9th, 1748-9, Jackson and Carter were removed from Newgate, as also Richard Mills, jun., from the New Gaol in Surrey, under a strong guard, to Horsham, in their way to Chichester. When they came to Horsham, the other five prisoners, viz., Richard Mills, sen., Benjamin Tapner, John Hammond, John Cobby and William Combleach (the latter committed only on suspicion), who were already in that gaol, were all put in a waggon, and conveyed from thence under the same guard as brought the others from London to Chichester, where they arrived on Friday, the 13th.

On their arrival there they were all confined, being well secured with heavy irons, in one room, except Jackson, who being extremely ill, was put into a room by himself, and all imaginable care was taken of him, in order to keep him alive (for he was in a very dangerous condition) till he had taken his trial.

Having thus brought the prisoners to Chichester, and put them in safe confinement, we shall leave them there for the present, till we meet them again on their trials, of which we are enabled to give the most authentic account of any that has been, or may be, published. After that, we shall attend the prisoners while under sentence of condemnation, and truly relate whatever appeared remarkable in their carriage or demeanour; and then bear them company to the place of execution, where we shall take particular notice of their behaviour and dying words.

But, previous to this, it will be necessary to give some account of the journey of the judges from London to Chichester, in order to rectify some mistakes that were made in the accounts published of it in the public prints.

The judges set out from London on Friday, January the 13th, and arrived at the Duke of Richmond's house at Godalming in Surrey that evening, where they lay that night, and the next day they set out for Chichester, and were met at Midhurst by his Grace the Duke of Richmond, who entertained their lordships with a dinner at his hunting-house near Charlton. After which they proceeded on their journey, and got into Chichester about five o'clock, and went directly to the Bishop's Palace. It was reported, though very erroneously, that they were guarded in their journey by a party of horse, both thither and back again; but they had none but their own attendants, except a few servants of his Grace the Duke of Richmond, the judges, counsellors, and principal officers being in six coaches, each drawn by six horses.

On Sunday morning, the 15th, they went to the Cathedral, accompanied by the Duke of Richmond, the

Mayor and Aldermen of the Corporation, where an excellent sermon was preached suitable to the occasion, by the Reverend Mr. Ashburnham, Dean of Chichester.

We shall now proceed to give an account of what passed at Chichester during their trials ; only observe first, that William Combleach, the gardener (whom we have before observed to have been committed only on suspicion, by his own idle talk, which, no doubt, gave a just foundation for his said commitment) was not ordered to be indicted, nor from the mouths of the witnesses on the trials was his name more than barely mentioned.

* * *

Chichester, January 16th, 1748.

This morning between eleven and twelve o'clock, the judges assigned to hold the assize by special commission, viz., the Hon. Sir Michael Foster, Knt., one of the judges of His Majesty's Court of King's Bench ; the Hon. Edward Clive, one of the Barons of His Majesty's Court of Exchequer : and the Hon. Sir Thomas Birch, Knt., one of the Judges of His Majesty's Court of Common Pleas ; went from the Bishop's Palace, preceded by the High Sheriff of the County, with the usual ceremonies, to the Guildhall, where they were met by his Grace the Duke of Richmond, Sir Richard Mill, Sir Cecil Bishop, Sir Hutchins Williams, Barts., John Butler, Esq., Robert Bull, Esq., and others of the commissioners named in the commission for that purpose ; and after having opened the said commission, and the same having been read, the gentlemen who were summoned to be of the grand jury, were called over, and the following twenty-seven, who were present, sworn., viz. :

Sir J. Miller, Bart., foreman.　William Mitford, Esq.
Sir M. Fetherstonhaugh, Bart.　James Goble, Esq.
Sir Thomas Ridge, Knt.　John Cheal, Esq.
John Page, Esq.　William Leeves, Esq.
George Bramston, Esq.　Richard Nash, Esq.
William Battine, Esq.　Thomas Fowler, Esq.
John Winker, Esq.　William Peckham, Esq.
Edward Tredcroft, Esq.　William Bartlet, Esq.
William Winker, Esq.　John Hollest, Esq.
Samuel Blunt, Esq.　Francis Peachey, Gent.
William Pool, Esq.　John Laker, Gent.
Peckham Williams, Esq.　William Peachey, Gent.
Thomas B. Bilson, Esq.　John Pay, Gent.
Thomas Phipps, Esq.

As soon as they were sworn, Mr. Justice Foster gave a most learned and judicious charge, taking notice among other things, that this commission, though it did not extend to all the crimes which are cognizable under the general commissions which are executed in the common circuits; yet it did not differ from other commissions granted for holding the assizes, so that they must proceed on this commission in the same method of trial as was usually done in commissions of assizes; that this commission was only to enquire of murders, manslaughters and felonies committed in the county of Sussex, and the accessaries thereto, and therefore the Grand Jury could not take notice of anything else but what was specified in the said commission.

Then his lordship was pleased to say, that the several murders and other crimes, committed by armed persons gathered together contrary to all law, in this and the neighbouring counties, loudly demanded the justice of the nation; and for that reason his Majesty had been pleased to entrust his lordship and brethren with his special commission, that public justice might be done upon the offenders against the public laws of the kingdom, and that the innocent might be released from their confinement.

His lordship likewise took notice of the dangerous confederacies that had been formed for many years past in Sussex and its neighbouring counties, for very unwarrantable and very wicked purposes; even for robbing the public of that revenue which is absolutely necessary to its support, and for defeating the fair trader in his just expectations of profit; and which, without mentioning more, are the necessary unavoidable consequences of that practice which now goes under the name of smuggling; and this, his lordship said, was not all, for this wicked practice had been supported by an armed force; and acting in open daylight, in defiance of all the law, to the terror of his Majesty's peaceable subjects; and had gone so far in some late instances, as deliberate murders, attended with circumstances of great aggravation, in consequence of those unlawful combinations.

His lordship likewise said, that in case of a murder, wherever it appeared that the fact was committed with any degree of deliberation, and especially where attended with circumstances of cruelty, the usual distinction between murder and manslaughter could never take place; for the fact is, in the eye of the law, wilful murder, of malice prepense; and involves every person concerned, as well those aiding and abetting as those who actually commit the fact, in the same degree of guilt.

His lordship was pleased further to take notice, that where a number of people engage together with a felonious design, every person so engaged, and present aiding and abetting in the fact, is considered as a principal in the felony ; and the reason the law goes upon is this, that the presence of every one of the accomplices gives countenance and encouragement to all the rest ; so that consequently the fact is considered, in the eye of the law, and of sound reason too, as the act of the whole party, though it be perpetrated by the hands only of one ; for he is considered the instrument by which the others act.

And when we say that the presence of a person at the commission of a felony will involve him in the guilt of the rest, we must not confine ourselves to a strict, actual presence as would make him an eye or ear witness of what passes. For an accomplice may be involved in the guilt of the rest, though he may happen to be so far distant from the scene of action, as to be utterly out of sight or hearing of what passes.

For instance ; if several persons agree to commit a murder, or other felony, and each man takes his part : some are appointed to commit the fact, others to watch at a distance to prevent a surprise, or to favour the escape of those who are more immediately engaged ; the law says, that if the felony be committed, it is the act of all of them ; for each man operated in his station towards the commission of it, at one and the same instant. And so much doth the law abhor combinations of this kind, especially where innocent blood is shed, that a man may, in judgment of the law, be involved in the guilt of murder, when possibly his heart abhorred the thoughts of it. For if numbers of people assemble in prosecution of an unlawful design, with a resolution to stand by each other against all opposers, and a murder is committed by one of the party in prosecution of that design, every man so engaged at the time of the murder, is, in the eye of the law, equally guilty with him that gave the stroke.

"Many cases might be put which come under this rule. I will confine myself to a few which the present solemnity naturally suggests.

"For instance: Numbers of people assemble for the purpose of running uncustomed goods, or for any of the purposes which now go under the term of smuggling, with a resolution to resist all opposers (and the riding with fire-arms and other offensive weapons is certainly an evidence of that resolution); numbers of people, I say, assemble in this manner and for this purpose. They are met by the officers of the revenue; one of the party, *in the prosecution of this unlawful design*, fires on the King's officer, and kills him or any of his assistants: the whole party is, in the eye of the law, guilty of murder, though their original intention went no further than smuggling; for that intention being unlawful, the killing in prosecution of that intent is murder, and every man engaged in it partakes of the guilt. The act of one, in prosecution of their common engagement, is considered as the act of all.

"I will go one step further: the party assembled in the manner and for the purposes I have mentioned, is met by the King's officers, and an affray happens between them; during the affray one of the party fires at the King's officers, but misses his aim, and kills one of his own party, perhaps his nearest relation or bosom friend (if people of that character are capable of true friendship). This is murder in him and in the whole party too. For if a man upon malice against another strikes at him and by accident kills a third person, the law, as it were, transfers the circumstance of malice from him that was aimed at to him that received the blow and died by it. And consequently, in the case I have just put, the person who discharged the gun being guilty of murder, all his accomplices are involved in his guilt; because the gun was discharged in prosecution of their common engagement, and it is therefore considered as the act of the whole party.

"What I have hitherto said regards those who are present in the sense I have mentioned, and abetting the fact at the time of the commission of it. But there are others who may be involved in the same guilt, I mean the accessaries before the fact. These are all people who by advice, persuasion or any other means, procure the fact to be done, but cannot be said, in any sense, to be present at the actual perpetration of it.

"These persons are involved in the guilt, and liable in the case of wilful murder to the same punishment as the principal offenders are.

"I am very sensible, gentlemen, that I have been something longer than I needed to have been, if I had spoken barely for your information. But on this occasion I thought it not improper to enlarge on some points, that people may see the infinite hazard they run by engaging in the wicked combinations I have mentioned: and how suddenly and fatally they may, being so engaged, be involved in the guilt of murder itself, while perhaps their principal view might fall very short of that crime."

His lordship having ended his charge, two bills of indictment were presented to the grand jury, one for the murder of William Galley, sen., a custom-house officer in the port of Southampton, and the other for the murder of Daniel Chater, of Fordingbridge, in the county of Hants, shoemaker; when, as soon as the grand jury had received the bills, they withdrew to the council chamber in the North Street; and the following persons were sworn to give evidence before them, who immediately after their being severally sworn in court, went and attended the grand jury, viz., William Steel, alias Hardware, and John Race, alias Raise (two accomplices in the said murders), Mr. Milner, collector of the customs at the port of Poole; Mr. Shearer, collector of the customs at the port of Southampton; William Galley, son of the deceased William Galley; Edward Holton, George Austin, Thomas Austin, Robert Jenkes, Joseph Southern, William Garrat, William Lamb, Richard Kent, Ann Pescod, William Scardefield, Edward Soanes, Mrs. Chater, the widow of the deceased Daniel Chater, John Greentree, George Poate and Mr. Brackstone. And then the court adjourned until nine o'clock the next morning.

Chichester, Jan. 18, 1748-9.

The judges went to the court this morning about nine o'clock, and the court being sat, the seven following prisoners, viz., Benjamin Tapner, John Cobby, John Hammond, William Jackson,* William Carter, Richard Mills the younger and Richard Mills the elder, were put to the bar (the grand jury having returned both the bills found into court), and arraigned upon the indictment for the murder of Daniel Chater; the three first as principals, and the other four as accessaries before the fact.

The clerk of the arraigns called upon the several prisoners at the bar to hold up their hands, which being

---

* Jackson was so ill that he was obliged to be brought in a chair; and likewise was permitted to have a chair, and sat during the time of both his trials.

done, he read the indictment aloud, which was as follows, viz. :—

"That you, Benjamin Tapner, John Cobby and John Hammond, together with Thomas Stringer and Daniel Perryer, not yet taken, not having the fear of God before your eyes, but being moved and seduced by the instigation of the devil, upon the 19th day of February, in the 21st year of his present Majesty's reign, with force of arms, at the parish of Harting, in the county of Sussex, in and upon one Daniel Chater, being then and there in the peace of God, and his said Majesty, feloniously, wilfully, and out of your malice aforethought, did make an assault; and that you, the said Benjamin Tapner, a certain cord or rope made of hemp, of the value of sixpence, which you the said Benjamin Tapner had then and there in your hands, about the neck of him the said Daniel Chater, then and there with force and arms, feloniously, wilfully, and out of your malice aforethought, did put, bind and fasten ; and that you, the said Benjamin Tapner, with the rope aforesaid by him about the neck of the said Chater, so put, bound and fastened as aforesaid ; him the said Chater, then and there with force and arms, feloniously, wilfully, and out of your malice aforethought, did choke and strangle, of which said choking and strangling of him the said Chater, in manner aforesaid, he the said Chater did then and there die. And that you the said John Cobby, and John Hammond, together with Thomas Stringer and Daniel Perryer, both not yet taken, at the time of the felony and murder aforesaid by him the said Benjamin Tapner, so feloniously, wilfully, and out of his malice aforethought, done, perpetrated and committed, as aforesaid, then and there feloniously, wilfully, and out of your malice aforethought, were present, aiding, abetting, comforting and maintaining the said Benjamin Tapner, the said Daniel Chater in manner and form aforesaid, feloniously, wilfully, and out of his malice aforethought to kill and murder. And so that you the said Benjamin Tapner, John Cobby, John Hammond, together with Thomas Stringer and Daniel Perryer, not yet taken, the said Daniel Chater in manner and form aforesaid, then and there with force and arms, feloniously, wilfully and out of your malice aforethought, did kill and murder against his Majesty's peace, his crown and dignity. And that you, Richard Mills the elder, Richard Mills the younger, William Jackson and William Carter, together with John Mills, Thomas Willis and Edmund Richards, not yet taken, before the felony and murder aforesaid, by them the said Benjamin Tapner, John Cobby, John Hammond, Thomas Stringer and Daniel Perryer, in manner and form aforesaid, feloniously, wilfully, and out of your malice aforethought, done, perpetrated and committed (to wit) upon the said 19th day of February, in the 21st year aforesaid, at the Parish of Harting aforesaid, in the county of Sussex aforesaid, them the said Benjamin Tapner, John Cobby, John Hammond, Thomas Stringer, and Daniel Perryer, the felony and murder aforesaid in manner and form aforesaid, feloniously, wilfully, maliciously, and out of your malice aforethought, to do, perpetrate, and commit, feloniously, wilfully, and out of your malice aforethought, did incite, move, instigate, stir up, counsel, persuade and procure against his Majesty's peace, his crown and dignity.

To which indictment they severally pleaded Not Guilty.

This being done, William Jackson and William Carter were arraigned upon the other indictment as principals in the murder of William Gally, otherwise called William Galley.

Which indictment the clerk of the arraigns read aloud to them as follows : That you, William Jackson and William Carter (together with Samuel Downer, alias Howard, alias Little Sam, Edmund Richards, and Henry Sheerman, alias Little Harry, not yet taken), not having the fear of God before your eyes, but being moved and seduced by the instigation of the devil, upon the 15th of February, in the 21st year of his present Majesty's reign, with force and arms, at Rowland's Castle in the County of Southampton, in and upon one William Gally, otherwise called William Galley, being then and there in the peace of God and his said Majesty, feloniously, wilfully, and out of your malice aforethought, did make an assault, and him the said William Galley, upon the back of a certain horse, then and there with force and arms, feloniously, wilfully, and out of your malice aforethought, did put and set, and the legs of him the said William Galley, being so put and set upon the back of the said horse as aforesaid, with a certain rope or cord made of hemp, under the belly of the said horse, then and there with force and arms, feloniously, wilfully, and out of your malice aforethought, did bind, tie and fasten ; and him the said William Galley, being so put and set upon horseback as aforesaid, with his legs so bound, tied, and fastened under the horse's belly as aforesaid, with certain large whips, which you had then and there in your right hands, in and upon the head, face, neck, shoulders, arms, back, belly, sides, and several other parts of the body of him the said William Galley, then and there with force and arms, feloniously, wilfully, and out of your malice aforethought, for the space of one mile, did whip, lash, beat and strike ; by reason whereof, the said William Galley was then and there very much wounded, bruised and hurt ; and not being able to endure or bear the misery, pain and anguish, occasioned by his having been so whipped, lashed, beat, and struck, as aforesaid, and by his being so wounded, bruised, and hurt, as aforesaid, then and there dropped down the left side of the said horse, on which he then and there rode, with his head under the horse's belly, and his legs and feet across the saddle upon the back of the said horse, upon which you, the said William Jackson and William Carter, together with Samuel Downer, otherwise Howard, otherwise Little Sam, Edmund Richards, and Henry Sheerman, otherwise Little Harry, not yet taken, then and there, untied the legs of the said William Galley ; and him the said Galley, in and upon the same horse then and there, with force and arms, feloniously, wilfully, and out of your malice aforethought, did again put and set, and the legs of him the said William Galley, being again so put and set upon the said horse as last aforesaid, with the same rope or cord under the belly of the said horse, you then and there, with force and arms, feloniously, wilfully, and out of your malice aforethought, under the horse's belly did again bind, tie, and fasten ; and him the said William Galley* being again so put and set upon the said horse, as last aforesaid, with his legs so bound, tied and fastened under the horse's belly, as last aforesaid, with the said whips which you had then and there in your right hands, as aforesaid, in and upon the head, face, neck, arms, shoulders, back, belly, sides, and several other parts of the body of him the said

* Chater, as well as Galley, was tied on the same horse, and in the same manner with him, yet in the indictment it only mentioned the name of Galley.

William Galley, you then and there with force and arms, feloniously, wilfully, and out of your malice aforethought, for the space of half a mile further, did again whip, lash, beat, and strike; by reason whereof he the said William Galley was then and there much more wounded, bruised and hurt, and not being able to endure or bear the misery, pain, and anguish occasioned by his having been so whipped, lashed, beat, and struck, in manner, as aforesaid; and by his being so wounded, bruised, and hurt, in manner as aforesaid, did then and there drop a second time from off the said horse, with his head under the horse's belly, and his legs and feet across the saddle. Upon which you the said William Jackson and William Carter, together with the said Samuel Downer, otherwise Howard, otherwise Little Sam, Edmund Richards and Henry Sheerman, otherwise Little Harry, not yet taken, then and there again untied the legs of him, the said William Galley, and him, in and upon another horse, behind a certain other person, did then and there with force and arms, feloniously, wilfully, and out of your malice aforethought, put and set, and the said William Galley, being so put and set on horseback, as last aforesaid, with the same whips which you had then and there in your right hands as aforesaid, in and upon the head, face, neck, arms, shoulders, back, belly, sides, and several other parts of the body of the said William Galley, did then and there with force and arms, feloniously, wilfully, and out of your malice aforethought, for the space of two miles further, until you came into the parish of Harting, in the county of Sussex aforesaid, again whip, lash, beat, and strike, by reason whereof the said William Galley was then and there much more wounded, bruised and hurt; and not being able to endure or bear the misery, pain and anguish occasioned by his having been so wounded, bruised and hurt, in manner as aforesaid, then and there in the parish of Harting aforesaid, got off the said horse ; upon which you the said William Jackson and William Carter, together with Samuel Downer, otherwise Howard, otherwise Little Sam, Edmund Richards and Henry Sheerman, otherwise Little Harry, not yet taken, him the said William Galley, in and upon another horse, whereon the said Edmund Richards, then and there rode, with the belly of him the said William Galley across the pommel of the saddle, on which the said Richards then and there rode, then and there with force and arms, feloniously, wilfully, and out of your malice aforethought, did put and lay ; but before you had gone the space of eighty yards further, William Galley, not being able to bear the motion of the said horse, on which he was so put and laid as last aforesaid, by reason of having been so whipped, lashed, beat and struck as aforesaid ; and by reason of his being so wounded, bruised and hurt, in manner as aforesaid, then and there tumbled off the horse, and fell upon the ground in the common highway there, by which fall he the said William Galley, was then and there much more wounded, bruised and hurt ; whereupon you the said William Jackson, William Carter, together with Samuel Downer, otherwise Howard, otherwise Little Sam, Edmund Richards and Henry Sheerman, otherwise Little Harry, not yet taken, him the said William Galley in and upon another horse by himself, then and there with force and arms, feloniously wilfully, and out of your malice aforethought, did put and set ; but the said William Galley not being able to sit upright on the said last mentioned horse, he the said

Henry Sheerman, otherwise Little Harry, did then and there get upon the same horse behind him, the said William Galley, in order to hold him on; but after you the said William Jackson, and William Carter, together with Samuel Downer, otherwise Howard, otherwise Little Sam, Edmund Richards, and Henry Sheerman, otherwise Little Harry, not yet taken, and the said William Galley had rode on a quarter of a mile further together, in manner aforesaid, he the said William Galley, not being able to sit upon the said horse, or ride any further upon the same, through the great misery, pain and anguish, occasioned by his having been so whipped, lashed, beat and struck, as aforesaid; and by his being so wounded, bruised and hurt, in manner as aforesaid, then and there tumbled off the said horse, on which he was so put and set as last aforesaid, and again fell to the ground; and as he tumbled and fell, the said Henry Sheerman, otherwise Little Harry, who rode behind the said William Galley, and upon the same horse with him, in manner aforesaid, then and there with force and arms feloniously, wilfully, and out of his malice aforethought, give to him the said William Galley, a most violent thrust and push; by reason whereof the said William Galley then and there fell, with much more weight and force to the ground than otherwise he would have done; and was thereby then and there much more wounded, bruised and hurt. And that by reason of the said binding, tying and fastening, of him the said William Galley, by you the said William Jackson, and William Carter, together with Samuel Downer, otherwise Howard, otherwise Little Sam, Edmund Richards and Henry Sheerman, otherwise Little Harry, not yet taken, in manner and form aforesaid; and of the whipping, lashing, beating and striking, of him the said William Galley, by you, in manner and form aforesaid; and of the several wounds, bruises and hurts, which he the said William Galley received from such whipping, lashing, beating and striking in manner aforesaid; and other wounds, bruises and hurts which he, the said William Galley so received from the several falls which he so had from off the said horse, on which he was by you so put, set and laid, in manner aforesaid; and of the said thrust and push which he the said Henry Sheerman, otherwise Little Harry, so as aforesaid, gave him the said William Galley, as he the said William Galley so tumbled and fell from off the said horse, as last aforesaid; he the said William Galley, at the parish of Harting aforesaid, in the county of Sussex aforesaid, did die. And further, that you the said William Jackson, and William Carter, together with the said Samuel Downer, alias Howard, alias Little Sam, Edmund Richards and Henry Sheerman, alias Little Harry, not yet taken, him the said William Galley, with force and arms in manner and form aforesaid, feloniously, wilfully, and out of your malice aforethought, did kill and murder, against his Majesty's peace, his crown and dignity."

The indictment being read to them, Mr. Justice Foster acquainted the prisoners they might each of them challenge twenty of the panel, without shewing cause; but if they challenged more, they must shew a reasonable cause for so doing; and that if they agreed to join in their challenges they might be tried together, but if they did not, they would be tried separately; and left them to act in that behalf as they should see proper.

The prisoners then consulted among themselves for a

little while, and then agreed to join and be tried
together. And then the jury were sworn, and charged
by the Clerk of the Arraignments, whose names were
as follows, viz. :—

John Burnard, foreman,	John Hipkins,
William Faulkner,	William Hobbs,
Richard North,	John Shotter,
William Halsted,	Thomas Stuart,
Henry Halsted,	William Poe,
John Woods,	Christopher Wilson.

The counsel for the King were Henry Banks, Esq.,
Sidney Strafford Smythe, Esq., and two of his Majesty's
counsel learned in the law ; also Mr. Burrel, Mr.
Purkes, and Mr. Steele, recorder of Chichester.

Mr. Steele opened the indictment, as soon as the jury
were sworn, against the prisoners ; after which Mr.
Banks very judiciously and learnedly laid down the
facts attending the murder, which we choose to give
our readers in his own words.

Counsel for the King : "This is an indictment
against the seven prisoners at the bar, for the murder
of Daniel Chater. It is against the three first, viz.,
Benjamin Tapner, John Cobby and John Hammond, as
principals in that murder, by being present, aiding,
abetting and assisting therein; and against Thomas
Stringer and Daniel Perryer as principals also, and
who are not yet apprehended. And it is against the
prisoners, William Jackson, William Carter and
Richard Mills the younger, as accessaries before the
murder ; and also against three others as accessaries
before the fact, viz., John Mills, another son of Richard
Mills the elder, Thomas Willis and Edmund Richards,
not yet taken and brought to justice.

"Although this indictment hath made a distinction between the several prisoners, and divided them into two classes, of principals and accessaries, yet the law makes no distinction in the crime. And in case all the prisoners are guilty of the charge in this indictment, they will be all equally liable to the same judgment and punishment.

"In the outset of this trial I shall not enlarge upon the heinousness of murder in general; nor shall I dwell upon those circumstances in aggravation attending this in particular. When I come to mention those circumstances of cruelty and barbarity, I doubt not but they will have all that effect upon the jury which they ought to have—to awaken and fix your attention to every part of the transaction, and to balance that compassion which you feel for the prisoners, though they felt none for others. The effect I mean these circumstances should and ought to have, is to clear the way for that justice which the nation expects, from your determination and verdict.

"To comply with this general demand of justice upon the prisoners, his Majesty, in order to give the prisoners the earliest opportunity of proving their innocence and of wiping off this foul suspicion of murder they now lie under, or if guilty of a breach of the laws of God and man, that they may suffer the punishment due to their guilt, has been pleased, by a special commission, to appoint this trial to be before their lordships, not less knowing in the laws than tender and compassionate in the execution of them.

"I cannot here omit taking notice of the unhappy cause of this fatal effect, now under your consideration. Every one here present will, in his own thoughts, anticipate my words and know I mean smuggling.

Smuggling is not only highly injurious to trade, a violation of the laws, and the disturber of the peace and quiet of all the maritime counties in the kingdom ; but it is a nursery for all sorts of vice and wickedness ; a temptation to commit offences at first unthought of ; an encouragement to perpetrate the blackest of crimes without provocation or remorse ; and is in general productive of cruelty, robbery and murder.

" It is greatly to be wished, both for the sake of the smugglers themselves and for the peace of this county, that the dangerous and armed manner now used of running uncustomed goods was less known and less practised here.

" It is a melancholy consideration to observe, that the best and wisest measures of Government, calculated to put a stop to this growing mischief, have been perverted and abused to the worst of purposes. And what was intended to be a cure to this disorder has been made the means to increase and heighten the disease.

" Every expedient of lenity and mercy was at first made use of to reclaim this abandoned set of men. His Majesty, by repeated proclamations of pardon, invited them to their duty and to their own safety. But instead of laying hold of so gracious an offer, they have set the laws at defiance, have made the execution of justice dangerous in the hands of magistracy, and have become almost a terror to Government itself.

" The number of prisoners at the bar, and of others involved in the suspicion of the same guilt, the variety of circumstances attending this whole transaction, the length of time in the completion thereof, and the general expectation of mankind to be informed of every minute circumstance leading and tending to finish the scene of horror, will necessarily lay me under an obligation of taking up more time than will be either agreeable to the court or to myself.

" To avoid confusion in stating such a variety of facts with the evidence and proofs thereof, and to fix and guide the attention of the gentlemen of the jury to the several particular parts of this bloody tragedy, at last completed in the murder of Chater, I shall divide the facts into four distinct periods of time.

" 1st. What happened precedent to Chater's coming to a public house, the sign of the White Hart, at Rowland's Castle in Hampshire, kept by Elizabeth Payne, widow, upon Sunday, the 4th of February, 1747-8.

"And this period of time will take in the occasion and grounds of the prisoners' wicked malice to the deceased and the cause and motive of his murder.

" 2nd. What happened after Chater's arrival at the widow Paine's, to the time of his being carried away from thence by some of the prisoners to the house of Richard Mills the elder, at Trotton in Sussex.

" This will disclose a scene of cruelty and barbarity, previous to Chater's murder, and show how active and instrumental the prisoners Jackson and Carter were therein.

" 3rd. What happened after Chater was brought to the house of Richard Mills the elder, to the time of his murder, upon Wednesday night, the 17th of that February.

" This will take in the barbarous usage of Chater at Mills' house ; a consultation of sixteen* smugglers in what manner to dispose of Chater, and their unanimous resolution to murder him : and will shew Tapner, Cobby

---

* There were sixteen in the whole, with Race and Steel, the two admitted evidence for the King.

and Hammond to be principals therein, and the other four prisoners to be accessaries.

"4th, and last period, takes in the discovery of Chater's body in a well, where he was hung, with the proofs that it was the body of Chater.

"In the opening of this case, it will be impossible for me to avoid the frequent mention of one William Galley, also suspected to have been murdered: and for whose murder two of the prisoners, viz., Jackson and Carter, are indicted, and are to be tried upon another indictment.

"But the murder of Galley is not the object of your present consideration, nor do I mention his name either to aggravate this crime, by taking notice of his murder also, nor to inflame the jury against the prisoners at the bar; but I do it for the sake of method, and for the purpose only of laying the whole case before the jury; for the story of Chater's murder cannot be told without disclosing also what happened to Galley, his companion and fellow-sufferer.

"To begin with the first period of time. Some time in September, 1747, a large quantity of uncustomed tea had been duly seized by one Captain Johnson, out of a smuggling cutter, and by him lodged in the custom-house at Poole, in the county of Dorset.

"In the night of the 6th of October following, the custom-house of Poole was broken open by a numerous and armed gang of smugglers; and the tea which had been seized and there lodged, was by them taken and carried away.

"This body of smugglers, in their return, passed

through Fordingbridge, where Dimer,* one of that company, was seen and known by Chater. Dimer was afterwards taken up upon suspicion of being one of those who had broken open the custom house, and was in custody at Chichester for further examination, and for further proof that he was one of that gang.

" And in order to prove the identity of Dimer, and that he was one of the gang, Daniel Chater, a shoemaker at Fordingbridge (the person murdered), was sent in company with, and under the care of, William Galley, a tide-waiter of Southampton, by Mr. Shearer, collector of the customs there, with a letter to Major Battine, a Justice of Peace for Sussex, and surveyor general of the customs for that county. Sunday morning, the 14th of February, 1747-8, Galley and Chater set out from Southampton, with Mr. Shearer's letter, on their journey to Major Battine's house, at East Marden, in the neighbourhood of Chichester.

" At the New Inn at Leigh,† in Havant parish, in Hants, Chater and Galley met with Robert Jenkes, George Austin, and Thomas Austin, and having shewed them the direction of the letter to Major Battine, they told them they were going towards Stansted, where Chater and Galley were informed Major Battine then was ; and said they would go with them, and shew them the road. Their direct way to Stansted lay near Rowland's Castle ; but Jenkes and the two Austins carried them

---

* In the former part of this account we called his name Dimer otherwise Diamond, for he was as frequently called by the one as the other, but as he was named by the counsel Dimer, we shall keep to that name where he was so called.

† Mr. Banks omitted here speaking of his calling first on Mr. Holton in the village of Havant, but that will appear in its proper place.

to Rowland's Castle that Sunday about noon, where this cruel plot was first contrived, and in part carried into execution.

"The malice conceived by the prisoners against Chater appears not to have arisen from any injury, or suspicion of injury, done by the deceased to the prisoners. But because Chater dared to give information against a smuggler, and do his duty in assisting to bring a notorious offender to justice, he was to be treated with the utmost cruelty, his person was to be tortured, and his life to be destroyed. What avail the laws of society, where no man dares to carry them into execution? Where is the protection of liberty and life, if criminals assume to themselves a power of restraining the one, and destroy-the other.

"Having mentioned the motive of the prisoners in this murder, I shall now open to you a scene of cruelty and barbarity, tending to the murder of Chater, begun at Rowland's Castle, by the two prisoners Jackson and Carter, in company with others, and from thence continued, until Chater was brought to the house of Richard Mills the elder, at Trotton, upon Monday morning the 15th of February, before it was light.

"And here you will observe how cruelly and wickedly, in general, the gang assembled at Rowland's Castle behaved; and in particular, how active Jackson and Carter appeared in every step of this fatal conspiracy.

"Soon after Chater and Galley, and the three others, had arrived at Rowland's Castle, the widow Payne suspected Chater and Galley intended some mischief against the smugglers; and for that purpose enquired of George Austin who the two strangers were, and what their business was. He privately informed her they were going to Major Battine with a letter. She desired he would either direct the two strangers to go a different way from Major Battine's, or would detain them a short time at her house, until she could send for Jackson, Carter and others. And she immediately sent her son William for the prisoner Jackson; and soon afterwards ordered her other son Edmund to summon the other prisoner Carter, and Edmund Richards, Samuel Howard, Henry Sheerman, William Steel and John Race, who all lived near Rowland's Castle; and accordingly they all came, as also did Jackson's and Carter's wives. They were immediately informed by the widow Payne of what she suspected, and had been informed concerning the two strangers. Jackson and Carter being very desirous of seeing the letter to Major Battine, got Chater out of the house, and endeavoured to persuade him to let them see the letter, and to inform them of the errand to Major Battine. But upon Galley's coming out to them, and interposing to prevent Chater's making any discovery, they quarrelled with Galley, and beat him to the ground; Galley complained of this ill-usage, and said he was the King's officer, and to convince them shewed his deputation.

"Chater and Galley were very uneasy at this treatment, and wanted to be gone; but the gang insisted upon their staying; and in order to secure and get them entirely in their own power, they plied them with strong liquors, and made them drunk; and then carried them into another room to sleep.

"During the two hours Galley and Chater slept, the letter was taken out of Chater's pocket; whereby it appeared that Chater was going to give information against Dimer. The secret being thus disclosed to the gang, the next thing to be considered of by the smugglers, was how to save their accomplice Dimer, and to punish Chater and Galley for daring to give information against him. For that purpose, whilst Chater and Galley were asleep, several consultations were held.

" It was proposed first to put Galley and Chater out of the way, to prevent their giving information against Dimer; and to that end it was talked of murdering them, and flinging them into a well, a quarter of a mile from Rowland's Castle, that was in the horse pasture; but the proposal was overruled, fearing a discovery, as the well was so near Rowland's Castle.

" The next thing proposed was secretly to convey Chater and Galley into France, at that time at war with England.

" The second scheme was, for all present to contribute threepence a week for the maintenance of Chater and Galley, who were to be confined in some private place, and there subsisted until Dimer should be tried; and as Dimer was done unto, so Chater and Galley were to be dealt with.

" The third and last proposal was to murder both.

" With a view and intention to execute this last, and the most cruel proposal, Jackson went into the room about seven that evening, where Chater and Galley lay asleep, and awaked them. They both came out very bloody, and cut in their faces; but by what means, or what Jackson had done to them, does not appear. They were immediately afterwards forced out of the house by Jackson and Carter; the others present consenting and assisting; Richards, one of the company, with a cocked pistol in his hand, swore he would shoot any person through the head who should make the least discovery of what had passed there.

" Chater and Galley were put upon one horse; and to

prevent their escape, their legs were tied under the horse's belly; and both their legs tied together; and the horse was led by William Steel. After they had been thus carried about one hundred yards from Rowland's Castle, Jackson cried out to Carter and the company, " Lick them, d......n them, cut them, slash them, whip them." Upon which, they whipped and beat them over their heads, faces, shoulders, and other parts of their bodies, for the space of near a mile. With this cruel treatment they both fell down under the horse's belly, with their heads dragging upon the ground. They were again put on the horse, and tied as before; and whipped and beat with the like severity, along the road for upwards of half a mile. And when they cried out through the agony of their pain, pistols were held to their heads, and they were threatened to be shot, if they made the least noise or cry. Being unable to endure this continued and exquisite pain, and to sit on horseback any longer, they fell a second time to the ground. By this inhuman usage, they were rendered incapable of supporting themselves any longer on horseback. Galley was afterwards carried behind Steel, and Chater behind Howard, the prisoners Jackson and Carter, with the rest of the company, still continuing their merciless treatment of Chater and Galley, but instead of whipping, they now began to beat them on the heads and faces with the butt-ends of their whips, loaded with lead. When they came to Lady Holt Park, in Sussex, Galley almost expiring with the torture he had undergone, got down from behind Steel; and it was proposed to throw him alive into a well adjoining to that park; in which well Chater was three days after hanged by the same gang. Galley was then thrown across the pommel of the saddle and carried before Richards. He was afterwards laid along alone upon a horse, and supported by Jackson, who walked by him, and was at last carried before Sheerman, who supported him by a cord tied round his breast. When they came to a lane called Conduit-lane, in Rogate parish, in this county, Galley in the extremity of anguish, cried out, " I shall fall ! I shall fall !" upon which Sheerman swore, " D......n you, if you will fall, do then;" and as Galley was falling he gave him a thrust to the ground ; after which Galley was never seen to move, or heard to speak more.

" Jackson, Carter, and the others, in order to prevent a discovery of the murder of Galley, went about one o'clock on the Monday morning, to the Red Lion at Rake, in Sussex, a public house, kept by William Scardefield, whither they carried Chater all over blood, and with his eyes almost beat out ; and also brought the body of Galley. They obliged Scardefield to shew them a proper place for the burial of Galley ; and accordingly he went with Carter, Howard, and Steel, to an old fox earth, on the side of a hill near Rake, at a place called Harting Coombe, where they dug a hole and buried Galley.

" The same morning, and long before it was light, whilst some were employed in the burial of Galley, Jackson and Sheerman carried Chater to the house of Richard Mills the elder, at Trotton.

" I am now come to the third period of time : from Chater's arrival at the house of Richard Mills the elder, to his murder upon Wednesday night, the 17th of February.

"And here it is that Richard Mills the elder appears to be privy and consenting to the intended murder of Chater. A private house was thought much more

proper and safe for the confinement of Chater, than a
public house, at all times open to every man; and
therefore Chater was to be removed from Scardefield's.
The prisoners and their companions being no strangers
to Old Mills, but his intimate acquaintance, and confederates in smuggling; where could Chater be so
secretly imprisoned, as at the private house of the elder
Mills? and where could he be more securely guarded
than under the roof of one of their gang? With these
hopes and reliance, and in full confidence of the secresy
and assistance of Old Mills, Chater was brought to his
house by Jackson and Sheerman. When they came
there, they told Old Mills they had got a prisoner; he
must get up and let them in; upon which Old Mills
got up, and received Chater as his prisoner, whose face
was then a gore of blood, many of his teeth beat out,
his eyes swelled and one almost destroyed. I shall
here omit one or two particular circumstances, which
the witnesses will give an account of; which shew that
Old Mills was also void of all tenderness and compassion.

" Chater was received by him as a prisoner, and a
criminal; and therefore was to be treated as such. Old
Mills's house itself was thought too good a prison for
him; and therefore he was soon dragged into a skilling
or out-house, adjoining to the house, wherein lumber
and fuel was kept. And although Chater was in so
week and deplorable a condition as to be scarce able to
stand, yet to prevent all chance and possibility of his
escape, he was chained by the leg with an iron chain,
fastened to a beam of the out-house; he was guarded
night and day, sometimes by Sheerman, and sometimes
by Howard, who came there that Monday evening.
Thus he continued in chains until he was loosened for
his execution. But lest he should die for want of

sustenance, and disappoint their wicked designs, he was to be fed and just kept alive, until the time and manner of his death was determined. During the whole time of this imprisonment, Old Mills was at home and in his business as usual. He betrayed not the trust reposed in him. He acquainted nobody with what had happened, nor with whom he was entrusted; but like a gaoler, took care to produce his prisoner for execution.

" On Wednesday, the 17th of February, there was a general summons of all the smugglers then in the neighbourhood, at Scardefield's house, who had been concerned in breaking open the custom house at Poole, to meet that day at Scardefield's. Upon which notice, all the prisoners (except Old Mills) came that day to Scardefield's. And there were also present John Mills, another son of Old Mills, Edmund Richards, Thomas Willis, Thomas Stringer, Daniel Perryer, William Steel and John Race; Howard and Sheerman still continuing at Old Mills's, and there guarding Chater. It was at this consultation at Scardefield's unanimously agreed by all present that Chater should be murdered.

" This was a deliberate, serious, and determined act of minds wickedly and cruelly disposed, and executed with all the imaginable circumstances of barbarity.

" At this meeting Tapner, Cobby and Hammond were first concerned in, and became privy and consenting to, this murder. And there also Richard Mills the younger first became an accessary to this murder; but he was so eager in pursuit of it, that he particularly advised and recommended it; and said he would go with them to the execution, but he had no horse. And when he was told that the old man (meaning Chater) was carried by a steep place in the road to Rake, he said—'If I had been there, I should have called a council of war, and he should have come no farther.'

" About eight o'clock on that Wednesday evening, all who were present at the consultation at Scardefield's (except Richard Mills the younger, John Mills and Thomas Willis) went from Scardefield's to the house of Old Mills, where they found Chater chained, and guarded by Howard and Sheerman.

" They told him he must die, and ordered him to say his prayers. And whilst he was upon his knees at prayers, Cobby kicked him ; and Tapner, impatient of Chater's blood, pulled out a large clasp knife, and swore he would be his butcher, and cut him twice or thrice down the face, and across the eyes and nose. But Old Mills in hopes of avoiding the punishment due to his guilt, by shifting Chater's execution to another place, said—' Don't murder him here : carry him somewhere else first.'

" He was then loosened from his chains, and was by all the prisoners (except Mills the father and his son), and by all the gang that came from Scardefield's, carried back to that well, wherein Galley had before been threatened to be thrown alive. Jackson and Carter left the company some small distance before the others came to the well ; but described the well to be fenced round with pales and directed them where to find it ; and said—' We have done our parts,' meaning we have murdered Galley ; ' and you shall do yours,' meaning you shall murder Chater.

" Tapner, in order to make good what he had before said, after Chater had been forced over the pales which fenced the well, pulled a rope out of his pocket, put it about Chater's neck, fastened the other end to the pales, and there he hung Chater in the well until he was dead, as they all imagined.

"They then loosened the cord from the rail of the pales, and let him fall to the bottom of this well, which was dry; and one of the accomplices imagined he heard Chater breathe, and that there were still some remains of life in him.

"To put an end to a life so miserable and wretched, they threw pales and stones upon him. This was the only act that had any appearance of mercy and compassion ; and it brings to my remembrance the saying of the wisest of men, fully verified in this fatal instance of Chater's murder—'The mercies of the wicked are cruelties.'

"I am now come to the fourth and last period of time.

"And here it is observable, that although Providence had for many months permitted this murder to remain undiscovered, yet it was then disclosed and brought to light when the appointed time was come, and an opportunity given to apprehend and bring to justice many of the principal offenders.

"Upon the 17th of September last, search was made in pursuance of information given, for the body of Chater. And the body was found with a rope about its neck, covered with pales, stones and earth, in that well I have before mentioned, close by Lady Holt Park, in a wood called Harrass Wood belonging to Mr. Carryll.

"By the length of time, from February to September, the body was too much emaciated to be known with any certainty. But by his boots, clothes and belt, there also found, it evidently appeared to be the body of the unfortunate Chater.

"I have now opened to you the substance of all the most material facts : and should the proofs support the truth of those facts, no man can doubt the consequence thereof, that Chater was murdered, and the prisoners were his murderers."

Mr. Smith, another of the King's counsel, also spoke as follows, viz. :—

"The crime they are charged with is one of the greatest that can be committed against the laws of God and man, and in this particular case attended with the most aggravated circumstances.

"It was not done in the heat of passion, and on provocation, but in cold blood, deliberately, on the fullest consideration, in the most cruel manner, and without any provocation. The occasion being as you have heard, only because he dared to speak the truth.

"This prosecution, therefore, is of the utmost importance to the public justice of the nation, and to the safety and security of every person; for if such offenders should escape with impunity, the consequence would be, that no crime could be punished. It would teach highwaymen and all other criminals, to unite in the manner those men have done, and whoever received injuries from them would not dare to take any steps towards bringing them to justice, for fear of exposing themselves to the revenge of their companions.

"Our constitution, therefore, which must be supported by a regular administration of justice, and a due execution of our laws, depends, in some measure, on bringing such offenders to condign punishment; and it is to be hoped a few examples of this kind will restore the peace and tranquillity of this county.

"In stating the facts, I shall point out to you the share which every one of the persons at the bar had in this murder.

"In October, 1747, the custom-house at Poole was

broken open; the smugglers who did it, on their return, passed through Fordingbridge, where Chater saw Dimer among them; and having declared so was obliged to make oath of it; on which information Dimer was committed to goal for further examination : and on the 14th of February, Chater was sent by the collector of Southampton, in company with Galley, with a letter to Mr. Battine, Surveyor General of the customs, in order that Chater might see if the man in goal was the same person he saw at Fordingbridge.

" These two men, having enquired their way at the New Inn at Leigh, one Jenkes undertook to direct them, and carried them to widow Payne's, at Rowland's Castle, who saying she feared they were going to do the smugglers some mischief, sent for Carter and Jackson, Steel, Race, Richards, Sheerman and Howard, who, having made Galley and Chater drunk, and seen the letter to Mr. Battine, consulted what to do with them. Some proposed to murder them, others to send them prisoners to France, and others to confine them, till they saw what had become of Dimer, and to treat them as he was dealt with.

" Having sent Jenkes away, these poor men were left absolutely in the power of the smugglers; and indeed, into worse hands they could not have fallen; had they been taken in battle they would have had quarter, and been treated with humanity; had they fallen into the hand of enemies of those nations who give no quarter, their lot would have been immediate death; but as it was their hard fate to fall into the hands of smugglers, to have neither quarter or immediate death, but they were reserved to suffer the most cruel usage for several days and afterwards murdered.

" These poor wretches, after having been beat and

abused at Payne's by Carter and Jackson, and the rest of the gang, were carried away by force, both set on one horse, with their legs tied under the horse's belly, and whipt and beat by direction of Carter and Jackson, till they fell; then they were set up again in the same manner, and whipt and beat again, till they fell a second time; and were then set on separate horses, and used in the same manner, till Galley had the good fortune to be delivered by death from their cruelty; after which they carried Chater, who was bloody and mangled with the blows and falls he had received, to Scardefield's, at the Red Lion at Rake, who observed Jackson's coat and hands bloody; and while Carter and the rest buried Galley, Jackson and Sheerman carried Chater to old Mills's in the night, between the 14th and 15th of February, where he was chained by the leg in the skilling, or out-house, till the Wednesday night following, and Sheerman and Howard guarded him.

" Imagine to yourselves the condition of this unhappy man, certain to die by their hands, uncertain only as to the time, and the cruel manner of it: suffering for three days and three nights pain, cold and hunger; and what was infinitely worse, that terror and anxiety of mind which one in his situation must continually labour under; he must doubtless envy the condition of his companion Galley, who by an early death was delivered from the misery he then endured.

" On Wednesday following, the 17th of February, all the prisoners at the bar (except Old Mills) met at Scardefield's, and there were present also seven more; at which meeting it was unanimously agreed by all present to murder Chater; and Young Mills particularly advised it; and said if he had a horse he would go with them and do it; and either then, or at another meeting at

Scardefield's, when Carter and Jackson said, that as
they came along, they brought Chater by a steep place
thirty feet deep, Young Mills said, 'If I had been there I
would have called a council of war, and he should have
come no further.'

" This being determined, the prisoners Tapner, Cobby,
Hammond, Carter and Jackson, together with five more
of that company went to Old Mills's, where they found
Chater chained and guarded by Sheerman and Howard,
and told him he must die ; he said he expected no other.
Tapner then said he would be his butcher, and, taking
out a knife, cut him across the eyes and nose ; on which
Old Mills said, ' Don't murder him here, but take him
somewhere else first.'

" Tapner, Cobby, Hammond, Carter, Jackson, and the
rest, who came there together, with Sheerman and
Howard, then carried him away to murder him : Sheerman, Howard and Richards, having been concerned in
Galley's murder, said the rest should kill Chater, and
therefore went away to Harting ; Carter and Jackson
having been likewise concerned in Galley's murder,
when they came to Lady Holt Park Gate, turned in
there, and left the others ; having first told them, ' The
well is a little way off, you can't miss it ; 'tis fenced
round with pales, to keep the cattle from falling in.'

" Tapner, Cobby, Hammond, Carter, Jackson, and the
rest, went then to the well, where Tapner put a rope
round Chater's neck to hang him ; and some of the
pales being broken down, Chater would have crept
through. Tapner would not let him, but made him climb
over the pales, weak as he was, and then hanged him in
the well about a quarter of an hour, till they thought
him dead ; then having drawn him up till they could
take hold of his legs, they threw him headlong into the

well; and fancying they heard him breathe or groan, threw posts and stones in upon him, and went their way.

" The terror of this act of cruelty had spread through the country, stopt every person's mouth who had it in their power to give any information ; so that the body was not found till September, when it was so putrified and consumed as not to be known but by the belt, and which Chater's wife will prove to be her husband's. If there was any doubt as to the identity of the man, we could shew likewise, that being examined by the smugglers just before he was murdered, he said his name was Daniel Chater.

" It appears therefore from this state of the case that all the prisoners are guilty of the indictment ; Tapner was present at the consultation at Scardefield's, and was the person who hanged him ; Cobby and Hammond were present at the consultation, helped to carry him to the well, and were present at the murder, and therefore equally guilty with Tapner as principals ; Carter and Jackson took him away by force from Payne's, and the treatment of him there on the road shewed an intention from the first to murder him, though perhaps the particular death he was to suffer was not then agreed on. They were afterwards present at the consultation at Scardefield's, where it was resolved to murder him, and went almost to the well with him ; and when they parted, gave those who murdered him particular directions to the well. Young Mills was also at the consultation, and particularly advised and directed the murder, in which he declared he would have joined if he had a horse. Old Mills, though he kept no public-house, receives this man brought in the night, in a bloody and deplorable condition. Chater is chained in his out-house from Sunday night till Wednesday ; yet

Old Mills never discovers it to any person, or uses any means to deliver him, which is a strong evidence of his knowledge of their design; and when Tapner declared he would be his butcher and cut him, Old Mills expresses no disapprobation of the murder, does not dissuade him from it, but desires him ' not to do it there, but carry him somewhere else first,' which shews his approbation of the fact; though to secure himself he would have had it committed at some other place.

" This, gentlemen, is the fact, which shews that securing themselves and their companions was not their principal aim; were it so, they would have murdered this man as soon as they had him in their power; but their motive seems to have been revenge, and a disposition to torture one who should dare to give any information which might bring them or their friends into danger.

"After hearing the whole evidence, if these men appear innocent, God forbid they should be found guilty; and I would not have the cruel circumstances of the fact incline you to believe anything we suggest that is not supported by the strongest proof; but if the fact is proved beyond a possibility of doubt to be in the manner we have stated it, I am sure you will do your duty, and by a just and honest verdict deliver your country from men so void of humanity."

The king's counsel having finished what they had to premise, proceeded to call the witnesses for the crown in support of the charge; the first witness called was Mr. Milner, collector of the customs at Poole, who deposed that about the 17th of October, 1747, he had advice that the custom-house was broken open; upon which he hastened thither, and found the outer door burst open, and the other door broken in pieces; that the room wherein some run tea was lodged, that was taken by Captain Johnson, was broken open, and all the tea carried away, excepting a little bag containing about four or five pounds.

Mr. Shearer, collector of the customs at Southampton, was next called, who deposed that in February last he received a letter from the commissioners of the customs, acquainting him that one John Dimer was committed to Chichester gaol on suspicion of breaking open the custom-house at Poole, with directions to send the deceased Daniel Chater, who could give some information against Dimer, to Justice Battine, the Surveyor-General, and to acquaint Justice Battine with the occasion of his sending Chater; that he accordingly sent Chater with a letter addressed to Justice Battine, under the care of one William Galley, a tidesman in the port of Southampton; that they set out on Sunday morning, the 14th of February last. He could not take upon him to say how Chater was dressed, but he remembered he rode upon a dark brown horse, and had a great coat on, with another coat under it, and upon the under coat a belt; he could not recollect how Galley was dressed, but remembered that he was mounted upon a grey horse.

The next witness called and sworn was William Galley, the son of the deceased William Galley, who deposed that he remembered his father's setting out upon this journey to Justice Battine, in February last; that he saw the letter to Justice Battine the night before his father set out, and saw the directions; he remembered the dress his father had on: it was a blue great coat, with brass buttons covered with blue, a close bodied coat, of a light brown colour, lined with blue, with a waistcoat and breeches of the same, and that he rode on a grey horse; he remembered that Daniel Chater, a shoemaker at Fordingbridge, set out at the same time with his father, and had on a light surtout coat, with red breeches, and a belt round him, and rode upon a brown horse; that this was the last time he ever saw his father alive, and that he never saw Chater since.

Edward Holton was next called and sworn, who deposed that on the 14th of February last he saw Daniel Chater and another person, whom he took to be Mr. Galley, at his own house at Havant, in the county of Hants; that he knew Chater very well, and had some conversation with him; that Chater told him he was going to Chichester upon a little business, and then went out to Galley, and brought in a letter, which was directed to William Battine, Esq., at East Marden; upon which he (the witness) told him he was going out of the way; Galley wished he would direct them the way, that he directed them to go through Stanstead, near Rowland's Castle; and that they said they should be back again the next day.

George Austin being called and sworn, deposed that on Sunday, the 14th of February last, he saw two men, one mounted on a brown horse and the other on a grey, at the New Inn at Leigh, in the parish of Havant; that they came to the New Inn when he was there and enquired the way to East Marden, to which place he was going to direct them, when one of the men who had a blue coat on, pulled a letter out of his pocket, which he (the witness) looked at, and seeing it was directed to Justice Battine at East Marden, he told them they were going ten miles out of their way, and that he and his brother, Thomas Austin, and his brother-in-law, Robert Jenkes, were going part of their road, and would

conduct them the best they could; that they went no
further together than to a place called Rowland's
Castle, to a public house which was kept by the widow
Payne; the two strangers, Galley and Chater, called for
rum at the widow Payne's. This was about the middle
of the day, or something after. That the widow Payne
asked him if he knew these men, or whether they
belonged to his company; he told her they were going
to Justice Battine's, and that he was going to shew
them the way; she then said she thought they were
going to do harm to the smugglers, and desired him
to set them out of the way; which he refused. She
then seemed uneasy, and she and her son consulted
together; that her son went out, and the prisoner
Jackson came in a little time; that the prisoner
Carter and several more came thither soon
afterwards. He knew none but Jackson and
Carter*. That Jackson enquired where the two men
were bound for, and the man in the light coat answered
they were going to Justice Battine's, and from thence
to Chichester: but Carter was not by at that time; that
Galley and Chater had some rum, and Jackson called
for a mug of hot—which was gin and beer mixed, or
something of that kind—to the best of his knowledge
they all drank together; he did not see any ill-
treatment, nor either of the men bloody whilst he was
there; that he went away between two and three, and
left the two men there; the widow Payne called him
out of doors, and told him his brother Jenkes wanted
to speak to him; when he came out his horse was at
the hedge by the back door, and his brother said he

---

* The other five prisoners were not at Rowland's Castle, so
that Mr. Austin could have no knowledge of them.

wondered why the two men did not go away; upon which he went back again into the house, and his brother was uneasy because he did so; that the widow Payne advised him to go home, and said the two men would be directed the way: he was uneasy at going without them, because he saw so many men come in, and imagined they had a design to do some harm to them; that when he went away, Jackson and Carter were left with the two men, Galley and Chater, to the best of his knowledge; and Jackson, as well as the widow Payne, persuaded him to go home, saying it would be better for him. He was positive that Jackson and Carter were there, for he knew them very well.

The Court asked Jackson and Carter if they would ask the witness any questions,

To which they both answered they had no questions to ask him.

Thomas Austin was then called, who deposed that he was at the New Inn at Leigh on Valentine's Day last, with his brother George, where he saw two men who enquired the way to Justice Battine's; he went from thence with them to Rowland's Castle; they went to the widow Payne's at that place, and called for a dram of rum; the prisoners were not there at first, but in a little time Jackson came, and soon afterwards the prisoner Carter. That the widow Payne spoke to him at the outer door before either of the prisoners came and asked him if he knew the two men, and said she was afraid they were come to do the smugglers some mischief, and that she would send for William Jackson; accordingly her son went for him, and he soon came, and another little man and his servant. This witness further deposed that he saw in the house one Joseph Southern and the prisoner

Carter, but that Carter did not come so soon as Jackson. That Jackson struck one of the men who had a blue coat on, but they were all soon appeased, and then they all drank very freely, and he was drunk and went to sleep, and the two men were fuddled and went to sleep in the little room ; that about seven o'clock Jackson went into the room and waked the two men ; after they came out, the two men were taken away by Jackson and Carter, and one William Steel and Edmund Richards ; but he did not remember they were forced away, and did not see them upon the horses, nor did he ever see them any more ; this was between seven and eight o'clock.

Being asked whether he saw either of the men produce his deputation or heard any high words,

He said he did not ; that he was asleep the best part of the afternoon, and did not see any ill-treatment, but that one blow which he had mentioned.

Being cross-examined at the request of the prisoners,

He deposed that he did not know who the two strangers were, but they were the same two persons that his brother George had just spoken of, and had a letter for Justice Battine ; that one of them had a blue coat on, and rode upon a grey horse, and the other man rode upon a brownish horse ; that he did not see the direction of the letter, but he heard it read by Robert Jenkes.

The next witness produced was Robert Jenkes, who came with the two deceased men from Leigh to this house, along with George and Thomas Austin, who, being sworn, deposed : that he saw two men upon 14th February last, at the New Inn at Leigh, one of them upon a brownish horse, the other upon a grey, and dressed in riding coats ; that they were the same men that the witnesses George and Thomas Austin had spoken of; that they all went together to Rowland's Castle, and got there about twelve o'clock, and went into a house there which was kept by the widow Payne. He did not hear her give any directions to send for anybody; but the prisoners Carter and Jackson soon came thither; that whilst he was there he did not see any abuse, or observe that either of them were bloody, and that he had no conversation with Jackson further than that Jackson said he would see the letter which was going to Major Battine, and Carter, he believed, might say so too; when he wanted to go away, Jackson would not suffer him to go through the room where the two men were (for the two men were carried into another room), but Jackson told him if he had a mind to go, he might go through the garden to the back part of the house where his horse should be led ready for him; that he did so, and found his horse there and went away.

Being now particularly asked if he could say why Jackson refused his going through the room where the two men were, he answered he could not be certain, but believed it was for fear the two men should go away with him; and that he did not order his horse to be led round to the garden himself; and that George Austin and he went away together upon his horse, and that Jackson declared he would see the letter one of the men had in his pocket; and the witness saw the direction of it was William Battine, Esq., at East Marden.

Being cross examined by the prisoner Carter, whether Carter said he would see the letter, he answered that both Carter and Jackson said they would see the letter for Justice Battine; that he (the witness) did not order his horse to be carried to the back part of the house; and that Carter was by, when he was told by Jackson, that if he had a mind to go, his horse should be led to the back part of the house.

Joseph Southern deposed that on Sunday, the 14th February last, he saw Jenkes, the two Austins, and two other men coming from Havant towards Rowland's Castle. One of them had a blue coat on, and rode a grey horse; and he went to Rowland's Castle himself that day, and saw Jenkes, the two Austins, and the same two men sitting on horseback, drinking at the widow Payne's door; he stayed there best part of an hour, and saw them and several other persons in the house; that he saw Carter and Jackson in the house whilst he stayed there; he sat down and drank a pint of beer by the kitchen fire, but the other persons were in another room; that he saw the two men come out to the door and go in again, and one of them had an handkerchief over his eye, and there was blood upon it; that he met this man as he was going in, and heard him say to Jackson, " I am the King's officer, and I will take notice of you that struck me." That Carter was not present when this was said, but was in the house: the man who spoke thus to Jackson had a parchment in his hand; he likewise saw a letter in his hand, and heard him say he was going to Justice Battine with it; that he (the witness) went away between two and three o'clock, and did not know what became of the letter, nor had he heard either Jackson or Carter say what became of it.

This being all Mr. Southern had to say, and Jackson and Carter, though asked particularly if they would have him asked any questions, saying they had none, he was set down.

William Garret deposed that he was at the widow Payne's on the 14th of February last, and saw Jackson and Carter and two strangers there ; that one of them who had a blue coat on, had received a stroke upon his cheek, and the blood run down just as he came in ; this man was standing up by the back of a chair, and Jackson by him, and he heard Jackson say, "that for a quartern of gin he would serve him so again," by which he understood that Jackson had struck him before. He did not hear the man say he was the King's officer, but he heard Jackson say, "You a King's officer ! I'll make you a King's officer, and that you shall know." Then when he went away he left them all there.

The prisoners would not ask this witness any questions.

The next witness produced was William Lamb, who being sworn, deposed, that he went to the widow Payne's, at Rowland's Castle, on the 14th of February last, about four in the afternoon, and found Jackson and Carter there ; that before he went he saw one of the widow Payne's sons call Carter aside, at his house at Westbourne ; that there were several other people there (Rowland's Castle) in another room, amongst whom were Thomas Austin and two men that were strangers to him, one of whom had on a blue great coat. He further deposed that the two men who were strangers he understood were going with a letter to Justice Battine ; but that he saw no ill-treatment during the little time he stayed there. He said that during the time he was there Edmund Richards, one of the company, pulled out a pistol, and said that whoever should discover any thing that passed at that house, he would blow his brains out. But that Jackson and Carter, two of the prisoners, were not in the room when these words were spoken, as he verily believes. He saw, he said, the man in the blue great coat, pull a parchment out of his pocket, and he heard him tell the people he was the King's officer; his wig was then off, and there was blood upon his cheek; that he saw a letter, which he understood to be going to Mr. Battine; and Kelly and the prisoner Carter had it in their hands, but he did not know how they came by it; that he did not see the direction of the letter; but he observed it was broken open when he saw it in the hands of Carter and Kelly, and he understood, by the discourse of the company, that it was a letter which the two strangers were to carry to Mr. Battine, but he never heard it read.

The prisoners Carter and Jackson would not ask him any questions.

Richard Kent deposed, that he was at the widow Payne's on the 14th of February; that he saw Jackson and Carter, and many others, particularly two strangers, who he supposed were Galley and Chater; that they took the strangers out with them, and that Edmund Richards told him that if he spoke a word of what he had heard or seen he would shoot him; but Jackson and Carter were not in the room when Richards said this.

George Poate deposed that he was at Rowland's Castle on Sunday, the 14th of February last, about seven o'clock in the evening, and saw nine men there; Jackson and Carter were two of them; he stayed there about half an hour, and as soon as he came in he saw four or five men with great coats and boots on, most of them upon their legs, as if they were just going; he went and warmed himself by the kitchen fire, and soon after he heard the stroke of a whip, repeated three or four times, in a little room that was at the corner of the kitchen, but did not see who gave the blows, nor

who received them ; that he afterwards heard a strange
rustling of people, more than before, and saw seven or
eight men come into the kitchen; that he knew Jackson
and Carter, and William Steel, Edmund Richards, and
two that went by the names of Little Sam and Little
Harry; there were two other persons there, whom to
his knowledge he had never seen before or since, and
could give no account of them, nor did he observe how
they were dressed; that soon after he thought he heard
a blow, and saw Jackson in a moving posture, as if he
had just given a blow, and was drawing up his arm in
a proper form, as if he was going to give another; but
William Payne stepped up, and called him a fool and a
blockhead for so doing; upon which he sunk his arm,
and did not behave in a like manner any more in his
sight; that just as they were going out of doors, Jackson
turned round with a pistol in his hand, and asked for a
belt, or string, but nobody gave him either, and he put
his pistol into his pocket, and went away with the rest;
that by the trampling of horses he supposed they all
went on horseback, but which way he knew not; it
was between seven and eight o'clock, as nigh as he could
guess, when they went off; he did not hear any conversation about one of the strangers being a King's officer,
nor did he see the blow given, nor the person to whom
the other blow was going to be given.

The prisoners Jackson and Carter said they had no
questions to ask this witness.

Then his Majesty's counsel desired that John Raise,
otherwise Race, he being an accessary to the fact, should
be called, who appearing and being sworn, deposed, that
on Sunday, the 14th of February, he was at Rowland's
Castle between twelve and one o'clock at noon; that when
he came there he found Edmund Richards, William Steel,

the prisoners Carter, Jackson, and Little Sam, Richard Kelly, Jackson's wife, and Galley and Chater; he saw Jackson take Chater to the door, and heard him ask him if he knew anything of Dimer the shepherd, and Chater answered he did, and was obliged to go and speak against him; that Galley then went out to keep Chater from talking to Jackson; whereupon Jackson knocked Galley down with his fist; that Galley came in again, and soon after Jackson and Carter. When they were all come in, he (the witness) with the prisoners Jackson and Carter, and Edmund Richards, went into the back room; that there they enquired of Jackson what he had got out of the shoemaker (meaning Daniel Chater); that Jackson informed them that Chater said he knew Dimer and was obliged to come in as a witness against him; that then they consulted what to do with them (Chater and Galley)—this was about three o'clock in the afternoon : they first proposed to carry them to some secure place, where they might be taken care of till they had an opportunity of carrying them over to France; and that when this proposition was made, the prisoners Jackson and Carter, and Richards and himself were present. This resolution was taken to send them out of the way, that Chater should not appear against Dimer; and afterwards it was agreed to fetch a horse and carry them away; that Galley and Chater appeared very uneasy, and wanted to be gone; and thereupon Jackson's wife, to pacify them, told them that she lived at Major Battine's and her horse was gone for, and as soon as it came she would shew them the way to Mr. Battine's; that he (the witness) then went away, and saw no more of them that night.

Being cross examined at the request of the defendant's counsel, he said, " At this consultation there was nothing mentioned, as he remembered then, but the securing them in order to carry them to France."

This witness having gone thus far in his evidence, was set by for the present; the counsel for the crown declaring that they would call him again, to give an account of what passed on the 17th, when Chater was murdered, after they had examined the next witness.

Then William Steel, one of the accomplices in both the murders from beginning to end, was sworn, who deposed that he was sent for to the widow Payne's on Sunday, the 14th of February; that Jackson, Little Sam, one Kelly, and two men more, and Jackson's wife, were there when he came, which was about two o'clock in the afternoon, and soon afterwards Little Harry, Carter, Edmund Richards, John Race, the last witness, and Carter's wife came thither; he said he did not know how Carter or Jackson came to be there, but the widow Payne's son came and called him out, and said he must go to the Castle, his mother's, for there were two men come to swear against the shepherd; that when he came in he found the two strangers, Galley and Chater, and Jackson, Carter, Richards, and some others; and that they were in general sober, but they sat drinking together about two hours; that Jackson took Chater out of the house to examine him about Dimer; and after they had been out some time, Galley went out to them, but soon returned, and said Jackson had knocked him down; the witness saw he was bloody all down the left cheek; that Jackson was not in the room when Galley came in, but came in with Carter a little time afterwards; that then Galley, addressing himself to Jackson, said he did not know any occasion Jackson had to use him in that manner, and that he should remember it, and took down his name in Jackson's presence. Galley likewise said he was an officer, and shewed his deputation to the people that were in the room.

This witness, continuing his deposition, said Galley and Chater began to be very uneasy, and wanted to be going, but that the prisoners Jackson and Carter, and the rest of them that were smugglers, persuaded them to stay, and be pacified, and all things should be set right; and the company continued drinking till Galley and Chater were quite fuddled, and were carried into a little inner room to sleep; this was about four or five o'clock, and they continued in the little room two or three hours; the rest of the company sat drinking all the while, consulting what to do with Galley and Chater. The prisoners Jackson and Carter, and Little Sam, Little Harry, Richards, and the witness were at the consultation. It was proposed to put them (Galley and Chater) out of the way, because they should not appear against the shepherd, meaning Dimer; after which it was proposed to throw them into the well in the horse pasture, about a quarter of a mile from Rowland's Castle, but that it was thought not convenient to put them into a well so near, for fear of discovery.

Here the question was particularly asked Steel, the witness, which of them it was that proposed the murdering them directly and flinging them afterwards down the well; to which he replied, he believed he might.

After this it was next proposed to join and each man to allow them threepence a week, and to keep them in some secret place till they saw what became of Dimer, and as Dimer was served, so these two people (Chater and Galley) were to be served. This was talked of

while Chater and Galley were asleep and there was no
other proposal made as he heard at that time : but
while they were talking of these things, the wives of
Carter and Jackson said it was no matter what became
of them (Galley and Chater), or what was to be done
with them ; they ought to be hanged, for they were
come to ruin them, meaning the smugglers. He then
said that about seven o'clock Carter and Jackson went
into the inner room and waked Galley and Chater, and
brought them out of the room very bloody and very
drunk ; he did not see what passed in the room, but
was sure they did not go in so bloody, and he believed
Jackson and Carter had kicked and spurred them, for
they had put on their boots and spurs ; that then
Jackson and Carter brought them (Galley and Chater)
out into the kitchen ; and took them through to the
street door all very bloody, when they set Galley the
officer upon a brown or black horse and Chater up
behind him ; that Jackson, Carter and Richards put
them on horseback, and tied their legs under the horse's
belly and also their legs together ; then they tied a line
to the bridle, and he (the witness) got upon a grey
horse and led them along ; that just after they had
turned round the corner about 70 or 80 yards from the
house, Jackson cried out " Whip them, lick the dogs,
cut them." It was then dark, and the company
whipped and lashed them with their horse-whips, some
on one side and some on the other with great violence,
on the face and head and other parts of the body, and
continued doing so while they rode about half a mile to
a place called Woodash, or Wood's Ashes ; that there
they alighted and Little Sam gave all the company a
dram or two, but none to Galley and Chater ; that as
they were mounted again Jackson and Carter cried out,

of Aldsworth,

William Jackson   b. Hampshire,
b. circa 1699   1871
(Roman Catholic)   d. 16th January 1749
visited the
White Hart at Rowlands Castle

Callum (mobile)
07736 945525

"D...n them, lick them, whip them," and they were whipped as before for about a mile further, and then they fell down under the horse's belly, with their heads upon the ground and their legs over the saddle; upon which Jackson and Carter and some of the others of the gang dismounted and untied Galley and Chater, and immediately set them up again, and their legs were tied together in the same posture, and the company went on whipping them as before till they came to a place called Dean,* which was about half a mile further. They were beat very much, and in the judgment of the witness, it was almost impossible they should sit their horses; that when they came to Dean somebody of the company pulled out a pistol and said he would shoot them (Galley and Chater) through the head, if they made any noise whilst they went through the village. He could not tell who it was that threatened to shoot them, but apprehends it was done for fear the people in the village should hear them. They went on at a foot pace, and after they got through Dean they were whipped again as before; and when they came near a place called Idsworth, they fell down again under the horse's belly, and then some of the company loosed them, and set up the officer (Galley) behind him (the witness), and Chater behind Little Sam, and in this manner they proceeded towards Lady Holt Park, which is near three miles from Idsworth, whipping Galley and Chater as before. But the lashes of their whips falling upon the witness as he sat before Galley, he (the witness) could not bear the strokes, and therefore he cried out, and then they left off whipping Galley in that manner.

---

* The name of the place is Goodthrop Dean, a little village.

This witness further said that Galley sat upon the horse till they got to Lady Holt Park, and then being faint and tired with riding, he got down; and then Carter and Jackson took him, one by the arms and the other by the legs, carried him towards a well called Harris's Well by the side of Lady Holt Park; and then Jackson said to Carter " We'll throw him in the well," to which Carter replied " With all my heart;" and Galley seemed very indifferent what they did with him; but some of the company saying 'twas a pity to throw him into the well, Jackson and Carter set him up behind the witness again and Chater was still behind Little Sam. They went on in this manner till they came to go down a hill, when Galley was faint and tired, and could not ride any further and got down there; upon which Carter and Jackson laid him on a horse before Edmund Richards, with his belly upon the pommel of the saddle. They laid him across the horse because he was so bad that they could not contrive to carry him in any other manner, and they carried him so for about a mile and a half from the well; that then Richards, being tired of holding him, let him down by the side of the horse; and Carter and Jackson put him upon the grey horse that he (the witness) was upon, and the witness got off. They set him up, his legs across the saddle and his body lay over the horse's mane; that in this posture Jackson held him on and he did not remember that anybody else held him at that time; that they went on for about half a mile in this manner, Galley crying out all the time " Barbarous usage! barbarous usage! for God's sake shoot me through the head or through the body." He (the witness) thought Jackson was at this time pinching him by the private parts, for there were no blows given when he cried so;

that Chater was still with the company behind Little Sam, and they went on for about two miles and a half further, the company holding Galley by turns on the horse until they came to a dirty lane, at which place Carter and Jackson rode forwards, and bid the rest of the company stop at the swing gate beyond the water till they should return. Jackson and Carter left them here and went to see for a place proper for taking care of Chater and Galley, but soon came to them again at the swing gate and told them that the man of the house whither they went was ill and that they could not go thither, by which he understood that they had been in the neighbourhood to get entertainment. It was then proposed to go forward to one Scardefield's, and Little Harry tied Galley with a cord and got up on horseback behind him in order to hold him up on the horse, and they went on till they came to a gravelly knap in the road at which place Galley cried out " I shall fall! I shall fall!" whereupon Little Harry said, " D...n you, then fall," and gave him a push, and Galley fell down and gave a spirt, and never spoke a word more. He (the witness) believed his neck was broke by the fall; that they laid him across the horse again and went away for Rake to the sign of the Red Lion, which was kept by William Scardefield; that Chater was behind Little Sam and was carried to Scardefield's house and was very bloody when they came to Scardefield's; that Jackson and Little Harry went from Scardefield's with Chater about three o'clock in the morning and Jackson afterwards returned to Scardefield's and said he had left Chater at Old Mills's, and that Little Harry was left to look after him that he might not escape. This was Monday, the 15th of February, and they remained all that day at Scardefield's; that the prisoner

Richard Mills the younger was there on that day, and upon hearing from Jackson and Carter that they had passed by a precipice thirty feet deep when they had Chater with them, he said, " If I had been there I would have called a council of war on the spot, and he (Chater) should have gone no further," or to that effect.

That two or three days afterwards the company met at Scardefield's again, to consult what to do with Chater ; that the prisoners John Race, Carter and Jackson, the prisoner Richard Mills the younger (a son of the prisoner Richard Mills the elder), Thomas Willis, John Mills (another son of old Mills), the prisoners Tapner, Cobby, Hammond, and Thomas Stringer, Edmund Richards, and Daniel Perryer, and he (the witness) were consulting what to do with Chater, and John Mills* proposed to take him out, and load a gun, and tie a string to the trigger, and place him (Chater) against the gun, and that they should all of them pull the string, to involve every one of them in the same degree of guilt ; but this proposal was not agreed to.   Then Jackson and Carter proposed to carry him back to the well near Lady Holt Park, and to murder him there, which was agreed to by all the company ; but Richard Mills the younger and John Mills said they could not go with them to the well, because they had no horses ; and as it was in their (the other persons') way home, they might do it as well without them ; and so it was concluded to murder Chater, and then throw him into the well.

As soon as it was agreed amongst them to murder Chater and fling him down the well, they went away

---

* The witness was not certain whether it was John Mills, or his brother Richard Mills, that made the proposal.

for Rake to the house of the prisoner Richard Mills the
elder, and found Chater in a back skilling or out-house,
run up at the back of Mills's house, a place they usually
put turf in; where they found him chained with an
iron chain to a beam in the skilling; that Chater was
bloody about the head, and had a cut upon one of his
eyes, so that he could not see with it : that the prisoner
Richard Mills the elder was at home, and fetched out
bread and cheese for them to eat, and gave them drink ;
that the house is a private house, no alehouse ; that
they all of them went to and again, between the house
and the skilling, and that the prisoner Richard Mills
the elder was at home all the while; that the prisoner
Tapner bid Chater go to prayers, and pulled out a large
clasp knife, and swore he would be his butcher ; and
while Chater was at prayers, he cut him across the eyes
and nose, and down his forehead, so that he bled to a
great degree. He was ordered by some others of the
company to say his prayers, for they were come to kill
him, and kill him they would ; and some of the company
were then in the skilling, and the rest of them were in
the house, but no one interposed to save his life ; that
he (the witness) was in the skilling when Chater was
advised to say his prayers and was cut, and that Chater
was chained by the leg at the time.

When they had kept him there as long as they
thought fit, someone unlocked the chain and set him on
horseback, and Race, Richards, Little Harry, Little
Sam, the prisoners Tapner, Stringer ; the prisoners
Cobby, Hammond and Perryer ; the prisoners Jackson,
Carter, and the witness, set out with him to Lady Holt
Park, to carry him down to the well ; that when they
came to a place called Harting, Richards, Little Harry
and Little Sam went back ; and when the rest came to

7

the white gate by Lady Holt Park, Carter and Jackson left them, but first told them they must keep along a little further, and they could not miss the well, for there were white pales; that it was about 200 yards further, some pales on the right hand of it, and that there were pales round the well. They went on, found the well by the direction given them, and carried Chater with them; that then Tapner, Hammond, Stringer and Cobby got off their horses, and Tapner pulled a cord out of his pocket, and put it about Chater's neck, and led him towards the well. Chater seeing two or three pales down said he could get through, but Tapner said, "No, you shall get over," and he did so with the rope about his neck; they then put him into the well and hanged him, winding the rope round the rails, and his body hung down in the mouth of the well for about a quarter of an hour; and then Stringer took hold of his legs to pull him aside, and let his head fall first into the well, and Tapner let the rope go, and down fell the body into the well head foremost; that they stayed there for some time, and one of the company said he thought he heard him breathe or groan; on this they listened, and being of the same opinion, went to one Combleach, a gardener, who was in bed, and asked him to lend them a ladder and a rope, for one of their company had fallen down the well; which he readily did, not thinking, as the witness verily believed, any otherwise. They brought the ladder with them, but as it was a long one they could not get it down the well through the hole in the breach of the pales; when they all tried to raise it up and put it over the pales; but then, not having strength sufficient, they laid that part of their design aside; and looking about them found a gate post or two, which they threw into the well and then left him.

Steel, the witness, being cross-examined as to this, said, he never heard the prisoner say he would not have them murder the man, and added, that he was sure he must hear them talk of murdering while they were at his house.

John Race being called again, said: That after he had left the company at the widow Payne's on the 14th of February, he met some of the same company and others, on the Wednesday evening following, being the 17th of February, at Scardefield's, at Rake; that the prisoners, Richard Mills the younger, Carter, Jackson, Tapner, Cobby, and Hammond, with Steel, Richards, Little Sam, Daniel Perryer, John Mills and Thomas Willis, were there; and it was proposed at that meeting to murder Chater. He could not say who first made the proposal, but to the best of his knowledge, it was either Carter or Jackson, and it was agreed to by all the company; it was not then resolved how it was to be done, but only in general, that he was to be murdered and thrown into a well; that they went to the house of Richard Mills the elder, to join Little Harry, who was left there to take care of Chater, and found Chater chained by the leg upon some turf in a skilling, at the back side of the house; that the prisoner, Richard Mills the elder, was at home, and ordered his housekeeper to fetch bread and cheese, and some household beer, for any of them to eat and drink that would, and was sure that old Mills knew that they came for Chater; that Tapner and Cobby were very earnest to go and see Chater; and Tapner having his knife in his hand, said, "This knife shall be his butcher"; and thereupon the prisoner, Richard Mills the elder said, "Pray do not murder him here, but carry him somewhere else before you do it"; that Old Mills said this on seeing that Tapner had his knife in his

hand, and hearing him declare it should be his (Chater's)
butcher; that they then went out into the skilling, and
found Chater sitting upon some turf, and Tapner
ordered him to say his prayers; whilst he was repeating
the Lord's Prayer, Tapner cut him over the face with
his knife, and Cobby stood by kicking and damning
him. This, too, was whilst the poor man was saying
the Lord's Prayer. That Chater asked them what was
become of Galley, and they told him he was murdered,
and that they were come to murder him. Upon which,
Chater earnestly begged to live another day; that Cobby
asked him his name, and whether he had not formerly
done harvest-work at Selsey? To which he answered
that his name was Daniel Chater, and that he had har-
vested at Selsey, and there he became acquainted with
Dimer. That Little Harry unlocked the horse lock
that was on his (Chater's) legs, and Tapner, Cobby and
Stringer brought him out of the skilling, and set him
upon Tapner's mare, in order to carry him to the well,
to be there murdered, and thrown in; and that all the
company knew at that time what was to be done with
him; that they rode about three miles towards the well,
and sometimes whipped Chater with their horsewhips;
and Tapner observing that he bled, said, "D......n his
blood, if he bloods my saddle, I will whip him
again." When they came to Harting, Carter, Jackson,
Richards, Little Sam, Little Harry, and Steel said, "We
have done our parts, and you (meaning the rest of the
company) shall do yours." By which they meant, as he
took it, that they had murdered Galley, and that the
rest should murder Chater; and Richards, Little Sam
and Little Harry, stopped there, and did not accompany
them any further; the rest went on towards the well,
but Carter and Jackson stopped before they came to it,

and told them the well was a little further off, describing it to them, and told them they could not miss finding it, for it had some white pales by it, and that it was not above 200 yards further, and then Jackson and Carter left them; that he (the witness) and Tapner, Cobby, Stringer, Hammond, Perryer and Steel, came to the well, got off their horses, and took Chater off his horse, the witness was not certain which; and either Tapner or Cobby put a cord round his neck; that there was a "shord" in the pales about the well, and he heard Chater say he could get through there, but Cobby or Tapner said, "D......n you, no; you shall not, you shall get over"; that Tapner wound the cord round the pales, and Chater being put into the mouth of the well, hung by the neck for about a quarter of an hour, and then they loosened the rope, and turned the body, so that it fell into the well head foremost. They stayed there till some of the company thought they heard him breathe or groan, and then went to get a rope and a ladder at one Combleach's, a gardener; that they met Jackson and Carter and told them what they had done, and that they were going to get a rope and a ladder, for Chater was not quite dead; that they all could not raise the ladder; so they got some old gate-posts and stones and threw them down upon him into the well, and then left him.

The prisoner Hammond desired the witness might be asked whether when they were at Old Mills's, he did not offer to ride away, and make a discovery, but was prevented by the company.

Race said he never heard him say anything about it; but one of the company, which he believed was Richards, did threaten any of the rest who should refuse to go to the murder of Chater.

Ann Pescod deposed, that two men came to her father's on the 15th of February, about one o'clock in the morning, and called for her father ; that she asked one of them his name, and he said it was William Jackson. Her father who was then very ill, said they might come if they would ; that Jackson did come in, and asked if they could not bring a couple of men there for a little while, to which she answered " No," because her father was ill ; and thereupon Jackson turned to the other man, and said, " We cannot think of abiding here, as the man is so ill," and so they went away. She saw that Jackson's hand was bloody.

She was ordered to look at the prisoners Jackson and Carter, and see if they were the two men that came, and she said Jackson was one, for that she took particular notice of him, his hand being bloody, and that she verily believed Carter was the other.

Then the King's Counsel called William Scardefield, who deposed that he kept the Red Lion, at Rake, in the parish of Rogate, and that in the night, between the 14th and 15th of February, Jackson and Carter, with Steel and Richards, came to his house and called out to him, " For God's sake get up and let us in " ; then he let them in, and saw they were bloody. He asked them how they came to be so ; and they said they had an engagement and lost their goods, and some of their men they feared were dead and some wounded. That they said they would go and call them that were at the other public-house ; and while he was gone into the cellar, he heard horses come to the door ; and some of the men went into the kitchen, some into the brew-house, and some into the parlours. That he saw two or three men in the brewhouse, and there lay something like a man before them in the brewhouse, by the brewhouse door, and he heard them say he was dead. That some of them calling for liquor, he carried a glass of gin into the parlour, and saw a man standing upright in the parlour, with his face bloody and one eye swelled very much. That Richards was in the parlour with the man, and objected to his coming in, and Carter and Jackson and three others were then in the brewhouse, and Steel was with them. After they had drunk three mugs of hot, they got their horses out and sent him down for some brandy and rum, but when he came up with it they were gone 20 yards below the house, though several of them came back to drink, one or two at a time. That he did not know what became of the man that he saw in the parlour ; but he observed they separated into two companies ; that one of the company, a little man, asked him if he did not know the place where they formerly laid up some goods ; and the prisoner Carter came back, and said they must have a lantern and spade. That Richards fell in a passion because he refused to go along with them, and upon seeing him coming towards them with a light, the company parted : that he saw a horse stand at a little distance, and there seemed to him to be a man lying across the horse, and two men holding him on, and he believed the person he saw lying across the horse was dead, but he was not nigh enough to see whether he was or not. That when they came to the place, one of the little men began to dig a hole ; and it being a very cold morning, he, the witness, took hold of the spade and helped to dig ; and in that hole the company buried the body that lay across the horse. That on the Wednesday or Thursday following, about twelve or one at noon, the prisoners Jackson and Carter, and all the rest of the company came again to his house; and the prisoners Richard Mills the younger, and his brother John, were sent for, and came to them.

Edward Sones proved that on the 16th or 17th of September last he found the body of a dead man in a well in Harris's Wood, within 200 yards of Lady Holt House, and that there were two pieces of timber over the body. That he went immediately to get the coroner's inquest, and when he came back he saw the man had boots on, and there was a rope about his neck; that the well is by Lady Holt Park, in the county of Sussex.

Mr. Brackstone produced the boots and a belt that were taken off the body, and given him by the Coroner.

Mrs. Chater, the widow of Daniel Chater, deposed that she remembered her late husband set out from Southampton on the 14th February last, and that she had never seen him since that time; she looked upon the belt produced by Mr. Brackstone, and said she knew it was the same belt her husband had on when he set out from home, by a particular mark in it; and she believed the boots produced were likewise her husband's.

Mr. Sones proved also, that the horse which Chater set out upon was found about a month afterwards and delivered to the owner.

The King's Counsel submitted it here.

Mr. Justice Foster acquainted the prisoners that the King's Counsel, having gone through their evidence, it was now time to offer what they could in their own defence.

He repeated to each of the prisoners the particular facts the evidence had charged him with, and asked them severally what they had to say to clear themselves of that charge.

To which the prisoner Tapner said he did not know that they were going to murder the man, but Jackson and Richards threatened to kill him if he would not go with them, and he received three or four cuts from Hammond or Daniel Perryer, but he did not know which; that Richards and another man tied the rope; and he denied that he drew a knife and cut Chater across the face.

Mr. Justice Foster told him, that supposing he was threatened in the manner he insisted on, yet that could be no legal defence in the present case; and that in every possible view of the case, it was infinitely more eligible for a man to die by the hands of wicked men, than to go to his grave with the guilt of innocent blood on his own head.

Cobby said he did not know what they were going to do with the man, that he never touched him, and he knew nothing of the murder.

Hammond said when he understood what they were going to do, he wanted to go off and make a discovery; but the company prevented him; and that by the company he meant all the prisoners.

Richard Mills the elder, said he did not know what they were at, and did not think they would hurt the man; and did not know he was chained till after they were gone away.

Richard Mills the younger, said he knew nothing of the matter, and never saw either of the men (Galley and Chater) in his life; he acknowledged that he was at Scardefield's house, but said he knew nothing of the murder, and denied the charge; that Scardefield was the only witness he had, for he (Scardefield) knew when he came, and how long he stayed there.

Jackson said, the man who said he would be Chater's

butcher, was his butcher, and nobody else, that he (Jackson) was not by when he was murdered, and was not guilty of it.

Mr. Justice Foster cautioned him not to deceive himself, and told him that with regard to the present charge, it was not necessary that he should have been present at the murder; he was not charged with being present, but as an accessary before the fact in advising and procuring the murder to be done: and that was the fact he was called upon to answer.

Carter said that when he went to the widow Payne's, he only thought they were going to carry the men out of the way, till they saw what should become of Dimer, and that he never laid hands upon them; and went along with the company to prevent mischief.

Scardefield, the witness, was then called again, and Richard Mills the younger, being asked whether he would ask him any questions, only desired he might be asked what time he came to his house, and how long he stayed there; to which Scardefield answered, that Mills came to his house about half an hour after one; stayed there about an hour and a half, and went away on foot.

The rest of the prisoners said they had not any witnesses.

Upon which, Mr. Justice Foster opened to the jury the substance of the indictment as before set forth; and told them that whether the prisoners or any of them were guilty in manner as therein they are severally charged, must be left to their consideration, upon the evidence that had been laid before them.

That in order to enable them to apply the evidence to the several parts of the charge, it would be proper for him first to acquaint them how the law determines in cases of this nature; that with regard to the persons charged as principals, wherever several persons agree together to commit a murder, or any other felony, and the murder or felony is actually committed, every person present aiding and abetting is, in the eye of the law, guilty in the same degree, and liable to the same punishment as he who actually committed the fact. And the reason the law goes upon is this, that the presence of the accomplices gives encouragement, support and protection to the person who actually commits the fact; and at the same time contributes to his security.

That it is not necessary that the proof of the fact, in cases of this nature, should come up to the precise form of the indictment; for if the indictment charges that A did the fact, and that B and C were present, aiding and abetting, if it be proved that B did the fact, and that A and C were present aiding and abetting, they will be all guilty within the indictment.

That accessaries before the fact are those who, not being present in any sense of the law at the time the fact is committed, have advised or otherwise approved the fact to be done. These persons, in the case of wilful murder, will be liable to the same punishment as those who committed the murder by their instigation, advice or procurement.

He then summed up the evidence very largely, and applied it to the case of the several prisoners, and concluded, that if upon the whole, the jury should be of opinion that either of the principals (Tapner, Cobby, Hammond, or the others charged as principals in the indictment) did strangle the deceased, and that the prisoners Tapner, Cobby, and Hammond were present aiding and abetting, they will be within this indictment.

And if they should be of opinion that the prisoners charged as accessaries before the fact, did advise, consent to, or procure the murder, they likewise will be guilty within this indictment, though they were not present when the fact was committed.

The jury, after some little consideration, gave their verdict, that Tapner, Cobby, and Hammond were guilty of the murder, as laid in the indictment: And

Richard Mills the elder, Richard Mills the younger, William Jackson, and William Carter, were guilty, as accessaries before the fact.

Chichester, January 18*th*, 1748-9.

The Judges being in court, the prisoners who were convicted yesterday were all put to the bar; but Cobby, Hammond, Tapner, and the Mills's were set aside, and Jackson and Carter set forward in order to be tried for the murder of William Galley.

Then the Clerk of the Arraigns bid William Jackson and William Carter to hold up their hands, which they did, and he then read over to them the indictment on which they had been arraigned the day before, as principals in the murder of William Galley, and to which they had pleaded Not Guilty.

Mr. Steele opened the indictment to the jury, and Mr. Bankes, the King's Counsel, spoke to much the same purport as he had done the day before.

Mr. Smythe, another of the King's Counsel, spoke as follows, viz.: " I shall only add a word or two, to explain why these two men, who were convicted yesterday as accessaries before the fact to the murder of Chater, and thereby liable to suffer death, should be tried a second time as principals for the murder of Galley :

"The reasons for it are, in the first place it will be necessary to convict them as principals for the murder of Galley, otherwise the accessaries to that murder, either before or after the fact, cannot be convicted.

"Another reason is, as the intention of all prosecutions, as well as punishments, is not so much to revenge and punish what is past, as to deter others from committing the like crimes, it may be of service to the public to have every circumstance of this cruel transaction disclosed, to shew how dangerous to their neighbours, and to the country in general, those persons are who are concerned in smuggling, and how much it concerns every man to use his utmost endeavours to suppress, and bring them to justice. And it may have another good effect in preventing persons from engaging in that lawless practice when they see it consequently engages them in crimes, which at first they might never intend; for I believe, if these unhappy men had been told when they first began smuggling, that the time would come when they would coolly bathe their hands in the blood of two innocent men, bad as they now are, they would then have been shocked and startled at the imagination of it; yet the men are so naturally led from one vice to another, that having once transgressed the laws of their country, they have insensibly arrived at such a height of wickedness, as to commit this heinous crime without the least hesitation or remorse."

After which the following witnesses were called for the Crown, viz.:—

Mr. Milner, Mr. Shearer, William Galley, son of the deceased, were severally produced and sworn, and Mr. Milner, Mr. Shearer, William Galley gave the same evidence as on the former trial; as did Mr. Edward Holton of the deceased and Chater's calling on him at his house at Havant, on Sunday, the 14th of February, 1747-8.

Robert Jenks also proved upon the trial the same as he did upon the former, with this addition :

That when they were at the widow Payne's, Jackson and Carter both said they would see the letter for Justice Battine, because they thought the men were going to swear against the smugglers ; that both Jackson and Carter hindered him from going through the room where the two men were ; and that one of the men had on a blue great coat.

Being cross-examined at the request of Carter, whether he hindered him from going through the room,

Answered that both the prisoners did.

Joseph Southern, William Lamb, William Garrett and George Poate, proved the same as upon the former trial.

John Race, to the first part of his evidence relating to his transactions at the widow Payne's, added, that the blood ran down from Galley's head and face, on Jackson knocking him down ; and that Jackson and Carter were not fuddled when he went away.

Being asked if he was certain the two prisoners were present at Rowland's Castle at the consultation that was had to take the men Galley and Chater away and confine them, said, Yes, he was sure they were both present.

William Steel, to his former evidence, added, that whilst they were at the widow Payne's, Jackson said, that if any of the gang went away from them, he would shoot them through the head, or through the body, or serve them as bad as the two men should be served.   That he supposed Jackson meant by this, that he would murder any of their own company, or use any of them as ill as they did the officer and Chater, if they left them ; that when the company left off whipping Galley with their thongs and lashes of their whips, as mentioned in the former trial, because the lashes of the whips reached this witness, they beat him with the butt-end of their whips, which were very heavy, and loaded with lead, till one of their whips was beat all to pieces. That the gravelly knap, where Galley was pushed off the horse, when he died, was in Conduit-lane, in Rogate parish ; and Little Harry pushed him in the back, and shoved him down ; and that Jackson and Carter, Little Sam, and Richards, were in company when he died ; and that they laid his body upon a horse, and one man held him on one side, and another on the other side, and so they led the horse along. That Carter and Jackson went before to call Scardefield up, and when they came there, they laid Galley's body down in the brewhouse, at Scardefield's, and carried Chater into another room ; that they drank every one a dram, and Jackson and Carter asked Scardefield if he knew any place to bury that man in, and he said " No." But they said he must go with them ; and they got a spade, and a candle and lantern, and they laid Galley on horseback again, and he (the witness), Carter, Little Sam and Scardefield, went back for about a mile, and he held the horse whilst Scardefield, Carter and Little Sam went to find the place to bury him in ; and when they had found it, Carter and Sam came back to him, and left Scardefield to dig the grave. They went and buried him there, and returned back to Scardefield's again ; that Jackson told them that whilst they were burying Galley, he and Little Harry went to carry Chater to Old Mills's ; that they buried Galley two or three feet deep in the heart of a sand pit. The time at which they buried him was about three or four o'clock in the morning.

Being cross examined, and asked by Carter, whether he (Carter) struck Galley; answered that they all struck him.

Being asked at the request of the prisoners' Counsel, what was the consequence of that thrust which Little Harry gave Galley, when he fell the last time; answered that he thought by the fall Galley's neck was broke, because as soon as he was down he gave himself a turn, and stretched out his hands and legs, and never stirred or spoke afterwards; that Galley was not falling till Little Harry gave him the push. Said that he did not know the parish of Rogate, or that the place where Galley died was within that parish, any otherwise than that he had been there since, and several people said it was the parish of Rogate.

Mr. Staniford, who was Counsel for the prisoners, moved, that the place where Galley died was not in the county of Sussex, and therefore the prisoners must be acquitted of this indictment; for that the present special commission, by which their lordships were trying the prisoners, was only to enquire into murders and felonies committed in the county of Sussex.

Whereupon the Counsel for the King replied that they would undertake to prove the place in the county of Sussex; and for that purpose William Steel was then asked whether the gravelly knap where Galley died was in the county of Southampton or in the county of Sussex; answered that he could not tell. That he had never heard, as he remembered, what county that place was in, but he was carried thither last Friday to see the place, and he shewed to some people then present the spot of ground where Galley fell off the horse and died, and he believed he should know one of the men that were with him.

John Aslett being called up, Steel said he was one of the men that was there.

Aslett was then sworn, and proved that he was with Steel and some dragoons on Friday last ; that Steel pointed down to the ground with a stick, and said, " There the man died " ; that he (the witness) took particular notice of that place, and is sure it was in the parish of Harting in Sussex ; that he now lives at Harting, and was born and bred just by, and had lived there ever since he was a lad, and served the offices of surveyor and constable.

Steel, being cross-examined, was asked how he could remember the place so as to be sure of it ; said he knew the place very well again by the little gravelly rising of the ground.

William Scardefield proved the same as in the former trial, with the following facts relating to the burial of Galley : that one of the gang asked him if he knew the place where they laid up some goods about a year-and-a-half ago, and he told them he did ; upon which the man said, " You must go along with us," but the witness told him his wife was ill, and he could not leave the house ; and then Carter came in and asked for a lantern, and Edmund Richards told him he must go with them, to which he replied, if he must go, he must ; that when he came down the hill a little way from his own house, he saw two companies, one on the right and the other on the left ; that Carter, Steel, and a short man he did not know, went on to the place, and one of them came up after him, and he told him where it was ; upon which they brought the horse up to a rough kind of a dell, and the short man fell a-digging, and it being a very cold night, he (the witness) took the spitter and dug to keep himself warm; there seemed to him to be a man upon the horse, and it fell into the pit like a dead man, and they covered it up; and he verily believed it to be the body of a man, but he did not help to put it in, and was about three or four yards from it; he never went nigh the ground afterwards, and did not see the body of a man upon the horse afterwards, or anywhere else; that the earth was thrown over the pit, and the short man did most of the work; and he did not enquire, or choose to ask any questions about it.

Edward Sones proved the finding the body of a dead man, in a fox earth, within three-quarters of a mile of Rake; there were boots upon the legs, and a glove upon one hand; that the body was much perished, and had a waistcoat and breeches on.

John Greentree produced a coat which he took up beyond Harting Pond in the public road, on the 15th of February last, and swore that there were some writings and a letter-case in the pocket, which he said he should know if he was to see them again.

Upon this a parchment was delivered into court by Justice Battine, and shewn to the witness, who said it was the same that he found in the coat pocket.

It was then read, and appeared to be a deputation under the commissioners of the customs, dated April, 1731, appointing Galley to be a tidesman in the port of Southampton.

William Galley, son of the deceased, looked at the coat which the witness produced, and proved it to be a coat his father had on the 14th of February, 1747-8, when he set out with Chater for Major Battine's to carry a letter to the Major.

John Greentree was called again, and said that the coat was very bloody when he found it.

The King's counsel submitted it here, upon which the prisoners being called upon to make their defence,

The prisoner Carter said he never intended to hurt the man, and never struck him, and only intended to carry him away to take care of him till they knew what became of Dimer; and that he had not any witnesses.

The prisoner Jackson said little or nothing, only that he did not kill the man, nor did he know who did.

The prisoners having neither of them any witnesses to produce, Mr. Justice Foster opened to the jury the substance of the indictment, as before set forth, and told them that where several people joined to do an act in itself unlawful, and death ensues from anything done in prosecution of that unlawful design, they will be all considered as principals in murder, if they were all present aiding or abetting therein; that it was not necessary that each of the prisoners at the bar should be guilty of every single abuse that was offered to the deceased in the long series of barbarities the witnesses of the crown had laid before them; if all or any of these abuses contributed to his death, and the prisoners at the bar were engaged in the several designs against him, and present aiding and abetting the others, they will be guilty within this indictment.

He summed up the evidence very largely, and applied it to the case of the prisoners; and then left it to the consideration of the gentlemen of the jury.

The jury, after some little consideration together, gave their verdict, that William Jackson and William Carter were both Guilty.

The counsel for the crown then moved for judgment; and all the seven prisoners being set to the bar, and severally asked what they had to say why judgment of death should not pass on them, Old Mills said he had nothing to say, only that he knew nothing of the murder of Chater.

Young Mills said he was not at Scardefield's a quarter of an hour; and that it was by accident he called there, and that he knew nothing of the murder.

Hammond and Cobby said they were compelled to stay by Richards and Jackson, and that they would have made their escape, but could get no opportunity to do so.

Tapner said he did not cut Chater across the face, neither could he tell who did.

Jackson and Carter said that they had nothing more to say than what they had already said,

And none of the prisoners or their counsel having anything to offer in arrest of judgment, Mr. Justice Foster spoke to them as follows:—

" Benjamin Tapner, John Cobby, John Hammond, William Jackson, William Carter, Richard Mills the elder, and Richard Mills the younger, you have been convicted upon very full and satisfactory evidence of the murder of Daniel Chater; three of you as principals, and the rest as accessaries before the fact.

" And you, William Jackson and William Carter stand further convicted as principals in the murder of William Galley.

" Deliberate murder is most justly ranked amongst the highest crimes human nature is capable of; but those you have respectively been convicted of, have been attended with circumstances of very high and uncommon aggravation.

" The persons who have been the objects of your fury, were travelling on a very laudable design, the advancement of public justice. For this they were beset in their inn, tempted to drink to excess, and then laid asleep in an inner room, while a consultation was held in what manner to dispose of them : and in the end a resolution was taken to carry them to some distant place and to dispatch them by some means or other.

" In consequence of this resolution they were set on horseback, and exercised with various kinds of cruelty for many hours together, till one of them sunk under the hardships he suffered and died upon the road.

" The other was carried to a place of safe custody, there kept chained on a heap of turf, expecting his doom for three days. During this dreadful interval, a second consultation was held, and a resolution taken to dispatch him too ; not a single man of thirteen who were present offering a word in his behalf.

" He was accordingly hurried to his death ; and though he begged earnestly to live but one day longer, that small respite was denied him. I will not repeat every circumstance : but I cannot forbear putting you in mind of one. When the poor man was told he must die that very night, some of you advised him to say his prayers, and accordingly he did address himself to prayer.

" One would have hoped that this circumstance should have softened your hearts, and turned you from the evil purpose you were bent upon. Happy had it been for you, if you had then reflected, that God Almighty was witness to every thing that passed among you, and to all the intentions of your hearts !

" But while the man, under great distraction of thought, was recommending his soul to mercy, he was interrupted in his devotion by two of you in a manner I scarce know how to repeat.

" I hope your hearts have been long since softened to a proper degree of contrition for these things; and that you have already made a due preparation for the sentence I am now to pass upon you.

" If you have not, pray lose not one moment more. Let not company, or the habit of drinking, or the hopes of life divert you from it; for Christian charity obliges me to tell you that your time in this world will be very short.

" Nothing now remains but that I pass that sentence upon you which the Law of your Country, in conformity to the Law of God, and to the practice of all ages and nations, has already pronounced upon the crime you have been guilty of. This court doth therefore award that you, Benjamin Tapner, William Carter, John Hammond, John Cobby, Richard Mills the elder, Richard Mills the younger, and William Jackson, and each of you shall be conveyed from hence to the prison from whence you came, and from thence you shall be led to the place of execution, where you shall be severally hanged by the neck, until you shall be dead, and the Lord have mercy upon your souls."

Having now completed the trials of these seven bloody criminals, I shall next give you the short Appendix which has been published by three of the clergymen who attended them after their conviction, and who have signed their names to the same, after which I shall give a much fuller account of their wicked lives and behaviour.

After sentence, the prisoners were carried back to Chichester gaol. The court were pleased to order them all for execution the very next day, and that the bodies of Jackson, Carter, Tapner, Cobby, and Hammond, the

five principals, should be hung in chains. Accordingly,
they were carried from the gaol, to a place called the
Broyle, near Chichester; where, in the presence of a
great number of spectators, on Thursday, the 19th day
of January last, about two o'clock in the afternoon, all
of them were executed, except Jackson, who died in
jail, about four hours after sentence of death was pronounced upon him.

The heinousness of the crimes of such notorious
offenders may possibly excite in the reader a desire to
be informed of their respective behaviour whilst under
sentence of death, and at the place of execution; to
satisfy which is subjoined the following authentic
account, under the hands of the several clergymen who
attended them alternately in gaol, and together at the
place of execution :—

" The first time I went to the malefactors under condemnation, being the evening after sentence was passed
upon them, I prayed with them all ; viz., Carter, Tapner,
Cobby, Hammond, and the Mills's (Jackson being dead
just before I went to the gaol) but many persons being
present, I had no opportunity of saying any thing
material, and therefore told them I would visit them
early the next morning, which I did accordingly.

" After prayers, I talked with them about their
unhappy condition, and the heinous crimes that brought
them into it. I asked them if they desired to receive
the Sacrament ; they all and each of them desired that
I would administer it to them ; accordingly I attended
them again, about ten o'clock, for that purpose ; and
during the whole time of my performing that office,
they all behaved with great decency and devotion,
especially Carter and Tapner.

" Afterwards I put the following questions to them,

and desired they would be sincere in their answers as dying men ; first, whether they did not acknowledge the sentence that was passed upon them to be just, and what they highly deserved ?   Carter, the most sensible and penitent amongst them, first answered, Yes ; as did afterwards Tapner, Cobby, and Hammond ; but the two Mills's did not.

"Secondly, I asked them whether they forgave everybody ; they all and each answered they forgave all the world.   Tapner then owned that Edmund Richards and another were the cause of his ruin, but yet forgave them.

"Carter laid his ruin to Jackson for drawing him from his honest employment.

"JOHN SMYTH,

"Curate of St. Pancras, in Chichester."

"Both Carter and Tapner, a few hours before their execution, confessed to me that they with several others assembled together with a design to rescue Dimer out of Chichester gaol ; that the only person amongst them who had arms was Edmund Richards ; but that being disappointed by a number of persons who had promised to join them from the East, their scheme was frustrated and their purpose carried no further into execution ; that one Stringer* was at the head of this confederacy, but not present with them at the time of their assembling together.

"SIMON HUGHES,

"Vicar of Donnington in Sussex."

---

* This Stringer is Thomas Stringer, who stands indicted as a principal in the murder of Daniel Chater, but is not yet taken.

" Benjamin Tapner, of West Stoke, in Sussex, labourer, son of Henry Tapner, of Aldingbourne, Sussex, bricklayer, aged 27, before he was turned off, owned the justice of his sentence, and desired all young persons to take warning by his untimely end, and avoid bad company, which was his ruin. When in gaol, before he was brought out for execution, he said he did not remember he put the rope about Chater's neck.

" William Carter, of Rowland's Castle, thatcher, son of Wm. Carter, of East Meon in Hants, aged 39, at the place of execution and in gaol, confessed the justice of the sentence passed upon him, and acted more suitably to a person in such unhappy circumstances than any of them ; he likewise at the gallows, cautioned every one against those courses that had brought him to so shameful an end.

" Tapner and Carter, when all the ropes were fixed, shook hands, but what or whether any words then passed between them, was not heard.

" Richard Mills the elder, of Trotton, in Sussex, colt-breaker, son of —— Mills of List, in Hants, labourer, aged 68, was unwilling to own himself guilty of the fact for which he died, and said he never saw Chater ; but being asked whether he never heard him, as he was confined so long in the next room to that in which he generally sat, made no answer.

" Richard Mills the younger, of Stedham, coltbreaker, son of the aforesaid Richard Mills, aged 37, would willingly have been thought innocent ; and it being put to him whether he made that speech about the council of war, &c., and whether he was not at the consultation, denied both ; but in the latter Tapner confronted him, and said, ' Yes, young Major, you was there ;' to which Mills replied, ' Ay, for a quarter of an hour or so,' or to that purpose. It so happened that his rope was first fixed to the gallows, and a considerable time was taken up in fixing the rest, which interim he might have much better employed than he did in gazing at the spectators, and then at the hangman (while tying the ropes of the other malefactors) till the cart was almost ready to drive away.

"John Cobby of Sidlesham, in Sussex, labourer, son of James Cobby of Birdham, in Sussex, carpenter, aged 30, appeared to be very dejected, and said but little in gaol, and little at the gallows.

"John Hammond of Bersted, in Sussex, labourer, son of John Hammond of the same place, labourer, aged 40, seemed likewise very much dejected, and had little to say for himself, excepting his pretending that the threats of Jackson, Carter and the rest, were the occasion of his being concerned in the murder.

"Cobby's excuse was much the same.

"They all, except the two Mills's, seemed sensible of the heinous nature of the crime for which they died, and behaved as became men in their unhappy condition, more particularly Carter; but the Mills's, father and son, appeared hardened and unaffected, both in the gaol and at the gallows, especially the son, who seemed by his behaviour, even when his rope was fixed to the gallows, to be as little moved at what he was about to suffer, as the most unconcerned spectator. However, just before the cart drove away, he and his father seemed to offer up some prayers to God.

"R. SANDHAM,
"Vicar of Subdeanry in Chichester.

"JOHN SMYTH,
"Curate of St. Pancras."

As Jackson died so soon after condemnation, no other account can be given of him, than he was of Aldsworth, near Rowland's Castle, in Hampshire, labourer, aged about 50 years ; and that being very ill all the time of his trial, as he had been for a considerable time before, was shocked at the sentence of death, and the apprehensions of being hung in chains, to such a degree as hastened and brought on his death before he could pay the forfeit of his life in that ignominy to which he was most deservedly doomed, and more particularly due to him as a ringleader in the most cruel and horrid barbarities and murders.

He professed the Romish religion some years before his death, and that he died a Roman Catholic may very reasonably be presumed from a printed paper that was found carefully sewed upon a linen purse in his waist-coat pocket immediately after his death, supposed to be a popish relique, and containing the following words, viz. :—

"Sancti tres Reges
Gaspar, Melchior, Balthasar,
Orate pro Nobis nunc et in Hora Mortis Nostræ.
Ces Billets ont touche aux trois Testes de S. S. Roys
a Cologne.
Ils sont pour Des Voyageurs, contre Les Malheurs de Chemins, Maux de Teste, Mal-cadaque, Fievres, Sorcellerie, toute sorte de Malefice, Morte subite."

In English thus :
"Ye three Holy Kings,
Gaspar, Melchior, Balthasar,
Pray for us now, and in the hour of death.
These papers have touched the three heads of the Holy Kings at Cologne.
They are to preserve travellers from accidents on

the road, headaches, falling sickness, fevers, witchcraft, all kinds of mischief and sudden death."

The body of William Carter was hung in chains in the Portsmouth road, near Rake, in Sussex; the body of Benjamin Tapner on Rook's Hill, near Chichester; and the bodies of John Cobby and John Hammond upon the sea coast, near a place called Selsea Bill, in Sussex, where they were seen at a great distance, both east and west.

The bodies of the Mills's, father and son, having neither friend or relation to take them away, were thrown into a hole, dug for that purpose, very near the gallows, into which was likewise thrown the body of Jackson. Just by is erected a stone having the following inscription, viz. :—

" Near this place was buried the body of William Jackson, a proscribed smuggler, who upon a special commission of Oyer and Terminer, held at Chichester, on the 16th day of January, 1748-9, was with William Carter, attainted for the murder of William Galley, a custom-house officer; and who likewise was, together with Benjamin Tapner, John Cobby, John Hammond, Richard Mills the elder, and Richard Mills, the younger, his son, attainted for the murder of Daniel Chater; but dying in a few hours after sentence of death was pronounced upon him, he thereby escaped the punishment which the heinousness of his complicated crimes deserved, and which was the next day most justly inflicted upon his accomplices.

" As a memorial to posterity, and a warning to this and succeeding generations,

" This stone is erected

" A.D. 1749."

Having now given an account of the behaviour of these seven bloody criminals, as occurred to the three clergymen who attended them after their receiving sentence of death, and who signed their names to the same; we shall now insert the account of their behaviour from the time of their being brought to Chichester gaol, to their execution, which account was taken by two persons who constantly attended on them, and is what occurred at the times the clergymen before-mentioned were not present; and are inserted to make this account complete.

The seven prisoners that were condemned, together with William Combleach the gardener, committed on suspicion of being concerned in the murder of Daniel Chater, were brought from Horsham gaol, in one waggon under a strong guard of soldiers, to Chichester, on Friday the 13th January, 1748-9.

Jackson being sick, was kept upstairs in a room by himself; and the other seven, William Combleach being with them, were put in a lower room, all ironed and stapled down, and well guarded; but behaved very bold and resolute, and not so decently as became people in their circumstances. They ate their breakfast, dinner and supper regularly, without any seeming concern, and talked and behaved freely to everybody that came to see them. Old Mills looking out of a window the day after they came there, which was market-day, young Mills said to Tapner, "D...n the old fellow, he will have a stare out."

1. Richard Mills, sen., was formerly well respected by the gentlemen of the county; but having had for many years concerns with the smugglers, and a smuggler himself, and having prevailed on his sons to go a-smuggling likewise, he lost most of his business

and character. He frequently said, that he was only sorry for his sons, for as to himself, he was under no trouble, for he was sure that he could not, according to the common course of nature, live above a year or two longer.

A few hours after sentence was passed upon him, a clergyman who lived near him, went to see him in the gaol, in order to discourse with him and bring him to a true sense of his deplorable condition; to which purpose he recommended him to make use of his few remaining moments in preparing for eternity. While the clergyman was thus seriously talking to him about the concerns of his soul, the old man interrupted him and said, " When do you think we shall be hanged ? " The gentleman, after reproving him for the little concern he discovered about the more important affairs of another world, told him he believed his time was very short, and that he thought his execution would be ordered some time the next day, but could not exactly say at what hour. Mills replied, that as to the murder it gave him but little trouble, since he was not guilty of it ; but as to the charge of smuggling, he owned he had been concerned in that trade for a great many years, and did not think there was any harm in it.

Being particularly asked, if he did not know that Chater was kept chained in his turf-house, he answered very indifferently, that he could not tell, he believed he did, but what was that to the murder ? But being told that his maid, Ann Bridges, had declared upon oath, that he got up when Jackson and Little Harry*

---

* Little Harry is Henry Sheerman, who was condemned at the last assizes at East Grinstead for the county of Sussex, for the murder of Galley ; and stood also indicted for the murder of

brought Chater to his house about three o'clock in the morning, and that he ordered her not to go into the turf-house, for there was a person there whom it was not proper she should see; he could not tell what to say, but stood seemingly dumbfounded; and an answer being pressed from him, he acknowledged that he did get up and let them in, and told Little Harry to carry him (Chater) into the turf-house, and chain him; and that he, as well as Little Harry, did look after him till the gang came and took him away the Wednesday night, but that he was no ways concerned in the murder; but at last he did acknowledge, that he did know they had agreed to carry Chater to the well by Lady Holt Park, and hang him, and throw him into it; and that Tapner took a cord for the purpose from his house.

Old Mills had been poor some time, and had left off smuggling, that is, going with the gangs to the seaside to fetch the goods, being sensible of the danger of going with others in a gang with firearms; but he got something by letting the smugglers bring anything to the house; and to blind the neighbours, he lived privately with his maid, Ann Bridges, and had, for upwards of a year, received alms from the parish, as he himself acknowledged.

2. Richard Mills, jun., had been concerned in smuggling for many years. He was a daring, obstinate, hardened fellow, and seemed capable of any mischief. He said to a gentleman, who went to see him, that he did not value death, but was not guilty of the murder

---

Chater, but was tried only on the first indictment. He was executed at Rake, near where Galley was buried, and there hung in chains. An account of him at his trial, under condemnation, and at the place of execution, will be inserted in the following pages.

of which he was accused, since he was not present when it was done; though if he had, he should not have thought it any crime to destroy such informing rogues. After his trial was over, two gentlemen going up to see him, they told him that his brother John,* who had been advertised in the Gazette as an accomplice in the murder of one Hawkins, and was likewise concerned in the murder of Mr. Chater, but not then taken, was seen following the judges over Hynd Heath, in their way to Chichester. "What," said Mills, "there has been no robbery committed upon the highway lately, has there ?" Upon which the person replied, "Not that I have heard of." Mills made answer, " I suppose Jack must take to the highway, for he has no other way to live, till an opportunity offers of his getting to France, which I heartily wish he may do." After their conviction on Tuesday night for the murder of Chater, he and the rest of them were remanded back to prison, and ordered to be brought down the next day, when Jackson and Carter were to be tried for the murder of Galley, and the whole to receive judgment, when Mills said, "What the d......l do they mean by that ? Could not they do our whole business this night, without obliging us to come again and wear out our shoes ? Well! if it must be so, the old man and I will go first, but I will give the old man the wall," as he accordingly did.

3. John Cobby seemed a harmless, inoffensive creature,

---

* This John Mills is the same person as went by the name of Smoker, who was condemned at the last assizes at East Grinstead, for the county of Sussex, for the cruel murder of Richard Hawkins, and is hung in chains near the Dog and Partridge on Slindon Common; and whose trial follows this account of the seven condemned at Chichester.

and being of an easy temper, it is supposed he was the more easily influenced to take on with the smugglers, though he declared he had not long been with them. He acknowledged that he was at the well when Chater was hung, and flung into it, and that he, as well as the rest, were all guilty of the crime for which they were condemned. He was very serious, and seemed very penitent ; owned he was a great sinner; begged pardon of God for his offences, and hoped the world would forgive him the injuries he had done to anybody.

4. Benjamin Tapner was born of very honest parents, who gave him good schooling; and he always lived in good repute, till being persuaded by Jackson and some others to follow their wicked courses : which he had done for something more than two years. He behaved all the time under his confinement more decently than some of the others, and frequently prayed very devoutly. He was always very reserved if mention was made of the cruelties he exercised on Chater. A gentleman, who desires his name may not be mentioned, went to see him on Tuesday evening, just after his conviction, who, taking him to one corner of the room, asked him if there was anything in the report of his picking Chater's eyes out, when he declared, as a dying man, he never made use of any weapon but his knife and whip ; and that he might in the hurry pick one of his eyes out with the point of his knife, for he did not know what he did, the devil had got so strong hold of him. He said he had been in many engagements with the King's officers, and been wounded three times ; and hoped all young people would take warning by his untimely fate, and keep good company, for it was bad company had been his ruin.

5. William Carter behaved himself very serious, and

said that Jackson had drawn him away from his honest employment to go a smuggling, which was the cause of his ruin ; and indeed his general character was very good except in that particular. He declared that these murders would never have happened, had not Mrs. Payne, at Rowland's Castle, sent for him and Jackson, and in some measure exasperated them against Galley and Chater, as being informers. This Mrs. Payne and her two sons are in custody in Winchester Gaol, in order to take their trials at the ensuing assizes, when it is hoped they will meet their just reward.

6. John Hammond was a hardened, obdurate fellow, and very resolute, and always had great antipathy against the King's officers and others concerned in suppressing smuggling ; and often would let drop words out of his mouth, and that he did not think it any crime in killing an informer; but when he came to receive sentence he began to cry very much. He frequently lamented the case of his wife and four children, and said that was all that touched him; and for dying he did not mind it.

7. William Jackson died in his room about 7 o'clock the same night he received sentence of death. He had been one of the most notorious smugglers living in his time ; and most of them, as well as Carter, gave him the worst of characters, and that he was even a thief among themselves ; for when he knew that any of them had got any run goods, he would contrive to steal them away from them. He reflected on himself, after receiving sentence, for what he had said on his defence, that Tapner only was guilty ; for he declared they were all concerned; and that when he had been concerned in the murder of Galley, he contrived to bring Cobby, Hammond, the three Mills's, Stringer, Tapner, and the

rest, to be concerned in the murder of Chater, lest they might, one day or other, run to the government, and make themselves an evidence, but by being guilty of murder, it would be an entire bar to them.

The afternoon preceding their execution, a person came to take measure of Jackson, Cobby, Hammond, Carter and Tapner, in order to make their irons in which they were to be hung in chains! which threw the prisoners into very great confusion, and they seemed under a greater concern than ever they had shewed before. But when old Mills and his son were told that they were exempted from that part of the punishment, they seemed to be mightily pleased at it, and contented to be hung only as common malefactors.

But it deserves particular notice, with respect to Jackson, that he was no sooner told that he was to be hung in chains, but he was seized with such horror and confusion, that he died in two hours afterwards; and though he was very ill before, yet it is believed that this hastened his end, and was the immediate cause of his death.

The foregoing accounts are a melancholy proof of the dreadful effects which are the fatal but too frequent consequences of the offence of smuggling—a crime which, however prejudicial to the kingdom in general, and to every fair trader in particular, perhaps may not, from an inattention to the many and monstrous mischiefs derived from it, have met with that general detestation and abhorrence it so highly deserves.

But a perusal of these sheets, shocking to every reader, cannot fail to alarm the nation, and open the eyes of all people, who must reflect with horror upon a set of dissolute and desperate wretches, united by a parity of inclinations and iniquities, formed into dangerous gangs and confederacies, that encouraged by numbers they might exercise cruelties and commit barbarities, which, abandoned as they were, they singly durst not attempt. Villains! not to be won by lenity, despising and rejecting proffered pardons, proceeding from crime to crime, till they arrived at the highest and, until now, unheard-of pitch of wickedness: who, not content with defrauding the King in his customs and revenues; not satisfied with violating the properties and possessions, pursued the lives of his subjects and servants, whose very blood could not satiate their malice—tortures were added to aggravate the pangs of death.

Before we take leave of these wretches, and begin upon the account of that most notorious villain and murderer, John Mills, and the rest, as promised, we think it will be very necessary to inform our readers of their several behaviours at the place of execution, not mentioned before in the account given by the three clergymen.

AT THE PLACE OF EXECUTION.

The prisoners were brought out of the gaol about two in the afternoon of Thursday, the 19th of January, 1748-9, being the day after receiving sentence, when a company of Foot Guards and a party of Dragoons were drawn out ready to receive them, and to conduct them to the place of execution, which was about a mile out of the town. The procession was solemn and slow; and when they came to the tree, they all, except the two Mills's, behaved a little more serious than they had done before.

Carter said the sentence was just on them all, for

they were all guilty, as charged in the indictments; and lamented the case of his wife and children, and said he hoped others would take warning by his untimely end.

The Mills's, as I observed before, seemed no ways concerned; and the young one said he did not value to die, for he was prepared, though at the same time he appeared so very hardened and abandoned.

The halter that was used for the old man was very short, the gallows being high; so that he was obliged to stand a-tiptoe to give room for it to be tied up to the tree: the old fellow saying several times while this was doing, "Don't hang me by inches."

Tapner appeared very sensible of his crime, and prayed aloud, and seemed, as I hope he was, very sincere and devout. He declared that Jackson, Cobby and Stringer held three pistols to his head, and swore they would shoot him if he did not go and assist in the murder of Chater, the old shoemaker, who was going to make an information against their shepherd, Dimer, otherwise Diamond; that they also extorted three guineas from him by the same way of threats, to repay Jackson and Carter what they had been out of pocket on that account. He said they were all guilty of the crimes laid to their charge; and that one T—ff, well known in Chichester, and Stringer, John Mills* and Richards (all not taken) were as guilty as himself; and as they deserved the same punishment, he hoped they would all be taken, and served the same as he was just going to be. He acknowledged cutting Chater across

---

* This is the John Mills, since executed and hung in chains on Slindon Common, Sussex, for the murder of Richard Hawkins, and of whom we shall give a particular account.

the face, but did not care to repeat any of the cruelties
he had exercised.

―――――

We are now come to the conclusion of the trials, and
the behaviour of those who were executed at Chichester,
and shall next proceed to those that were brought on
at the assizes at East Grinstead, where two of the same
gang were tried for murder, namely, Sheerman for that
of Galley, and John Mills, called Smoker, for that of
Hawkins, who was destroyed in as cruel and barbarous
a manner as either Galley or Chater.

After which we shall give an account of the trials of
the other smugglers, which were very remarkable for
the most notorious crimes with which they are charged,
such as murder, housebreaking, robberies on the
highway, &c. But as Sheerman was tried for the crime
for which several others had been already convicted, as
has before been related, we think this trial will most
properly follow those of his confederates, and with
whom he had been concerned throughout the whole
course of their villainies.

After which will follow the trial of John Mills,
who not only had a hand in the murder of Chater,
but likewise was a principal in that of poor Hawkins.

Henry Sheerman, otherwise Little Harry, was indicted
for the inhuman murder of William Galley, which the
said Sheerman, in company with several others, did
perpetrate and accomplish on the said William Galley,
by tying and fastening him on a horse, and then
lashing, whipping and beating him with their whips,
till the said Galley, no longer able to bear the cruel
scourges, fell with his head under the horse's belly, and
his feet across the saddle ; that being again set upright
on the horse, the said prisoner, with the rest, again

whipped, beat and bruised him, by the means of which he fell off the second time ; and being set on another horse, the said prisoner, with the others, again beat and whipped him, till the said Galley was so terribly bruised and wounded that, being ready to fall off the horse, the prisoner gave him him a push, and threw him to the ground, of which blows, wounds and bruises, and fall from the said horse, he died.

The counsel for the King upon this indictment were the same as were upon that against John Mills and John Reynolds, who after laying open and explaining to the court and jury the heinous nature of the offence and the pernicious consequences of smuggling, which generally brought on murder, robbery and other enormous crimes, they produced the following witnesses in support of the charge against the prisoner.

Mr. Shearer, collector of the customs at Southampton, deposed that he received a letter from the commissioners of the customs, informing him that one John Dimer was taken up on suspicion of being concerned with others in breaking open the custom-house at Poole and committed to Chichester gaol ; that thereupon he sent one Chater with a letter to Justice Battine under the care of the deceased William Galley, the 14th day of February was twelvemonth, and hired a grey horse for him to ride on.

William Galley, son of the deceased William Galley, deposed that he very well remembered that some time in February was twelvemonth, his father set out on a journey to Justice Battine ; that the night before he went he saw the letter and saw the direction upon it, which his father was carrying to the justice ; that his father was dressed in a blue great coat, lined with blue, with brass buttons, a light brown close-bodied coat trimmed with blue, his waistcoat and breeches the same, and rode upon a grey horse, and that he never saw his father afterwards.

George Austen deposed that on the 14th of February was twelvemonth, being at the New Inn at Leigh, he saw the deceased William Galley and another person on horseback, and hearing them enquire the way to East Marden, and shewing a letter they had for Justice Battine, he said that he and his brother, Thomas Austin, and his brother-in-law, Robert Jenkes, were going part of that road and would shew them the way; that he went with them to a place called Rowland's Castle, to a public house kept by one widow Payne; that being there Galley and his companion called for rum. That the widow Payne enquired of him if he was acquainted with these men, or whether they belonged to his company. He told her they were going to Justice Battine's; upon which she apprehended there was something in hand against the smugglers, several of whom came in soon afterwards.

John Race, otherwise Raise, an accomplice in the fact, deposed that on the 14th of February was twelvemonth, he was at Rowland's Castle; that when he came in, he saw there Edmund Richards, William Steel, Carter, Jackson, Little Sam, Richard Kelly, Jackson's wife, and the prisoner Henry Sheerman, together with Galley and Chater: that he saw Jackson take Chater to the door, and heard him ask him whether he knew anything of Dimer the shepherd, and Chater answering that he was obliged to appear against him, Galley came to them, to interrupt their talking, which Jackson resenting, struck him on the face with his fist. Being all come into the house again, Jackson related to the rest of them what Chater had said in relation to Dimer;

upon which they consulted together what to do with
Galley and Chater, and it was agreed by them all to
carry them to a place of security, till they should have
an opportunity of sending them to France; and that
the prisoner was present at this consultation.

William Steel, another of the accomplices in the fact,
deposed that on the 14th of February was twelvemonth
he was sent for to the widow Payne's; that when he
came there he found Jackson, Little Sam, Kelly, Carter,
Richards, Race and Little Harry; that he saw the two
strangers there, Galley and Chater, who were drinking
with the prisoner, and the rest of the smugglers; that
Jackson took Chater out of the house, and was followed
by Galley, who soon after returned with his face bloody,
having, he said, been knocked down by Jackson. That
Galley and Chater wanting to be gone, the prisoner,
with the rest of the smugglers persuaded them to stay,
and the company continued drinking till Galley and
Chater were quite drunk, and were led into a little
inner room to sleep; this was about four or five o'clock.
That in the meanwhile this witness, with the rest of
the smugglers, the prisoner being present, consulted
what to do with Galley and Chater; and it was
proposed to make away with them, and to that end, to
throw them into the well in the horse pasture, about a
quarter of a mile from Rowland's Castle; but upon
second thoughts that well was judged too near, and
might occasion a discovery. That then it was agreed
to allow three-pence a week each, and to keep them in
some private place till they saw what was the fate of
Dimer; and as Dimer was used, in the same manner
they agreed to use Galley and Chater. That about
seven o'clock Carter and Jackson went into the little
room, and having waked Galley and Chater, brought

them out all bloody; and he believed that Jackson and
Carter had kicked them with their spurs, which they
had just before put on; that they then brought Galley
and Chater out to the street door, and set them both
upon the same horse, and tied their legs together under
the horse's belly. That then he (the witness) got upon
a grey horse, and led that the deceased and Chater were
upon; that they had not gone above 80 yards, before
Jackson called out " Whip the dogs, cut them, slash
them, d...n them"; and then the company fell to
lashing and whipping them; while they rode about a
mile to a place called Wood's Ashes; that there they
all alighted, and the prisoner, Little Harry, gave each
of them a dram, but none to Galley and Chater; that
mounting their horses again, they fell to beating and
lashing the two men as violently as they had done
before, till they came to Dean, which was about half-a-
mile further; that then one of the company pulled out
a pistol, and swore he would shoot them (Galley and
Chater) through the head, if they made any noise while
they were passing through the village; when they were
got through Dean, they fell to whipping them again,
till they came almost to Idsworth, when Galley and
Chater fell again with their heads under the horse's
belly; upon which they parted them, and set up
Galley behind him (this witness), and Chater behind
Little Sam, and thus proceeded towards Lady Holt
Park, about three miles further, whipping them all the
way; but the lashes of their whips falling on this
witness, he cried out and they left off whipping Galley;
that being come to Lady Holt Park, Galley being faint
and tired, got off, and Jackson and Carter took him by
the arms and legs, and carried him to a well there, into
which they said they would throw him; but some of

the company interposing, they set him up behind this
witness, but went on till they came down a hill, and
Galley, not being able to ride any further, got down again;
upon which they laid him upon the pommel of the saddle,
across a horse before Richards, with his belly down-
wards, and in this manner carried him about a mile
and a half; that then Richards, being tired of holding
him, let him down by the side of the horse; that then
they put him upon the grey horse which this witness
rode upon, and this witness got off; they sat him up, his
legs across the saddle, and his body lay over the mane, and
Jackson held him on, and went on in this manner for
about half a mile, Galley crying out grievously all the
time, "Barbarous usage! barbarous usage! For God's
sake shoot me through the head or through the body;"
he (the witness) imagined that Jackson was squeezing
his privy parts. That they went on for two miles
further, and coming to a dirty lane, Carter and Jackson
rode forwards, and bad them stop at the swing gate till
they returned. Being gone a little while, they came
back again and said that the man of the house was ill
and could not entertain them. It was then proposed to
go to the house of one Scardefield at Rake, upon which
the prisoner tied Galley with a cord, and got up on
horseback behind him in order to hold him on; and
coming to a gravelly knap in the road, Galley cried out,
"I shall fall, I shall fall;" whereupon the prisoner then
said, "D...n you, then fall," and gave him a push, and
Galley fell down, gave a spirt and never spoke afterwards; he (the witness) believed his neck was broken
by the fall; that then they laid him across the horse
again, and went to the Red Lion at Rake, kept by
William Scardefield, whither they carried Chater all
over blood. That Jackson and the prisoner went from

Scardefield's with Chater, to Old Mills's, where he was left to the care of the prisoner, and in the meantime they buried Galley.

This witness was asked by the court whether the prisoner was present at the first consultation at the widow Payne's, and continued in the same company to the death of Galley, and he answered : " Yes, he was with them all the time."

Then William Scardefield was sworn, who deposed that the prisoner at the bar was with the rest of the smugglers at his house at Rake, when Galley was brought dead there, but went away with Chater, the other man who was all bloody.

The counsel for the King said they had a great many more witnesses, but they would rest the matter as it now was, and not give the court any further trouble.

The prisoner, being called upon to make his defence, said he had nobody to disprove the facts or speak to his character ; and said he was sent for to Rowland's Castle, though he did not know for what ; that when he came there he was threatened by Jackson, Richards and others that were there, that they would shoot him through the head if he would not go with and assist them in what they were going about, and that it was not in his power to make his escape from them.

The jury brought him in guilty.   Death.

Having now given the trial of Henry Sheerman, alias Little Harry, at East Grinstead, it will be necessary next to give an account of his life and behaviour under sentence of death, and at the place of execution, before we proceed to the trial of that notorious villain John Mills, alias Smoker, for the cruel murder of Richard Hawkins.

Henry Sheerman, alias Little Harry, about 32 years

of age, was born and bred up at West Strutton, in the county of Sussex, to husbandry, whose parents were people of good character, though of but middling circumstances; and gave him as good an education at school as they could afford; but he said he never minded his learning—his mind run more upon other things, so that he made but very little progress, though he could read very well and write a little.

He said that Jackson was the cause of his ruin, and the considerable gains that were allowed to those who were as servants to the master smugglers, seduced him to leave his honest employment and take on with them.

He often declared that he never was concerned in any other murder than that of Galley, for which he suffered; but being asked if he was not guilty of the other indictment that was against him, as being an accessary to the murder of Chater before the fact was committed, he evaded answering the question in full, and said he left the company and Chater, and did not go to the well where he was hanged and flung down; but on being interrogated, and informed it was the same thing, his knowing their intention of murdering Chater, though he did not go quite to the place, he said he did not know that the company, when he parted from them, were going to hang him in the well at Lady Holt Park, and then fling his body down it to prevent a discovery. He was asked if old Major Mills knew that Chater was confined in his turf house, and that they were going to murder him, because Old Mills partly denied it when he was executed on the Broyle near Chichester; he said that Old Mills was guilty of the whole affair laid to his charge, as being concerned in the murder of Chater; that Old Mills gave him the chain and horse-lock, to chain Chater to the beam, and went frequently to see

he was safe during his confinement there, and often told
Chater that he was a villain to turn informer, and he
would see he should be hanged to prevent his informing
any more ; and he declared, that when they took
Chater from Old Mills's house, that Old Mills knew that
they were going to hang him at the well by Lady Holt
Park, and that the resolution and agreement of him, Old
Mills, as well as the rest, was to fling his body down
there, it being a dry well, to prevent a discovery, and
that Old Mills himself said it was a very proper place,
for as it was a dry well, it might lie there an age before
anything could be discovered, and before that time it
would be rotted quite away to nothing.

Before we proceed any further, we shall inform the
reader what encouragement is given to seduce the
young people from their honest employments to turn
smugglers, which Little Harry declared.

The master smugglers contract for the goods either
abroad, or with the master of a cutter that fetches
them, for a quantity of teas (which they call dry goods)
and brandies, and the master of the cutter fixes a time
and place where he designs to land, and seldom or ever
fails being pretty punctual as to the time, if the weather
permits ; as the master smugglers cannot fetch all the
goods themselves, so they hire men whom they call
their riders ; and they allow each man half-a-guinea a
journey, and bear all expenses of eating and drinking
and horse, and allowance of a dollop of tea, which is
forty pound weight, being the half of a bag, the profit
of which dollop, even of the most ordinary sort, is worth
more than a guinea, and some sorts 25s. and some more ;
and they always make one journey, sometimes two, and
sometimes three in a week, which is indeed such a
temptation that very few people in the country can

withstand ; and which has been the cause of so many turning smugglers.

He said it was very hard work in going down to the sea-side to fetch the goods, and considering the hazard they run if taken, and of their own persons, as they are obliged to ride in the night only, and through the bye-ways, avoiding all the public roads as much as possible, people would not take on with them if it were not for the great profits that arise.

He said that all the smugglers, both masters and riders, drink drams to great excess, and generally keep themselves half drunk, which was the only thing that occasioned them to commit such outrages as they did sometimes ; and he gave the following account of the murders of Galley and Chater :—

That on Sunday the 14th of last February was twelvemonth, he was sent for to the widow Payne's, and informed that there were two men there who were going to make an information against John Dimer, that was in custody at Chichester, on suspicion of being concerned in breaking open the King's warehouse at Poole, that, as he was one concerned in the said fact, he readily went to hear what he could, and when he came there, he found Jackson, Richards, Steel (the evidence), and some more of the gang concerned in breaking open the said warehouse ; when Jackson said to him, " Harry, I have sent for you : here are two men have got a letter to Justice Battine, for him to take an information against Dimer ;" and that they (the smugglers) resolved to have the letter from them ; which he agreed to ; and after they had made the men drunk, Carter and Jackson went into the room where the men were put to sleep, and took the letter, which they read, and found the contents amounted to all they suspected ; that it was never proposed by any of them to hurt either Galley or Chater, but to keep them privately to prevent their giving the designed information, till the women, Carter's and Jackson's wives, proposed hanging them ; and then it was talked of carrying them to the well just by, and to hang them and fling them down it, but it was not agreed to ; neither did any of the men in his presence or hearing shew or intimate any inclination towards their so doing.

He said further, that they all drank pretty freely to make Galley and Chater drunk, and when they came to the resolution of carrying them both away, and concealing them till they knew what would be the fate of the shepherd Dimer, they were all more than half drunk ; that he verily believed none of them had any design of murdering them while they were at Rowland's Castle ; but Jackson, who was the drunkest of the company, called out to whip them, which was soon after they set out from Mrs. Payne's house, when Edmund Richards, who is not yet taken, began to lash them with his long whip ; and then they all did the same except Steel, who was leading the horse the two men rode on.

He said that the design of tying their legs under the horse's belly was for no other reason than to prevent their jumping off and running away, and making their escape, as it was night time ; which, if either of them should do, they would be all inevitably ruined.

The liquor they had drank, and giving way to their passion, urged them on to the cruelties they exercised on Chater; but when they found Galley was dead, it sobered them all very much, and they were all in a great consternation and surprise, and could not tell what to do, when they concluded to bury the body of Galley, and to take care of Chater.

He lamented the unhappy case of Chater during the time of his being chained in Old Mills's turf-house, but said, self-preservation obliged him to take care he did not get away, though he was all the time very uneasy, and said he declared his abhorrence to Tapner's cutting Chater across the face and eyes, and of Cobby's kicking him while he was saying the Lord's Prayer, and that he came out of the turf-house into the dwelling-house upon that account, not being able to bear hearing the poor man's expressions in begging for a few hours or minutes to make his peace with his Creator, at the same time the blood running all down his face. He said it was not Cobby alone that kicked Chater while he was at prayers, but also Richards and Stringer, who are both not yet taken.

Being asked why he did not give poor Galley and Chater a dram, as well as the smugglers, when they all got off their horses ; he said he was going to do it, but Richards, Carter and Jackson, all swore they would blow his brains out if he did. He acknowledged going away with them from Old Mills's in order to hang Chater according to agreement ; but seeing Tapner whip the poor man so cruelly, Chater at the same time being all over blood and wounds, his heart relented, and that was the only reason why he did not go with them, and be present at his murder.

At his trial he behaved with reservedness, but no way audacious, as some of the others were ; and after he had received his sentence, he began to bemoan his unhappy circumstances, and prayed very devoutly ; and confessed that he had been a very wicked liver ever since he turned smuggler.

He said he never was concerned in many robberies, as numbers of the smugglers had been ; and what gave him the most uneasiness was, the great scandal and vexation he had brought on his wife and family.

He was conveyed under a strong guard of soldiers from Horsham to Rake, near the place where Galley was buried, on the 20th day of March, 1749, and there executed, and afterwards hung in chains, as an example.

At the place of execution he behaved very penitent, and as became one in his unhappy circumstances, frequently saying that Jackson was the original person who was the cause of his ruin, and that he should not have gone to the widow Payne's that unfortunate day that Mr. Galley and Mr. Chater were there, had he not been sent for. He declared that at the time he gave Galley the push off the horse, when Galley fell down and died, he had no thought that that fall would kill him just then ; that he begged pardon of God and man, not only for that wicked action of his life, but for all others ; and then was turned off, crying to the Lord Jesus Christ to receive his soul.

We shall now proceed to the trials of John Mills, alias Smoker, John Reynolds, the master of the Dog and Partridge on Slindon Common, where Richard Hawkins was inhumanly murdered ; and then give an account of John Mills's wicked life, and behaviour at his trial, and under sentence of death ; and also of his confession, and last dying words at the place of execution.

John Mills, alias Smoker, together with Jeremiah Curtis, alias Butler, alias Pollard, and Richard Rowland, alias Robb (both not yet taken), was indicted for the murder of Richard Hawkins, in the parish of Slindon, in the county of Sussex, on the 28th day of January, 1748-9, in the 21st year of his Majesty's reign, by violently assaulting, sticking, beating, whipping and kicking, him, the said Richard Hawkins, over the face, head, arms, belly, and private parts : of which wounds, bruises, kicks and stripes he instantly died. And John Reynolds was indicted for aiding, assisting, comforting and abetting the said John Mills, alias Smoker, and Jeremiah Curtis, alias Butler, alias Pollard, and Richard Rowland, alias Robb (both not yet taken), in the murder of the said Richard Hawkins.

The counsel for the King were Mr. Staples, Mr. Steele, recorder of Chichester, Mr. Burrel, Mr. Smythe (one of the king's counsel, learned in the law, and member of Parliament for East Grinstead, in the county of Sussex), and Mr. Serjeant Wynn.

One of the counsel for the King having opened the indictment, Mr. Smythe observed to the court and jury that the practice of smuggling having prevailed all over the kingdom, particularly in that and the neighbouring counties, to so great a degree, and the persons concerned therein became so very audacious, that a great many murders were committed, and very barbarous ones too, upon such persons who should show the least inclination to prevent their pernicious practices. That the murder for which the present prisoners were indicted, was one of the most bloody and most cruel that ever was perpetrated in this, or any other civilized nation, except in two others that had happened in this county ; that the prisoner Mills seemed to have the honour of committing the first, and setting the example of this species of most terrible murders, though some persons who committed the other murder had been first brought to justice. That many people were induced to think smuggling was no crime at all, or if it was one, but a very small one, it was but cheating the King, and that was no harm ; not at all considering that it is a crime not only against the laws of the land, but against the law of God also, which commands all men to render to Cæsar the things that are Cæsar's. That smuggling was robbing the nation of that revenue which is appointed for payment of the national debt; and that every act of smuggling was defrauding every one of his Majesty's subjects that pay taxes, as they are obliged to make good all deficiencies. That when they shall hear the witnesses they will find that this evil practice was the original cause of this murder, and then he did not doubt but they would find the prisoners guilty.

Mr. Sergeant Wynn, after speaking of the nature of the crime, and that it was one of the consequential evils that attended smuggling, observed that most of the daring robberies that had been lately committed, were by these sort of men, who thought, or at least acted, as if they thought themselves above all law. That when they had called their witnesses, he did not doubt but they would give the jury such evidence as would induce them to believe the prisoners guilty, and consequently find them so.

Henry Murril deposed that some time in January last was twelvemonth, he was informed that some persons were at his house, enquiring after some tea they had lost, but could not tell who they were; that he went to young Cockrel's, who keeps a public-house at Yapton; where he saw Jerry Curtis and two others, drinking. Curtis was very angry; said some rogues had stolen two bags of tea from him, and d......n him, he would find it out, and severely punish those concerned therein; for d......n him, he had whipt many a rogue, and washed his hands in their blood; that Curtis had offered this deponent five guineas to get the tea again, or find out who had got it; and then said that if money could not get it, he would come sword in hand, and find it out and take it away.

Being asked by the court if the prisoner Mills was one of them that were with Curtis, said he could not tell.

Henry Titcomb deposed that one day in January last was twelvemonth, Curtis and Mills came to Mr. Boniface's barn, where he, the prisoner, and Richard Hawkins (the deceased) were at work; that Curtis called Hawkins out to speak with him; that he did not hear what passed between them, but that Hawkins went away with them; that a little while after, the same afternoon, he saw Hawkins riding behind Mills from Walberton towards Slindon, and never saw Hawkins the deceased afterwards.

John Saxby deposed that he was a servant to Cockrel the elder, of Walberton; that the day Hawkins (the deceased) was missing, Curtis, Mills, and Hawkins came to his master's house and drank together; that at going away, Mills bid Hawkins get up behind him, which he at first refused, saying he would not, without making a sure bargain; that they bid him get up for they would satisfy him, which Hawkins did; and this deponent never saw the deceased afterwards.

Thomas Winter, alias the Coachman, an accomplice, deposed that one day the latter end of January was twelvemonth, he, with Jerry Curtis, alias Pollard, were at the prisoner Reynolds's house, who kept the Dog and Partridge on Slindon Common; that Curtis presently went away from him, and promised to come to him again very soon, for he was to pay this witness some money he owed him; that this deponent stayed at the Dog and Partridge the rest of the day; that towards evening Richard Rowland, alias Robb, came to the

house, asked for his master Curtis, and stayed with
this deponent till night, when the prisoners Mills
and Curtis came; that Curtis called for Robb, and
said, "Robb, we have got a prisoner here"; then
Hawkins got down from behind Mills, and all went in
together, to a parlour in the prisoner Reynolds's house;
that they all, viz., Hawkins (the deceased), Curtis, Mills,
Rowland, otherwise Robb, and this deponent, sat down
together; that then they began to examine Hawkins
about the two bags of tea, which he denied, saying he
knew nothing of the matter; that Curtis said, "D......n
you, you do know, and if you do not confess I
shall whip you till you do, for, d......n you, I have
whipped many a rogue, and washed my hands in his
blood;" that the prisoner Reynolds came in when they
were urging the deceased to confess, and said to the
deceased, "Dick, you had better confess, it will be better
for you"; his answer was, "I know nothing of it."
After Reynolds was gone, Mills and Robb were angry
with the deceased; that Robb struck him in the face
and made his nose bleed, and threatened to whip him
to death; that Mills showed he was pleased with what
Robb had done, and again threatened the deceased, who
said, "If you whip me to death, I know nothing of it";
that then Mills and Robb made the deceased strip to
his shirt, then they began to whip him over the face,
arms and body, till they were out of breath, he all the
while crying out that he was innocent, and begged them,
for God's sake, and Christ's sake, to spare his life for the
sake of his wife and child; that when they were out of
breath, they pulled off their clothes to their shirts, and
whipped him again till he fell down; when he was
down they whipped him over the legs and belly, and
upon the deceased kicking up his legs to save his belly,

John Mills alias *Smoaker*, & *Rich.ᵈ Rowland* alias
Robb, Whipping *Rich.ᵈ Hawkins*, to Death, at y̌ *Dog* & *Par-*
-tridge on *Slendon Common*; & *Jeremiah Curtis*, & *Tho.ˢ Winter*
alias *Coachman*, Standing by Aiding & abetting y̌ Murder
of the said *Rich.ᵈ Hawkins*.

they saw his private parts; then they took aim thereat, and whipped him so that he roared out most grievously; that then they kicked him over the private parts and belly; they in the intervals asking after the tea; the deceased mentioned his father and brother, meaning the two Cockrels; that upon this Curtis and Mills took their horses, and said they would go and fetch them, and rode away, leaving the deceased with Robb and this deponent. That after they were gone, he and Robb placed the deceased in a chair by the fire, where he died.

Being asked by the court if the deceased was in good health when he came to the prisoner Reynolds's house, and if he believed he died of the ill usage he there met with, his answer was, "He was in good health when he came there, and was a stout man, and I am sure he died of the kicks and bruises he received from Mills and Robb."

He further deposed that when they found he was dead Robb locked the door, put the key in his pocket, then they took their horses and rode towards Walberton to meet Curtis and Mills; that in the lane leading to Walberton he met them, with each a man behind him; that he desiring to speak with them, the men behind them got off and stood at a distance. That this deponent asked Curtis what they were going to do with these two men, who answered, "To confront them with Hawkins." Then the deponent told him he was dead, and desired that no more mischief might be done, when Curtis replied, "By God, we will go through with it now." That this deponent begged that the two men might be sent home, for there had been mischief enough done already; that then Curtis bid the two men go home, and said when they wanted them they would

fetch them. That they rode all together to the prisoner
Reynolds's house, when Reynolds said to Curtis, "You
have ruined me," and Curtis replied he would make
him   amends.   That   then   they   consulted   what
to do with the body, when it was proposed to
throw him into the well in Mr. Kemp's park, and give
out that they had carried him to France ; that the
prisoner Reynolds objected to it, as that was too near,
and would soon be found. That they laid him on a
horse and carried him to Parham Park, about twelve
miles from Slindon Common, where they tied large
stones to him in order to sink the body, and threw him
into a pond belonging to Sir Cecil Bishop.

John Cockrel the younger deposed that the 28th day
of January last was twelvemonth, about ten o'clock
at night the prisoner Mills came to his house, called
for some ale, ordered his horse into the stable ; that
while he was in the stable Curtis came in, and
demanded two bags of tea, which he said his brother-
in-law had confessed he had got ; that this deponent
denied his having them, upon which Curtis beat him
with an oak stick till he was tired ; that after this they
took him with them to his father's at Walberton, where
they took his father and him with them, to carry them
to Slindon, on Mills's and Curtis's horses, one behind
each, and about a mile before they came to Slindon,
they met two men on horseback, who called to them,
and said they wanted to talk with them ; that then
they were ordered to get off from behind Curtis and
and Mills ; that after the two men had talked with
Curtis and Mills some time, Curtis bid them go home,
and when they wanted them they would fetch them.

John Cockrel the elder, being sworn, confirmed the
evidence as to being carried away, and afterwards let go.

Being asked by the court how long after his son-in-law (the deceased) was missing it was before he heard his body was found, said that in the April following he was sent for to Sir Cecil Bishop's; that there he saw the deceased Richard Hawkins mangled in a most terrible manner, having a hole in his skull; that he knew him by the finger next the little finger of his right hand being bent down to his hand.

Matthew Smith deposed that one night in January last was twelvemonth, he was at the prisoner Reynolds's house, the Dog and Partridge, on Slindon Common, and saw Curtis and Mills ride up to the door (Mills with a man behind him), and Curtis called out to Robb, and said, "We have got a prisoner"; and that then they all went in together into the back parlour.

Richard Seagrave, another witness, deposed that he lived at Sir Cecil Bishop's in Parham Park, and saw the body of a man taken out of a pond there, very much mangled and bruised; and was likewise present when John Cockrel the elder came there and said he knew the body to be that of his son-in-law, Richard Hawkins.

Jacob Pring, another witness, deposed that being at Bristol, he there fell in company with the prisoner Mills; that they came together from thence to his house at Beckenham in Kent; that on the road he asked him whether he knew of the murder of Richard Hawkins of Yapton; that he told him "Yes," and related to him the particular manner in which it was done, as follows: that in the beginning of January was twelve-month, they had two bags of tea stolen from the place where they had concealed some stuff, and suspecting Hawkins and the Cockrels to have it, he and Jerry Curtis went and fetched Hawkins from a barn where he was at work, and carried him to Reynolds's, on Slindon

Common, where Robb and Winter, commonly called the Coachman, were before them; that he and Robb whipped Hawkins with their horse-whips till he owned that the Cockrels had their tea; that then he and Curtis went and fetched the Cockrels, and as they were bringing them behind them on the road, Robb and Winter met them and told them that the man was dead whom they had whipped; that they then sent the Cockrels home and went and took Hawkins' dead body and carried it to Parham Park and threw it into Sir Cecil Bishop's pond.

Here the counsel for the King rested it.

The prisoner being called upon to make his defence, denied the murder, and said he left the deceased Richard Hawkins alive and well with Robb and Winter, when he and Curtis went to fetch the Cockrels, and how Hawkins came by his death he could not tell. This was Mills's defence.

The counsel for the prisoner Reynolds objected to the indictment, and said, though it might be extremely right with regard to the prisoner Mills, yet it was not so with regard to the prisoner Reynolds; for as Reynolds was indicted as a principal in the second degree, he should be concluded in the judgment as all principals are in murder. The court said this was a matter that might be offered in arrest of judgment, but not at that time.

The counsel, in his defence, said the prisoner Reynolds was no ways privy to or concerned in the said murder; that the persons who brought Hawkins to his house were in a room by themselves, and what they did there was without the privity or knowledge of the prisoner Reynolds, and that they should call witnesses to prove the same.

William Bullmar was called, who deposed that one day in January last was twelvemonth, he was at the prisoner Reynold's house with William Rowe in the kitchen; that he saw Curtis in the house, and heard there were other people with him in the new back parlour; that himself was there till twelve o'clock at night, and that the prisoner Reynolds was with him during all that time, excepting when he went to draw beer for his customers in the kitchen.

William Rowe deposed that he was at the prisoner Reynolds's house at the same time as the before-mentioned witness, that he saw Curtis and Mills in the house, and heard there were other people with them in the back room; that he stayed till twelve o'clock at night, during which time the prisoner Reynolds was with him except when he was called to draw drink for company.

The judge, after he had summed up all the evidence exactly in the manner it had been sworn, observed to the jury, that with regard to the prisoner Mills, the facts were proved extremely clear, as he had called no witnesses to contradict the evidence for the King in any shape; that with respect to the prisoner Reynolds it did not appear that he was in the party that committed the murder, but that he was at home at peace in his own house, when this transaction happened; if therefore, they believed the witness called on his behalf, they must acquit him, and the jury, without going out, found Mills Guilty, and acquitted Reynolds.*

---

* Notwithstanding James Reynolds was acquitted of the murder, yet as it appeared very plain that he concealed the murder, by knowing the same had been committed by the prisoner and the others who stand indicted for the same; as being present at the consultation for concealing the murder, and of burying the dead body, and advising therein, and his wife also being present, they are both indicted for the same, and are to be tried at the next assizes.

Mills's behaviour was very unbecoming one under his circumstances; but before we proceed to say anything more of this criminal, we will give the particulars of his being apprehended. The 31st January last, a proclamation was issued for the apprehending several notorious smugglers that were concerned in the murder of Richard Hawkins, of Yapton, naming this John Mills as one of them, promising his Majesty's pardon to anyone who should apprehend or give information of any of the offenders, although such informer was an outlawed smuggler, provided he was not concerned in any murder, or in breaking open his Majesty's warehouse at Poole. Now William Pring, who was a witness against the said Mills and the two Kemps, knowing himself to be an outlawed smuggler, yet not concerned in murder, nor in breaking open the warehouse at Poole, resolves, if possible, to get his own pardon by taking some of those offenders. To this purpose he applied to a great man in power, informing him that he knew Mills, and that if he could be assured of his own pardon, he would endeavour to take him, for he was pretty certain to find him either at Bristol or Bath, where he knew he was gone to sell some run goods. Being assured of his pardon he set out accordingly, and at Bristol unexpectedly found the two Kemps with him, whom he likewise knew as being notorious smugglers. They then began to talk about their affairs. Mills was in a proclamation for two murders, that of Chater and that of Hawkins. Thomas Kemp was advertised for breaking out of Newgate, and Lawrence Kemp was outlawed by proclamation, and both the Kemps were concerned in robbing one farmer Havendon.

After talking over matters together, and observing that all their cases were very desperate, Pring, as a

friend, offered his advice, by which he intended
to inveigle them into the snare he had laid for
them. He said, since they were all alike in
such desperate circumstances without any hopes of
mending their condition, he would have them go
with him towards London, and to his house at
Beckenham in Kent, and then consult together,
to go and rob upon the highway, and break
open houses in the same manner as Gregory's gang used
to do. Upon which they all agreed to come away
together; and upon the road, amongst other talk, Mills
owned that he was one of those who committed the
murder of Hawkins, and both the Kemps confessed that
they were concerned in robbing farmer Havendon, in
the manner it was proved upon their trials.

When they were all come to his house at Beckenham,
Pring then pretended that his horse being a very
indifferent one, he would go to town and fetch his mare,
which was a very good one, and would come back again
with all convenient speed, and then they would set out
together on their intended expeditions; for as their
horses were very good, and his but a bad one, it might
bring him into danger in case of a pursuit. Upon
which he set out, and they agreed to stay at his house
till his return; but instead of going to town, he rode
away to Horsham, where he applied to Mr. Rackster, an
officer in the excise there; who together with seven or
eight more, all well armed, set out for Beckenham, in
order to take them, where they arrived in the dead of
night, and found Mills and the two Kemps just going
to supper upon a fine breast of veal, and secured them.
They bound the arms of the two Kemps, but Mills
refusing to be bound in that manner, and being very
refractory, they were forced to cut him with one of their

hangers, before he would submit. They then brought them all three to the county gaol for Surrey, where they found Robert Fuller and Jockey Brown in custody for smuggling; and knowing that they had been guilty of many robberies on the highway in Sussex, they applied to the government for a Habeas Corpus, to carry them all five down to the assizes at East Grinstead, where, though they were each tried only upon one indictment, yet there was another indictment for murder, besides two for robbery against Mills, another for a robbery against Fuller, and two other indictments against the two Kemps, besides a number of other prosecutors, who were ready at East Grinstead to lay indictments against them, if there had been occasion.

John Mills, about 30 years of age, son of Richard Mills, of Trotton, lately executed at Chichester, was bred up to the business of a colt-breaker by his father. He said he had been a smuggler many years, and blamed Jeremiah Curtis, alias Pollard, who stands indicted for the same murder he was convicted of, and William Jackson, who was condemned at Chichester for the murders of Galley and Chater, as being the principal persons concerned in drawing him away from his honest employment.

Young Mills acknowledged himself a very wicked liver; but complained of the witnesses, that is, such of them as had been smugglers and turned evidences, and said that they had acted contrary to the solemn oaths and engagements they had made and sworn to among themselves, and therefore wished they might all come to the same end, and be hanged like him, and d.....ned afterwards.

John Mills stood indicted for two murders, besides robberies, as is before mentioned; but it is remarkable

that he committed both murders in twenty days ; that
of Hawkins, for which he was condemned, was
perpetrated on the 28th of January ; and the other,
that he was not tried for, which was the murder of
Daniel Chater, he committed the 17th of the following
month.

It having been said, as soon as Mills was convicted,
that the design of him and Curtis in fetching the two
Cockrels, the father and brother-in-law of Hawkins, to
the Dog and Partridge, was to serve them as they had
done Hawkins ; Mills being asked the question, at first
seemed very sulky ; but at last said, he believed that if
Winter and Robb had not met them and told them that
Hawkins was dead, they should have basted the
Cockrels well, when they had got them there ; so that
in all probability their lives were preserved by
Hawkins dying sooner than his murderers expected.

Jeremiah Curtis, alias Pollard, is at Gravelines in
France, and has entered himself into the corps of the
Irish brigades ; but Richard Rowland, alias Robb, he
imagined for very good reasons, was not out of the
kingdom ; and indeed he was seen and spoken to on
East Grinstead Common, which is near that town, the
latter end of the month of January last.

Being asked if he was upon Hind Heath on Saturday,
the 14th of January last, when the judges were going
over it to hold the assizes at Chichester on the special
commission, to try his father and brother, and the rest
of the smugglers then in custody, for the murders of
William Galley and Daniel Chater ; he said he was, and
two others were with him, but would not tell their
names ; that they had no manner of design against the
judges, or any body with them, neither did he or his
companions know or think of the judges coming at that

time, for they were upon other business; and that he
and his said two companions committed three robberies
that afternoon and evening, the nearest being upwards
of twelve miles from Hind Heath; but he refused to
name any particulars, declaring he thought he merited
d......ation if he was to discover any thing, by means of
which any of his companions might be apprehended and
convicted.

At the place of execution* he behaved himself much
more sedate than he had done before, during the small
time he lay under condemnation, and prayed very
devoutly; as he did indeed all the way from the gaol to
the place of execution, to which he was conveyed under
a strong guard of soldiers. He owned the fact of the
murder of Richard Hawkins for which he suffered; but
said when he went away with Curtis to fetch the two
Cockrels, he did not think the man was so near his
death.

He likewise acknowledged being present at the
consultation at Scardefield's, when it was agreed to
murder Daniel Chater, the shoemaker, who was at that
time confined in his father's skilling or turf-house; and
also that he was concerned with the two Kemps in
going with crape over their faces, and robbing farmer
Havendon, of Heathfield, in the county of Sussex.

He was pressed hard to make an ingenuous confession
of all the crimes he had been guilty of, but he refused;
and said he would inform them how far he was
concerned in anything that was known to the world
already, but nothing else.

Being then asked if he was with the gang when the

---

* He was executed on a gibbet, erected on purpose, on Slindon
Common, near the Dog and Partridge, and afterwards hung in
chains on the same gibbet.

King's custom-house at Poole in Dorsetshire was broken open, he said he was, for it was too well known to deny it.

Just before he was turned off, he declared he was sorry for his ill-spent life, and desired all young people to take warning by his untimely end ; and said that Richard Rowland, alias Robb, was only a servant to Curtis, and was ordered by Curtis to assist him in whipping poor Hawkins ; for the cruelties of which and the murder of Chater, and all other wicked actions of his life, he hoped God would forgive him ; declaring he died in peace with all mankind, and therefore hoped for forgiveness.

We will next proceed and give the trials in a concise manner, of Jockey Brown, the two Kemps, Fuller and Savage, all smugglers, and tried at the same assizes at East Grinstead, in Sussex, and then proceed and give an account of their wicked lives and conversation. And first we shall proceed on the trial of Jockey Brown.

John Brown, otherwise Jockey Brown, was indicted for assaulting and putting in fear John Walter, near Bersted, and robbing him of twelve guineas in gold and twelve pounds in silver, on the 12th of October, 1748.

John Walter deposed that riding along the road near Bersted, above seven o'clock at night, the 12th of October, he was stopped by four men ; two of them laid hold of the horse's bridle, and demanded his money, which he not delivering, the other two pulled him off his horse, one of them drew out a pistol, and the other aimed to strike at his head with a hanger, which he guarded with his stick ; in the meanwhile one of the other two took a canvas bag with the money in it out of his pocket, and afterwards cut his horse's bridle, and then they all rode off.

Thomas Dixon,* otherwise Shoemaker Tom, deposed that himself, the prisoner and two others, attacked the prosecutor in the road to Bersted, on the 12th of October, pulled him off his horse, and took from him a canvas bag, with upwards of twenty pounds of gold and silver in it. They afterwards rode about fourteen miles farther to a public house, where they shifted, meaning shared, the money among them all four.

Thomas Wickens deposed, that the night the prosecutor, Mr. Walter, was robbed, the last witness Dixon, the prisoner at the bar, and two others, came to his house about ten o'clock at night ; that they called for a private room, where they stayed drinking till twelve o'clock at night: that they had often been at his house, sometimes two, and sometimes three of them together, but at this time they were all together.

Sarah Wickens, wife of the last witness, deposed that the night Mr. Walter was robbed, the prisoner at the bar, Thomas Dixon and two others, came to their house at ten o'clock at night ; that they called for a pen and ink, and a private room ; that she waited upon them, and saw them telling out money in four parcels : that there was a great deal of silver and some gold, but could not tell what was the quantity.

The prisoner in his defence, said that the witness Dixon was a drunken, idle, good-for-nothing fellow, and deserved no credit to be given to what he should swear. But as he could call no witness to disprove the facts or justify his character, and Dixon's evidence being very

---

* This Shoemaker Tom had been a notoriouss muggler, but no murder being charged against him, he was by the court admitted an evidence.

circumstantially corroborated by Mr. and Mrs. Wickens, the jury found him Guilty. Death.

Lawrence Kemp and Thomas Kemp were indicted for forcibly entering the dwelling house of Richard Havendon, of Heathfield, disguised, and armed with firearms and cutlasses, putting him in fear of his life, and taking from his person eleven shillings and sixpence, and afterwards, with violence, seizing and carrying away from his dwelling house, thirty-five pounds in money, two silver spoons, three gold rings, a two-handled silver cup, and a silver watch in a tortoiseshell case, the 2nd of November, 1748.

Richard Havendon deposed that the 2nd November last, about seven at night, he heard somebody whistle at his door, and going out to see who was there, four men with crapes over their faces seized him, put a pistol to his breast, and said they wanted money ; upon which he gave them eleven shillings and sixpence out of his pocket ; but they said that would not do, and took him with them into the house ; when they came in they called for candles; and one of them holding a pistol to his breast, stayed with him below stairs, while the rest went up, where they stayed a considerable time, and then came down stairs with what they had got ; they then took him with them to the place where they had put their horses, and swore they would carry him away with them, unless he would tell them where the rest of his money was, for they were sure he had more than what they had got ; but when they were got upon their horses, they bid him good night, and went away and left him. When he came back to his own house again, he found they had broke open two doors, two trunks and a box, and taken away the money and things mentioned in the indictment. Asked what he was doing when they whistled at his door, said he was churning.

Francis Doe, an accomplice in the said robbery, being sworn, deposed that he, John Mills, alias Smoker (who was convicted for the murder of Hawkins), and the two prisoners at the bar, agreed to go and rob the prosecutor's house. That on the 2nd of November they all four, with their faces covered with crape, came to his house, and whistled at the door; that when the prosecutor came out, they seized him and demanded his money; that the prosecutor gave them eleven shillings and sixpence out of his pocket; that they then went into the house, and Lawrence Kemp, one of the prisoners, stood sentry over the prosecutor, whilst he, this witness, with Mills and Thomas Kemp, the other prisoners, went upstairs, forced open two doors, two trunks and a box, and took thereout several pieces of gold and silver, to the amount of five or six and thirty pounds, together with some rings, spoons and a watch. That when they came downstairs, they took the prosecutor with them to where their horses stood, and threatened they would carry him away with them unless he would discover where the rest of his money was, for they were sure he had more in the house. That upon his declaring he had no more, they let him go home, mounted their horses, and rode away. Upon shifting, that is, sharing the money, he had eight or nine pounds for his share. That Lawrence Kemp, one of the prisoners at the bar, was to sell the watch, rings, &c., and to divide the money between them, but he never did as he knew.

Jacob Pring deposed that he went down to Bristol to meet with and bring up John Mills, otherwise Smoker. That when he was there he met with the two prisoners at the bar, who agreed to come up with them. That on the road, talking together of their exploits, the two prisoners owned to him their robbing the farmer at Heathfield. That they said the old man was churning when they came to his house. That they craped their faces over, and took out of the house five or six and thirty pounds, besides a watch, rings, spoons, and a silver cup.

Being asked how they came to confess a robbery to him which must affect their lives, he said that he, the two Kemps, and Mills, alias Smoker, had agreed to go robbing on the highway, and to break open houses; that the prisoners bragged of this amongst other robberies they had committed.

Being asked by the court whether he had repented of the agreement he had so made, he said that he had no such intention, but that it was only a feint, and that he went down to Bristol on purpose to bring up Mills that he might be apprehended. That there meeting with the Kemps also, and hearing of this robbery at Heath-field, he resolved to do all in his power to allure them to his house, in order to get them and Mills apprehended.

The prisoners being called upon to make their defence, both said they knew nothing of the robbery; and the prisoner Thomas Kemp said that they never made any such confession to the evidence, Pring; that he, together with John Mills, alias Smoker, Francis Doe and Jockey Brown, were all the persons who robbed the farmer at Heathfield.

Being asked whether they had any witness to prove what they had asserted, or where they were when the robbery was committed, they said they had no witnesses, for that they had no "steady," meaning no certain place of abode, for two years past; upon which the jury found them both Guilty. Death.

Robert Fuller was indicted for assaulting William Wittenden in an open field, near the King's highway, putting him in fear of his life, and taking from the said William Wittenden seven shillings and sevenpence halfpenny, the 14th of November.

William Wittenden deposed that coming across a field near Worth, the prisoner at the bar, who was on horseback, stopped him and enquired the way to Worth; that this witness directed him; then the prisoner asked if he had any money; he answered, "No." The prisoner replied, "D......n you, you have, and I will have it," and then pulled out a pistol and put it to his breast; that then this witness pulled out a little bag, in which was seven shillings and sixpence in silver, and three halfpence, which the prisoner snatched from him, and then rode away.

Being asked by the court if he was sure the prisoner was the man that robbed him, answered he was very sure, and that he saw him ride by him the next day, in company with another man.

The prisoner in his defence said that the prosecutor declared, when he came to see him in the prison, that he did not know him; and to prove this called William Cooper, who, being sworn, deposed that the day before, the prisoner at the bar, with two other prisoners, were put into a room; that the prosecutor came in and said he knew nobody there.

The prosecutor being asked how many prisoners he saw in that room, said he saw but two, and that afterwards he went into another room, where all the prisoners were, and did not see anybody there that he knew, but, turning on his right hand, he saw the prisoner standing behind him, and he said, "That is the man that robbed me."

Mr. Rackster deposed that he was in the room the first time the prosecutor saw the prisoners; that there were indeed three prisoners in the room, but that the prosecutor saw but two, which stood before him, for the prisoner at the bar stood behind him, which was the reason that he did not see him then.

The prisoner being asked if he had any witnesses to his innocence or character, answered that he had none; upon which the jury found him Guilty. Death.

Richard Savage was indicted for stealing out of the Lewes waggon twenty-two yards three-quarters of scarlet cloth, twenty-six yards of blue cloth, the property of Thomas Friend, of Lewes, and a box, in which were contained two silk gowns and two guineas, the property of a person unknown, on April 5th, 1748.

Mr. Friend deposed that he knew his servant put up the cloth, and ordered it to be carried to the waggon.

William Brown, servant to Mr. Friend, deposed that he delivered the cloth to the carrier's man.

Matthew Comber, the carrier's man, said he received the cloth from the last witness. That on the 5th of April last he was set to watch the waggon all night at Chailey; that two men came up to him about ten o'clock at night, enquiring what waggon it was; on his telling them, they took him away about two hundred yards from the waggon, where one of them kept him prisoner with a pistol at his breast; that then came up seven more men, who got off their horses, and left them at some distance from the waggon, with one man to take care of them. That the rest of the men went up to the waggon, and cut the cords, threw off some woolpacks, and then threw some boxes and other goods out of the waggon; that they broke open the boxes, took out the goods, loaded their horses, and went away.

Thomas Winter, otherwise the Coachman, an accomplice, deposed that on the 5th of April, he and Shoemaker Tom, with the prisoner at the bar and several others, met at Deval's house at Bird's Hole, and agreed to go out and rob a waggon that was loaded with wrecked goods; that about ten o'clock at night they came all together upon Chailey Common, where they took the carrier's man prisoner, and one of them kept him so, while the rest went and rifled the waggon. That they broke open several boxes and parcels, and took away a large parcel of scarlet cloth, and another large parcel of blue cloth, and a box with two silk gowns and two guineas in it, with other goods. That after they had loaded their horses they rode away to Bird's Hole, near Devil's Ditch, where they shared the goods; that the prisoner at the bar was with them in the robbery, and had a share of the goods.

Thomas Dixon, otherwise Shoemaker Tom, another accomplice, deposed that he and Winter, and several others, met together at Deval's house, at Bird's Hole, and agreed to go and rob the waggon, as mentioned by the last evidence; that there they laid hold of the carrier's man, took him some distance from the waggon, and set one of their number as a guard over him; that they then plundered the waggon, and took the cloth and other things mentioned in the indictment; that having loaded their horses, they made the best of their way to Bird's Hole, and in a ditch near that place they divided the spoil.

Being asked by the court if the prisoner at the bar was with them at the time of their committing the robbery, said he believed he was, but was not sure; but that he was very sure that he was present at the time of sharing the goods, and that he had his share in the dividend; and that this witness sold his share to the last evidence, Thomas Winter.

The prisoner in his defence denied being any ways concerned in the robbery ; but had no witnesses to call to contradict the facts as sworn by the witnesses for the prosecution. The jury brought him in Guilty of single felony. Transportation.

Mr. Friend, the prosecutor of Savage, laid the indictment for single felony, because he did not care to take life away ; but the trial had not been over an hour, before he was informed by Winter and Shoemaker Tom that Savage had been concerned with them in many things, and that when Savage lived as a servant to Mr. Friend's brother, to look after and manage a farm for him, that was fallen upon his hands by a tenant leaving it, that Savage used to entertain them all, which was a gang of about twelve or thirteen, where they used to come with their goods, and he found the horses in hay and corn, and them with victuals and drink ; and they gave him tea and brandy for it, which he sold for his own use. He received sentence of transportation, but is ordered to be stopped in order to be tried next assizes for another fact.

Having now given an account of the trials of all the seven smugglers at East Grinstead, six of whom were executed for the several crimes of which they stood convicted, we shall now proceed to give an account of their behaviour and last dying words.

John Brown, alias Jockey Brown, about 33 years of age, was born of honest parents in the county of Sussex, who gave him a tolerable education, but he had followed smuggling for many years, and being apprehensive of being taken up for that crime, he absconded from his home and lurked about ; and being acquainted with Winter, commonly called the Coachman, Shoemaker Tom, who was evidence against him at his trial, Fuller, and the two Kemps, his fellow sufferers, and many more smugglers, many of whom were outlawed, they all agreed to rob on the highway, and break open houses, in order to support themselves, being afraid to go a-smuggling ; but they did that sometimes, when they could get anybody that they could trust to take the goods. He refused to make a general confession, but did not deny being concerned in robbing Mr. Walter on the highway near Bersted, for which he suffered.

He exclaimed against Mr. Wickens and his wife, who gave evidence against him at his trial, and said that he had never done them any harm.

He was taken up at first on suspicion of being a smuggler with Richard Mills, who was executed at Chichester, Richard Perrin, alias Payne, Thomas Kingsmill, alias the Staymaker, and William Fairall, alias the Shepherd, the three last now under condemnation in Newgate, for breaking open his Majesty's warehouse at Poole ; and being carried before Justice Hammond, in the Borough of Southwark, he committed them all five to the county gaol for Surrey, from whence he was removed by a Habeas Corpus to East Grinstead to take his trial.

He was not so very penitent as a person should be under his unhappy circumstances, but he frequently prayed to God to forgive him, and lamented most for the disgrace he had brought upon his family.

Lawrence Kemp and Thomas Kemp, two brothers, whose trials have been before related, refused to give an account of themselves, only that they were born near Hawkhurst, in Kent, and that they had been smugglers for many years and had committed many robberies, but said they never were concerned in any murder.

Thomas Kemp being asked if he was guilty of the indictment he was tried upon at the Old Bailey before he broke out of Newgate, he at first did not care to answer the question, but at last said he was.

They married two daughters of a farmer near Nettlebed, in Oxfordshire ; but as the father of the unhappy young women lives in good reputation, and the women themselves having the character of very virtuous persons, we think it improper to mention any particulars concerning them, their own misfortunes being sufficient trouble to them.

As to Thomas Kemp, he broke out of Newgate soon after he was tried and acquitted at the Old Bailey, being charged with a large debt due to the crown ; the circumstances attending his escape being somewhat more than common, we shall here insert them.

Thomas Potter and three other smugglers came into the press-yard of Newgate to see Thomas Kemp and William Grey, who was also one of the Hawkhurst gang, when they agreed at all hazards to assist in getting them out ; and accordingly the time was fixed (Kemp having no irons, and Grey had his so managed as to let them fall off when he pleased), and Potter and the other three came to the press-yard door, and rung the bell for the turnkey to come and let them in ; when he came and had unlocked the door, Potter immediately knocked him down with a horse pistol, and cut him terribly, when Kemp and Grey made their escape, and Potter and his companions got clear off without being discovered.

There were three other prisoners got out with them, but were taken directly, having irons on.

They were both very obstinate men, and could not be brought to think that smuggling was a crime, and when asked if they did not think robbing farmer Havendon, for which they were convicted, was a crime, they said they did, and begged pardon of him for it, but that if they had not been obliged to hide themselves from their home, for fear of being apprehended as smugglers, they should never have committed robberies.

Thomas Fuller, about thirty years of age, born in Kent, at first denied the robbery for which he was to suffer, and often said it was very hard to take away the life of a man on the single testimony of one person, who was to receive a reward for so doing; but the day before his execution he was brought to a confession of the fact, and acknowledged he did commit it in the manner it was sworn at his trial.

His wife attended him at his trial, and during his condemnation, for whose misfortunes he often declared himself sorry, and said he did not value death, but that he left her to the reproaches of a censorious world; but begged for God's sake, that nobody would reflect on her or any of her family, for none of them were ever privy to his wicked actions.

He acknowledged he had been a smuggler many years, and was as deeply concerned as most of them; but that he was not concerned in breaking open the King's warehouse at Poole, nor in the murders of Galley and Chater; but confessed he had been a very wicked sinner.

On Saturday, the 1st day of April last, they were all taken out of Horsham gaol and carried to the gallows, where they all seemed much more composed and devout than they had been before. None of them made any confessions, only desired all the spectators to take warning by their untimely end, particularly all young people.

After they had said their prayers some time, they were all tied up to the gallows and turned out of a cart, crying to the Lord to receive their souls.

We shall now give our readers, as we promised, an account of those four notorious smugglers, tried also at the assizes at Rochester, for the county of Kent, for divers robberies, and who were executed on Pickenden Heath, near Maidstone; whose method of robbing was going in the evening, disguised, and getting into houses, then binding all the family and robbing the same.

Stephen Diprose and James Bartlett were indicted, together with John Crumpton, not yet taken, for forcibly entering the dwelling-house of John Rich, of Linton, in the county of Kent, on the 31st of October last, putting him in fear of his life, and feloniously taking away 170*l.* in money, one small box and three gold rings.

The prosecutor deposed that about six o'clock in the evening on the 31st of October, somebody knocked at the door, and on his servant going to see who it was, four men rushed in, all disguised, with pistols and cutlasses in their hands. When they came in they demanded money, and asked him where his money was, upon which he desired they would be easy, and he would give them what he had. But they put one over him, and two of them went and rifled the house; and when they were gone he missed the money, &c., mentioned in the indictment.

Thomas Rogers, an accomplice in the fact, was next called, who deposed that he, the prisoners Stephen Diprose and James Bartlett, and John Crumpton, not yet taken, agreed to go and get some money upon the

31st October, and accordingly came to a resolution to go and rob Mr. Rich, of Linton. Accordingly they all set out, and when they came to Mr. Rich's door, Diprose knocked, and the door was soon opened, on which they all rushed in with firearms and cutlasses in their hands, and seized Mr. Rich and all his family, most of whom they bound, but who they were in particular he could not tell; that those who were not bound had one to stand guard over them, and two of the gang, Crumpton and James Bartlett, rifled the house; and that he believed they took away all the things mentioned in the indictment.

Being asked what he meant by saying he believed they took away all the things mentioned in the indictment, said that they did not give him nor Diprose a share of anything more than two gold rings and about seventy pounds in money; but that since that time he had heard by Crumpton that they took more money and goods at Mr. Rich's of Linton, which he and Bartlett had concealed.

Being asked if he was sure the prisoners at the bar were with him at the commencement of the fact, he said that they all agreed to go to Linton on purpose to rob Mr. Rich, imagining he had got a great deal of cash by him in his house.

Several of Mr. Rich's servants were then produced, who deposed to the like effect of the thieves coming to their master's house, and acting in the manner as was before related by the evidence Rogers; and some of them deposed further that the prisoners and Rogers were, they believed, three of the four men by their size and voices, that robbed Mr. Rich's house, and bound most of his family. Here the proof for the prosecutor was ended.

The prisoners being called on to make their defence, had little or nothing to say, only denied the fact, and said that Thomas Rogers was a very wicked fellow, and that they knew nothing of him; and supposed he swore this to get himself at liberty, and for the sake of the reward that was to be paid on their conviction; but having no witnesses to prove the contrary of what Rogers had sworn, and nobody appearing to give them the character of honest men; and it likewise appearing by the testimony of credible witnesses, that they and Rogers and Crumpton, who stand indicted for the same, were all acquaintance, and frequently together, and reputed all smugglers, the jury, without going out of court, brought them both in Guilty. Death.

William Priggs and James Bartlett (the same Bartlett convicted on the last indictment), were indicted for forcibly entering the dwelling-house of John Wright, of Snave, in the county of Kent, and taking from thence two bags of money containing containing 31l. 7s. 6d.

This fact was proved upon the prisoners by the prosecutor and his servants, and Rogers an accomplice; the prosecutor deposing he knew the prisoners again, and was sure they were the men that robbed him of the two bags of money mentioned in the indictment; he further deposed that when they came into his house they had all pistols and cutlasses in their hands, and swore they came for money, and " D..... n them," money they would have; that they bound him and his family, and one stood sentry with a pistol cocked in his hand, while the others went upstairs and took the money: that it was Priggs that stood sentry, while Bartlett and Rogers went and took the money.

The prosecutor further deposed, that when they had got the two bags which contained 31l. 7s. 6d., they swore they would blow his brains out if he did not tell them where the rest of his money was, for they were sure that was not all; that they would destroy the family if they did not confess where there was more money; but upon his declaring he had no more in the house, and they making him swear it, they went away and, on going, said if they stirred for two hours, or attempted to call out, they would murder them, and to that end should stay just by to watch.

Thomas Rogers, the same witness as was against Bartlett and Diprose on the last indictment, deposed that he and the two prisoners went and committed the robbery at Mr. Wright's house, at Snave, and bound Mr. Wright and his family, and took the two bags of money mentioned in the indictment; that they had crapes with them to put over their faces, but did not put them on at the committing this robbery.

Several other witnesses were produced, who confirmed what had been sworn by the prosecutor and Rogers the accomplice; and the prisoners having nothing to say or prove in contradiction to the evidence that had been given for the crown, only in general said they were innocent of the crime laid to their charge, the jury brought them both in Guilty. Death.

Thomas Potter was tried for stealing a horse; but as he so solemnly declared, and took the Sacrament just before his execution, that he knew nothing of the robbery, we shall omit the evidence, or the names of those concerned in the prosecution. The fact was sworn positively upon him, and he, not being able to prove the contrary, was found Guilty. Death.

While these men were under sentence of death, they were visited frequently by a reverend divine of the town of Maidstone, who endeavoured to bring them to a true and thorough repentance of all their past wicked lives and actions, being well assured that they had been smugglers many years, and that they had belonged to a gang, who committed many robberies, such as robbing houses in the same manner as the indictment had charged Diprose, Bartlett and Priggs; and also with having committed many robberies on the highway, besides other vile outrages, as well as smuggling.

They all behaved indifferently well under their unhappy circumstances, much better than those who had been smugglers generally did, and frequently prayed to God with great fervency, and were seemingly very sorry for their past misspent lives.

Thomas Potter, born at Hawkhurst, in Kent, twenty-eight years of age, declared he had been a very wicked sinner, and that he had been guilty of all manner of crimes except murder; which he declared he never was; though he confessed he did design to murder the turnkey of Newgate, when he went to get Grey and Kemp out of gaol; but that he was glad it happened no worse than it did, and that he often prayed the man might recover of the wounds he gave him; and that when he heard he was well again, he said it gave him great satisfaction.

He absolutely denied the fact for which he suffered, but acknowledged that he had committed crimes sufficient to have hanged him for many years past.

He refused to make any particular confession, but acknowledged that he had been a smuggler many years; and that he was well acquainted with the Kemps, Brown and Fuller: also with the Mills's, as likewise with Winter the Coachman, and Shoemaker Tom, who were both admitted evidences against their companions at Horsham.

William Priggs was born at Seling, in the county of
Kent, of very honest parents, who gave him a good
education in a common way, was about thirty years of
age, and had been a smuggler some years last past.

He acknowledged committing the fact for which he
died, as was sworn against him on his trial, and begged
pardon of the prosecutor for the great injury he had
done him; as also of others he had in any ways injured
in his life.

He solemnly declared that it was the evil gang he kept
company with that persuaded him to commit the fact
he died for, and said he never had been guilty of many
robberies, though he had been a smuggler many years.

The day before his execution he declared himself
truly penitent for all his wicked crimes he had been
guilty of, and said he freely forgave his prosecutor, as
he hoped for forgiveness from God.

He was asked if he knew of the robbery of the
Rev. Mr. Wentworth, of Brenset, in the county of Kent,
on the 19th day of December, when he declared he did
not; but that he had heard that one Butler was concerned; and for anything more concerning that affair
he did not know.

James Bartlett, aged forty-two years, was born of
very honest parents at Aknidge, in the county of Kent,
who gave him as much education as their circumstances
would allow them.

He acknowledged the fact for which he died, but said
as Priggs did, that it was evil company that he had
associated himself with that drew him in to commit
those wicked crimes.

He seemed very obstinate most of the time of his
being under condemnation, and would not acknowledge
himself guilty of any other robberies, but said he had

been a smuggler many years, and did not see any great crime in that.

He was particularly pressed to state if he was not concerned in any murders, particularly that of Mr. Castle, the excise officer, who was shot on Silhurst Common by a gang of smugglers, when he, with several other officers, had seized some run goods ; to which he would not give a positive answer, so that there were some grounds to think he was concerned.

He often said he had not the sin of murder to answer for; but one of his unhappy companions, and a fellow-sufferer, said he evaded the thing, by meaning that no person was ever murdered by his hands, but that Bartlett had been concerned where murder had been committed.

Stephen Diprose, born of honest parents, at High Halden, in the county of Kent, thirty-nine years of age, acknowledged himself guilty of the crime for which he was to suffer, and said he had been a wicked liver and a most notorious smuggler, having followed that employment for a great number of years; and that he never entertained a thought of smuggling being a crime till now, and that he was sincerely sorry for all his past iniquities.

He, as well as Priggs and Bartlett, laid the blame upon evil company, and said it was by the persuasion of some of his companions that he ever went a-robbing ; but just before he went out of the gaol to execution he confessed it was pure necessity that obliged him to it, as it was the case of the rest of his companions who were afraid of being apprehended for smuggling; which if it so happened, they were all dead men.

He said that he verily believed that the reason why so many notorious villianies and murders had been committed by the smugglers was owing to their not being safe in appearing publicly.

On Thursday, the 30th of March, they were conveyed from Maidstone gaol to Pickenden Heath, the usual place of execution.

There were three more criminals executed with them, that were likewise convicted at the same assizes at Rochester, viz. :—Samuel Eling, who was born at Stanmore, in Middlesex, about thirty-five years of age, and John Davis, born near Hertford Town, aged twenty-two, as companions, for a robbery on the highway on Bexley Heath ; and Richard Watson, born in Yorkshire, who would not tell his age, but supposed between thirty and forty, also for a robbery on the highway. These three criminals behaved themselves penitently at the gallows, as indeed they had done during the time of their lying under condemnation ; and Eling and Davis declared to the last moment they were both innocent, and that they had never been guilty of any felonies or robberies ; and forgave their prosecutor, as they expected forgiveness; and declared they died Protestants. Watson acknowledged his guilt ; and said little more than that he forgave all his enemies, and died in charity with all men.

At the place of execution they all behaved penitently. Potter declared to the last moment he did not commit the robbery for which he died ; and said he freely forgave his prosecutors, as he hoped for forgiveness for all his manifold sins, through his Redeemer Jesus Christ. Diprose said that his greatest consolation was, he never committed murder, or had been concerned at any time when murder had been committed. They none added anything to their former confessions, and having done praying and singing psalms, were turned off, crying to the Lord Jesus to receive their souls.

Having now finished the accounts of those smugglers, except Kingsmill, alias Staymaker, Fairall, alias Shepherd, Perrin, Glover and Lilliwhite, who were tried at the Old Bailey, for breaking open the King's custom-house at Poole, we shall next proceed to give their trials, and conclude this work with a particular account of their lives, and the last dying words of Kingsmill, Fairall and Perrin, who were executed at Tyburn, the first two named now hanging in chains in Kent.

As to the life of Kingsmill, it will appear to be very remarkable ; but for that of Fairall the like was never heard before, he being, even as he acknowledged himself, the most wicked smuggler living.

Thomas Kingsmill, alias Staymaker, William Fairall, alias Shepherd, Richard Perrin, alias Pain, alias Carpenter, Thomas Lilliwhite, and Richard Glover were indicted, and tried at the sessions-house in the Old Bailey, on Friday, the 4th of April, 1749, for being concerned with others, to the number of thirty persons, in breaking into the King's custom-house at Poole, and stealing out of thence thirty-seven hundredweight of tea, value 500*l.* and upwards, on October 7th, 1747.

The prisoners being severally arraigned, and pleading not guilty, the counsel for the King opened the nature of the indictment. Then Mr. Bankes and Mr. Smythe, two of his Majesty's counsel, spoke very particularly to the whole affair, shewing the enormity of the crime as being the most unheard-of act of villainy and impudence ever known, and proceeded to call the witnesses in support of the charge.

Captain William Johnson called and sworn: I have a deputation from the customs to seize prohibited goods. On the 22nd of September, 1747, I was stationed out of Stainham Bay, just by Poole. I was under the north shore and examined a cutter I suspected to be a smuggler. After quitting her I had a sight of the Three Brothers; I discovered her to the eastward, and after discovering her she put before the wind at N.N.W. I gave her chase with all the sail I could make; I chased her from before five in the afternoon till about eleven at night. After firing several shot at her, I brought her to. I went myself on board, and found she was loaded with tea, brandy and rum. The tea was in canvas, and oilskin bags over that, the usual packing for tea intended to be run; there was a delivery of it, forty-one hundredweight and three-quarters gross weight; there were thirty-nine casks, slung with ropes, in order to load upon horses, as smuggling brandy commonly is; there were seven persons in the cutter. I cannot say any of the prisoners at the bar were there. I carried these goods to the custom-house at Poole, and delivered them into the charge of the Collector of Customs there; the tea was deposited in the upper part of the warehouse; the brandy and rum were lodged in another part beneath.

William Milner, Esq., was next called and sworn: I am Collector of the Customs at Poole. On the 22nd or 23rd of September, Captain Johnson brought a vessel, whose name was given to me to be the Three Brothers. She had burthen two ton of tea, thirty-nine casks of brandy and rum, and a small bag of coffee. The tea was put in the upper part over the custom-house all together, except one small bag, which was damaged, which we put by the chimney. We made it secure; but it was taken away.

Q. Give us an account how it was taken away.

Milner. On the seventh of October, between two and three in the morning, I had advice brought me by one of the officers, that the custom-house was broken open; the staples were forced out of the posts; about five or six feet farther there was another door broken; at the door of my office the upper panel was broken in pieces, as if done with a hatchet, by which means they could more easily come at the lock, which was broken; and another door leading into the warehouse was also broken in pieces, so that there was a free passage made up to the tea warehouse, and the tea all carried off, except what was scattered over the floor, and one bag of about five or six pounds and the bag of coffee. They never attempted the brandy and rum.

Q. Did anybody ever come to claim the brandy and rum?

Milner. No, for it was condemned in the Exchequer.

Q. Was the tea in such sort of packages as the East India Company have?

Milner. No, sir, it was packed as is usual for run tea, and the brandy was in small casks all slung ready to fling over the horses.

The counsel for the crown having done examining Mr. Milner, proceeded to call several witnesses who were concerned in the fact; and in order that nothing but justice might be done, and the truth only appear against them, the witnesses were called in separately, so that Steel, who was the second, was not admitted into court till Race, who was the first examined, had gone through his evidence; and Fogden, who was the third and last examined, was likewise not suffered to go into Court till Steel had done.

John Race was called and sworn; who being asked if he knew the custom-house at Poole, answered, " I do know the custom-house at Poole."

Q. Do you know any thing of its being broken open?

Race. It was broken open soon after Michaelmas. I do not know the day of the month. It was a year ago last October. There was tea taken out of it.

Court. Look at the prisoners. Do you know either of them ?

Race. I know them all.

Court. Give us an account of what you know about it.

Race. I was not at the first meeting. The first time I was with them about it was in Charlton Forest, belonging to the Duke of Richmond : there was only Richard Perrin of the prisoners there then. We set our hands to a piece of paper to go and break open Poole custom-house, and take out the goods. It was Edmund Richards that set our names down ; some of them met there Sunday, but I was not then with them ; when we met on the Monday at Rowland's Castle, the prisoners were all there, except Kingsmill and Fairall, and were all armed when they met, with blunderbusses, carbines and pistols ; some lived thereabouts and some towards Chichester ; so we met there to set out altogether. When we came to the Forest of Bere, joining to Horndean, the Hawkhurst gang met us, the prisoners Kingsmill and Fairall being with them, and they were seven in number, and brought with them, besides the horses they rode on, a little horse, which carried their arms ; we went in company after we were joined, till we came to Lindhurst ; there we lay all day on Tuesday, then all the prisoners were there ; then we set out for Poole in the glimpse of the evening, and came to Poole about eleven at night.

Q. Were all the prisoners armed ?

Race. To the best of my knowledge all the prisoners were armed both at Horndean in the Forest of Bere, and at Lindhurst ; and when we came near the town of Poole, we sent two men to see if all things were clear for us to go to work, in breaking the warehouse, &c. The men were Thomas Willis and Thomas Stringer; Thomas Willis came to us and said "There is a large sloop laying up against the quay; she will plant her guns to the custom-house door, and tear us in pieces, so it cannot be done." We were turning our horses to go back, when Kingsmill and Fairall and the rest of their countrymen said, "If you will not do it, we will go and do it ourselves." This was the Hawkhurst gang. John and Richard Mills were with them; we call them the East-country people; they were fetched to help to break the custom-house. Some time after this, while we were consulting what we should do, Thomas Stringer returned and said the tide was low, and that the vessel could not bring her guns to bear to fire upon us. Then we all went forward to Poole. We rode down a little back lane on the left side the town, and came to the seaside. Just by this place we quitted our horses; Perrin and Lilliwhite stayed there to look after them.

Court. Why did you leave Perrin and Lilliwhite with the horses, more than anybody else?

Race. Because Perrin was troubled sometimes with the rheumatism, and not able to carry the goods so well as the rest; and Lilliwhite was a young man and had never been with us before."

Court. Well, go forward with your evidence.

Race. We went forward, and, going along, we met a lad, a fisherman; we kept him a prisoner. When we came to the custom-house, we broke open the door of the inside; and when we found where the tea was, we took it away. There was about thirty-seven hundredweight and three quarters. We brought it to the horses, and slung it with the slings, and loaded our horses with it ; the horses were two or three hundred yards off the custom-house. We sacked it in what we call horse-sacks to load.

Court. Were all the prisoners at the bar, or which of them, present at loading the horses ?

Race. All the five prisoners were there, I am sure ; and after we loaded all the horses, we went to a place called Fordingbridge ; there we breakfasted and fed our horses. There were thirty-one horses, and thirty men of us ; the odd horse was that for the East-countrymen to carry their arms upon.

The counsel for the King having done with this witness, those of the counsel for the prisoners got up ; and as Mr. Crowle was for Perrin, Mr. Carew for Glover, and Mr. Spilltimber for Lilliwhite, the court advised them to ask such questions only as related to the prisoners they were retained for.

Cross-examined by Lilliwhite's counsel.

Q. Did you see either of the prisoners assist in breaking the custom house ?

Race. I saw Fairall and Kingsmill carry tea from the custom-house to the horses. When we came back to a place called Brooke, there we got a pair of steelyards and weighed the tea, and equally divided to each man his share ; it made five bags a man, about twenty-seven pounds in a bag ; the two men that held the horses, which were Lilliwhite and Perrin, had the same quantity.

Q. Were you all armed—are you sure ?

Race. There were twenty of us all armed at Rowland's Castle. Richard Perrin had a pair of pistols tied round his middle.

Q. Had Lilliwhite arms ?

Race. Lilliwhite lay at my house on Sunday night,

and another man with him ; their horses were in my stable.

Q. Give me an answer to my question ; are you sure that Lilliwhite had arms about him when you left him to hold the horses ?

Race. I cannot tell ; I cannot be quite certain.

Q. Was Lilliwhite ever with you before or since that time ?

Race. No, never, as I know of ; I never heard he was a smuggler.

Cross-examined by Glover's counsel.

Q. Was Glover ever a reputed smuggler before, or did he ever act as such ?

Race. No, not as I know of, neither before nor since. Richard Perrin was the merchant that went over to Guernsey to buy this cargo of brandy, rum and tea. I paid him part of the money as my share to go. He told me, after the goods were taken and put on board another vessel, that he had lost the tea by the Swift privateer, Captain Johnson.

Q. Did you never hear that Glover was forced to go against his consent by Richards, his relation ?

Race. No, I did not hear any such thing. Edmund Richards brought him, and I never knew him do anything but this time.

Cross-examined by Perrin's counsel.

Q. Are you sure that Perrin was armed, particularly when he was with the horses ?

Race. Yes, he was, and was armed all the way we went from the Forest of Bere, and at that place too.

Q. You say Perrin was troubled with the rheumatism; why would you take a man with you that could not help you to carry off the goods ?

Race. I don't know ; I am sure he was with us, and had his share of tea when we divided it at Brooke.

William Steel was called, and appearing, was sworn.

William Steel. When I came home, I was told the goods were taken by Captain Johnson. The first time we met, I cannot say any of the prisoners were there. When we met in Charlton Forest at the Center-tree, I believe Richard Perrin was there ; there were a great many of us there ; this was some time in October ; we met to conclude about getting this tea out of Poole custom-house. We came to some conclusion there ; from thence we came to Rowland's Castle on a Sunday in the afternoon ; there were about twenty of us ; I think Thomas Lilliwhite was there.

Q. Were there any of your company armed ?

Steel. I cannot say there were any arms there on the Sunday. On the Monday, in the afternoon, some time before sunset, when we set out, every man was armed.

Q. How came they by their firearms ?

Steel. They had them from their own houses, as far as I know. I do not remember one man without : some had pistols, some blunderbusses ; all the Hawkhurst men had long arms slung round their shoulders, and Fairall, alias Shepherd, had a hanger. We went from Rowland's Castle, and when we came to the Forest of Bere we were joined by the Hawkhurst gang ; this was on a Monday night. The prisoners Kingsmill and Fairall were part of the Hawkhurst gang that joined us, and had with them a little horse which brought their arms and would follow a grey horse one of them rode on ; there were about seven of them. We went from Dean to Lindhurst, and when we set out from thence to Poole we were all armed ; we all looked at our firearms to see if they were primed.

Court. When you looked at your arms to see if they were primed at Dean, are you sure all the prisoners were there, or which of them ?

Steel. They were all five there at that time, and we went together till we came near Poole, when Stringer and Willis went forward to see how the way stood ; and when we came within about a mile of the town, Willis and Stringer* came and met us, and one of them said it was impossible to be done. We turned our horses again, and came to a little lane, and every man got off, and tied our horses up to a rail, which was put along a sort of a common. There were thirty-one horses; we left them under the care of Thomas Lilliwhite and Perrin ; we every man went to the custom-house, and broke it open. I and another went to the quay, to see that nobody came to molest us. When I came back again the custom-house was broken open ; they said it was done with iron bars. They were carrying the tea when the other man and I came to them.

Court. Who do you mean were carrying the tea ?

Steel. All that went on purpose to break the custom-house open ; I do not mean any in particular.

Court. Were any of the prisoners there ?

Steel. Yes : Glover, Kingsmill and Fairall, Lilliwhite and Perrin being still with the horses. When we came we found the strings and tied it together, and carried it away to a gravelly place. There we fetched our horses to the place, and loaded them and carried it away. Then we went to a place called Fordingbridge, where we baited and refreshed ourselves. We loaded, and went for a place called Sandy Hill; but at a place called

---

* Willis and Stringer stand both indicted for the murder of Galley and Chater.

Brooke, before we came to this place, we got two pair of steelyards and weighed the tea, and it came to five bags a piece.

Q. Did you carry the tea to your horses, or did you bring the horses to the tea?

Steel. We carried the tea to a plain place convenient for loading. Then we brought the horses forward to be loaded.

Here Race was called again—he had said they carried the tea to the horses.

Q. to Race. Did you carry the tea to the horses?

Race. I had been employed at the custom-house to tie up the tea; and when I came, the horses were with the tea.

Cross-examined by Lilliwhite's counsel.

Q. Did you ever know Lilliwhite before?

Steel. I have known him, and been acquainted with him four or five years.

Q. Who came there first, he or you?

Steel. He was there first.

Q. Was Lilliwhite ever a-smuggling with you before this time?

Steel. Not as I know of.

Q. Was he ever reputed a smuggler before this affair happened?

Steel. Not as I know of.

Q. Do you think when Lilliwhite went with you, that he knew what you were going about?

Steel. I think he did; we talked openly of it; but I cannot swear he did.

Q. Do not you know that Lilliwhite was asked only to take a ride with you, and that he did not know what you were going upon till you came to the Forest of Bere?

Steel. I cannot say any such thing; he joined us at Rowland's Castle.

Q. You say the Hawkhurst gang joined you at the Forest of Bere, and had a little horse with them?

Steel. Yes.

Q. What arms were upon that little horse?

Steel. I think there were seven long muskets on him.

Q. Were the arms for you?

Steel. We had arms before that; they were brought for their own use.

Q. Had Lilliwhite any arms when holding the horses?

Steel. I cannot say that he had.

Q. Did you all put down your names on a piece of paper to go upon this affair?

Steel. Each man's name was put down by Edmund Richards.

Q. Was Lilliwhite's name put down?

Steel. I cannot say it was.

Cross-examined by Glover's counsel.

Q. Was Glover ever concerned in smuggling before this?

Steel. No; I believe he never was before or since.

Q. Did you ever hear he went with reluctancy, and against his will?

Steel. As to that, I never heard he did; but I believe Richards forced him to it. This I know, Glover lived in Richards' house, and I believe Richards was the occasion of his going with us.*

Q. Who was your commander?

---

* Edmund Richards also stands indicted for being concerned in the murder of Galley and Chater.

Steel. There was nobody took the lead, one more than the other.

The counsel for the King then called Robert Fogden, who being come into court, was sworn.

Robert Fogden. I remember the time the tea was seized upon. I was at the consultation in Charlton Forest; there we concluded to go after the tea; there was a noted tree that stood in the forest, called the Center-tree. I do not know whether either of the prisoners were there. I was not at Rowland's Castle; I was with others of the company, on a common just below, for we met at both places, and then met altogether at a place appointed in the Forest of Bere.

Q. Were any of the prisoners at the house you was at?

Fogden. No, not one. At the Forest of Bere there were, I believe, all the five prisoners. We met together at a lone place there; we stayed there till the Hawkhurst men came to us; then there were thirty of us in number. The prisoners Kingsmill and Fairall were with the Hawkhurst gang, and were part of that gang.

Q. Were you all armed?

Fogden. To the best of my knowledge we were all armed.

Q. For what purpose did you meet there?

Fogden. We were going to fetch away the tea that had been taken from us by Captain Johnson, and lodged in the custom-house at Poole.

Q. How did you take it?

Fogden. By force; went from thence to Lindhurst; we got there in the night, just as it was light. We stayed there till near night again; then in the night we went to Poole, and went to the backside of the town, and left our horses in a little lane. I never was at

A Representation of ỹ Smugglers breaking open ỹ King's. Custom House at Poole.

Poole before this or since ; I believe we left our horses about a quarter of a mile out of town. We left them in care of two men, Perrin and Lilliwhite. Then we went and broke open the custom-house. I saw the door broken open with two iron bars.

Q. Where did you get them ?

Fogden. I cannot tell.

Q. Where did you find the tea lodged ?

Fogden. It was in the top of the warehouse.

Q. Were any of the prisoners at the bar concerned in it ?

Fogden. They were there, and did assist as the rest, except the two that held the horses. We brought the horses to a place near, and then carried the tea to them. It was a very narrow lane where we stopped first, and we brought the horses up to a more open place for loading.

Q. Did the prisoners at the bar help you load ?

Fogden. Yes, all of them.

Q. Did you put an equal quantity on each horse ?

Fogden. We distributed it as near as we could. There was our little horse that carried the arms had not so much as the other horses had on them. Every horse there was loaded with tea ; from thence we went to a little town called Fordingbridge ; at the next place we stopped, we weighed the tea with two pair of steelyards ; for we thought it was not equal, some was scattered out of some of the bags. Then we divided it as equally as we could ; they were quartern bags, each prisoner had five bags.

Q. When did you see Lilliwhite first ?

Fogden. In the forest ; I never saw him before.

Q. Was he there before or after you ?

Fogden. I cannot tell.

Q. Did you hear any threats, if any should discover this affair what should be done to them ?

Fogden. No, Sir.

Q. Had Lilliwhite arms when left with the horses ?

Fogden. I believe he had not.

Q. Was Lilliwhite ever with you a-smuggling before?

Fogden. No, never as I know of.

Q. Was Glover ever with you a-smuggling before ?

Fogden. No, never as I know of.

The counsel for the King resting their proof here, the prisoners were severally called upon to make their defence, when Kingsmill and Fairall said they had nothing to say, only that they knew nothing of the matter.

Perrin, having retained counsel for him, called the following persons to his character.

John Guy. I have known Perrin almost twenty years. He is a carpenter, and always bore a very good character among his neighbours. I never heard he neglected his business.

Q. Did you ever hear he was a smuggler ?

Guy. I have known him these fifteen or sixteen years, and he always bore a very good character. I never heard in my life of his neglecting his business and going a-smuggling.

Q. Did you never hear he was a smuggler ?

Guy. No, never, but by hearsay, as folks talk.

Richard Glover's defence: I was forced into it by my brother-in-law, Edmund Richards, who threatened to shoot me if I would not go along with him.

William Tapling. I have known Richard Glover twenty years; I never heard before this unhappy affair that he was a smuggler; I believe he never was before. I know his brother-in-law Richards, and that Glover was about two months with him. Richards is a notorious wicked, swearing man, and reputed a great smuggler; I cannot help thinking he was the occasion of Glover's acting in this.

Henry Hounsel. I have known Glover a child; he was a sober young lad; I never knew him otherwise, nor did I ever hear him swear an oath in my life.

Q. Did you never hear he was a smuggler?

Hounsel. Never before this. He lived with his father till the year 1744. His father dying, he followed his business till August, 1747. He went in the beginning of June to that wicked brother's house, and was there about two months. He went after that to live servant with the Rev. Mr. Blagden. After that he got into Deptford yard, and there he continued ever since, till taken up, articled to a shipwright. This affair was at the time he was at his brother-in-law's house.

John Grasswell. I have known Glover these twelve years and upwards; I believe he never was guilty of smuggling before this; his character is exceedingly good. I never knew him frequent bad company, or guilty of drinking or swearing an oath.

Woodruff Drinkwater. I have known Glover ever since he was born; I never heard he was reputed a smuggler either before or since, exclusive of this time; his temper is not formed for it at all, far from it; after his father died he was left joint executor with his mother (left in narrow circumstances); he often came to me on any little occasion for five or ten guineas; he always kept his word; after his mother married again, there was some difference in his family; he went into the country, and I was very sorry for him at his going to Richards's house, and I cannot think he was voluntary in this rash action.

Mr. Edmonds. I have known Glover ever since the 9th of April last; he came to me and was entered into his Majesty's yard at Deptford the day following; he bore a good character before, and during the time he has been with me he has behaved very well and sober; he obtained a good character of all that knew him; I have had as good an opinion of him as any man I know; he was with me till the day he was taken.

Mr. Dearing. I live in the parish where this young man was born. I go there for the summer season; I have known him about eighteen years; being informed of this bad thing, it made me come to London on purpose to say what I knew of him; we in the country had great reason to believe that bad man Richards had corrupted him; he was a well-behaved lad before this happened; his uncle came to me, and the young man came and begged of his uncle, that he would see out for some business for him, in some way or other, adding that he could not bear to live with Richards; I had just hired a servant, or I had taken him; just after this bad affair happened, and he was unfortunately drawn into it.

The Rev. Mr. Blagden. I live at Slindon, in Sussex. The prisoner Glover was my servant; I knew him and his family before; he behaved exceedingly well with me as any could, and if he were discharged from this I would readily take him again; he attended on religious service, public and private, constant; I never heard an ill word or an oath from his mouth, or anything vulgar.

Thomas Lilliwhite's defence: I was down in the country, and a person desired me to take a ride with him; I agreed upon it, not knowing where they were going; I had no firearms, nor was any way concerned.

Fra. Wheeler. I have known Lilliwhite about six

years; he always bore a very good character; was a worthy young fellow, and brought up in the farming under his father, who was a man in very good circumstances; he minded his father's business very diligently; I have known him refuse going out upon parties of pleasure, because he has had business of his father's to do; he married since this affair happened to a woman of fortune; I never heard him charged with any such crime as this before.

Sir Cecil Bishop. The prisoner married my housekeeper's daughter; had not he been a man of good character, I should not have been consenting to the match, which I was; she brought him a good fortune; he is a deserving young man, and I cannot think he would be guilty of such a crime knowingly.

The evidence being all finished, Sir Thomas Abney summed up the whole in a very impartial manner; taking notice that in the case of Lilliwhite, if they thought the evidence that had been given against him was not quite full, as to his going voluntarily with them, and that he was not armed with firearms, they might acquit him.

The jury went out of court, and in about a quarter of an hour returned into court, and gave their verdict as follows, viz. :—

Thomas Kingsmill, William Fairall, and Richard Perrin, Guilty. Death.

Thomas Lilliwhite, Acquitted.

Richard Glover, Guilty, but recommended to mercy.

Thomas Lilliwhite was immediately discharged out of court as soon as he was acquitted; and the other four received sentence of death the same day, together with the other four criminals who had been tried and convicted of divers felonies and robberies.

While under sentence of death, they all four, viz., Kingsmill, Fairall, Perrin, and Glover, behaved much better than they had done before ; and particularly Glover and Perrin were composed and resigned, and constantly prayed and sung psalms most of the night time ; but Kingsmill and Fairall were not so penitent as Glover and Perrin.

As for Kingsmill and Fairhall, they were reckoned two of the most audacious wicked fellows amongst the smugglers ; and indeed their behaviour while under condemnation, plainly shewed it.

The day they were brought to Newgate by Habeas Corpus, from the county gaol for Surrey, Fairall behaved very bold after declaring he did not value being hanged ; and said, " Let's have a pipe and some tobacco, and a bottle of wine, for as I am not to live long, I am determined to live well the short time I have to be in this world." He also behaved very insolently at his trial ; or more properly ignorantly, laughing all the time at the witnesses while they were giving their evidence ; and when taken notice of by the court, and reprimanded for his bad behaviour, it had no effect on him, for he continued his idle impudent smiles, even when the jury brought him in Guilty.

At the time when he received sentence of death, when Mr. Recorder, who passed the same on him, and the rest of the criminals, said these words, " and the Lord have mercy on your souls," he boldly replied, " If the Lord has not more mercy on our souls than the jury had on our bodies, I do not know what will become of them."

On Thursday, the 20th of April, 1749, the report of these four criminals was made to his Majesty by Richard Adams, Esq., Recorder, when Kingsmill,

Fairall, and Perrin were ordered for execution at Tyburn, on Wednesday, the 26th of the same month ; and his Majesty was pleased to grant his most gracious pardon to Glover, several favourable circumstances appearing in his favour ; and the court and jury having, after his trial, recommended him to his Majesty for mercy.

After the death warrant came down, Kingsmill and Fairall began to consider their unhappy circumstances more than they had done before, and always attending divine service at chapel, and prayed very devoutly, but retained their former behaviour of boldness and intrepidity, shewing no fear, and frequently saying they did not think they had been guilty of any crime in smuggling, or in breaking open Poole custom-house, as the property of the goods they went for was not Captain Johnson's or anybody else's, but of the persons who sent their money over to Guernsey for them.

Perrin, who was ordered only to be hanged and after-wards buried, and Kingsmill and Fairall being ordered to be hung in chains, Perrin was saying to them that he lamented their case : when Fairall replied smilingly, in the presence of many people, " We shall be hanging in the sweet air, when you are rotting in your grave."

The evening before their execution, after they came down from chapel, their friends came to take leave of them ; and Fairall smoked his pipe very heartily, and drank freely ; but being ordered to go into his cell to be locked up, said, " Why in such a hurry, cannot you let me stay a little longer and drink with my friends ; I shall not be able to drink with them to-morrow night."

I shall next proceed to give the little account of these

criminals as given by the ordinary of Newgate; and afterwards conclude this book with a relation of some of the most notorious actions committed by them, and which have been communicated by their confederates.

Thomas Kingsmill, alias Staymaker, aged 28, was born at Goodhurst, in Kent, a young fellow of enterprising spirit, and for some years past employed by the chiefs of the smugglers, the moneyed men or merchants, as they are usually amongst themselves called, in any dangerous exploits. As his character in general among his countrymen was that of a bold, resolute man, undaunted, and fit for the wicked purposes of smuggling, and never intimidated, in case of any suspicion of betraying their secrets, ready to oppose King's officers in their duty, and being concerned in rescues of any sort or kind, so he wanted not business, but was made a companion for the greatest of them all, and was always at that service when wanted and called upon.

He would own nothing of himself, and was scarce to be persuaded that he had done anything amiss by following the bad practices of smuggling.

He acknowledged he was present at the breaking open of the custom-house, and that he had a share of the tea; and said what was sworn at the trial was all truth; but that they must be bad men to turn evidence to take away other people's lives.

William Fairall, alias Shepherd, aged 25, was born at Horsendown Green, in Kent, bred to no business, but inured to smuggling from his infancy, and acquainted with most of the evil practices which have been used in those parts for some years past. In this behaviour he seemed equally as well qualified for the work as was Kingsmill, and it is generally believed that they were both concerned together in most of their undertakings.

Fairall at his trial seemed to shew the utmost daringness and unconcern ; even shewing tokens of threats to a witness, as he was giving his evidence to the court, and standing all the while in the bar with a smile or rather a sneer upon his countenance. He came also to the gang with Kingsmill to the Forest of Bere, and was one of the forwardest and most busy amongst the company. Yet he would not own any one thing against himself that he had done amiss, for which his life should be at stake. However, his own countrymen were glad when he was removed from among them, because he was known to be a desperate fellow, and no man could be safe who Fairall should once think had offended him.

Richard Perrin, alias Pain, alias Carpenter, aged 36, was born near Chichester, in Sussex ; being bred a carpenter, was looked upon as a good workman, and had pretty business till the use of his right hand being in a great measure taken away by being subject to the rheumatism, he thought proper to leave that trade, and take to smuggling. He was esteemed a very honest man, and was therefore often entrusted by others to go over the water to buy goods, and for himself ; he traded in that way for brandy and tea. And he was the man that went over for this very cargo of goods that was rescued from Poole Custom-house.

Having talked to the prisoners several times, each by himself, and also when they were altogether, neither of them all three would own anything ; but said they knew best what they had done, and for what was amiss they would seek God's forgiveness, and continued thus to declare to the last.

Having now given the ordinary of Newgate's short account of these criminals, I shall proceed to give some

account of such of their wicked actions as have come to
our knowledge.

About two years since William Fairall was apprehended as a smuggler in Sussex, and being carried
before James Butler, Esq., near Lewes, was ordered by
that gentleman to be brought to London, in order to be
tried for the same. They brought him quite safe to an
inn in the Borough overnight, in order to carry him
before Justice Hammond the next morning, but he
found means to escape from the guards; and seeing a
horse stand in Blackman Street, he got upon it and
rode away, though in the presence of several people.

He made the best of his way into Sussex, to his gang,
who were surprised at seeing him, knowing he was
carried to London under a strong guard but three days
before; but he soon informed them how he got away,
and his lucky chance of stealing the horse.

They were no sooner met than he declared vengeance
against Mr. Butler, and proposed many ways to be
revenged. First to destroy all the deer in his park,
and all his trees, which was readily agreed to; but
Fairall, Kingsmill and John Mills, executed on Slindon
Common, and many more of them, declared that would
not satisfy them; and accordingly they proposed to set
fire to his seat, one of the finest in the county of
Sussex, and burn him in it; but this most wicked
proposal was objected to by three of the gang, namely,
Thomas Winter, alias the Coachman, one Stephens and
one Slaughter, commonly called Captain Slaughter, who
protested against setting the house on fire or killing
the gentleman; and great disputes arose among them,
and they parted at that time without putting any of
their villainous proposals into execution; but Fairall,
Kingsmill and some more of the gang were determined

not to let their resentment drop, and accordingly they got each a brace of pistols, and determined to go and waylay him near his own park wall and shoot him. Accordingly they went into the neighbourhood, when they heard Mr. Butler was gone to Horsham, and that he was expected home that night, upon which they laid ready to execute their wicked design. But Mr. Butler, by some accident, happening not to come home that night, they were heard to say to each other, "D...n him, he will not come home to-night, let us be gone about our business"; and so they went away angry at their disappointment, swearing they would watch for a month together but they would have him.

This affair coming to Mr. Butler's knowledge, care was taken to apprehend them if they came again, and they, being acquainted therewith, did not care to go a second time without a number; but no one would join except John Mills and Jackson, who was condemned at Chichester for the murders of Galley and Chater, as not caring to run into so much danger; and they not thinking themselves strong enough, being only four, the whole design was laid aside.

On their being disappointed in their revenge against Mr. Butler, they were all much chagrined, and Fairall said, "D...n him, an opportunity may happen some time," that they might make an example of Mr. Butler, and all others that shall dare presume to obstruct them.

Thomas Winter, and several others of the smugglers, whose lives had been saved by turning evidence, said that Fairall and Kingsmill had been the occasion of carrying several officers of the customs and excise abroad from their families, for having been busy in detecting the smugglers, and seizing their contraband goods.

Fairall and Kingsmill were both concerned with the gang in Kent, viz., Diprose, Priggs and Bartlett, in all the robberies they committed; but as an account of those has been given before, we think it needless to make a repetition.

The morning of their execution they behaved very bold, shewing no signs of fear of death, and about nine o'clock, Fairall and Kingsmill were put into one cart, and Perrin in a mourning coach, and conveyed to Tyburn under a strong guard of soldiers, both horse and foot.

At the tree they joined in prayers very devoutly with the rest of the unhappy criminals who were executed with them, which being ended, and a psalm sung, they were turned off crying to the Lord to receive their souls.

The body of Perrin was delivered to his friends to be buried; and those of Fairall and Kingsmill were carried to a smith's shop in Fetter-lane, near Holborn, where they were put into chains, and afterwards put into two wooden cases made on purpose, and conveyed by some of the guards and the sheriff's officers for the county of Middlesex to Newcross turnpike in the county of Kent; where they were received by the officers to the sheriff of that county, who conveyed them to the places where they were ordered to be hung up, viz., Fairhall on Horsendown Green, and Kingsmill on Gowdhurstgore, at both which places they had lived.

Richard Glover, who had received his Majesty's pardon, was discharged out of Newgate on Wednesday, the 3rd of May, 1749.

We can with pleasure inform our readers, that notorious wicked fellow, Edmund Richards (so often named in this work, as being concerned in the murder of Galley and Chater, and also in forcing Richard Glover to go with him and the rest of the gang to break open Poole custom-house) is taken, and in safe custody in Winchester gaol, so there is no doubt but he will meet with a just reward for all his cruel and enormous crimes, at the next assizes for the county of Sussex, to which county gaol he will be removed by Habeas Corpus.

DIRECTIONS FOR PLACING THE PLATES.

A SERMON

PREACHED

IN THE CATHEDRAL CHURCH
OF CHICHESTER,

At a Special Assize held there, January 16, 1748-9,

By WILLIAM ASHBURNHAM, A.M.,

DEAN OF CHICHESTER.

———————

Job xxix., 14, 15, 16.

"I put on righteousness, and it clothed me: my judgment was as a robe and a diadem.

"I was eyes to the blind, and feet was I to the lame.

"I was a father to the poor : and the cause which I knew not I searched out."

THAT JOB was a person of great eminence both for his birth and station, that he had the supreme rule and government, or was at least a principal magistrate of the place he dwelt in, appears plainly from this chapter, whence the text is taken. "When I came in presence," says he, " the young men saw me, and hid themselves, and the aged arose and stood up ; the princes refrained talking, and the nobles held their peace ; I sat as chief, and dwelt as a king in the army, and all men gave attention to my words, and kept silence at my counsel."

But whatever was the particular state of this illustrious person, whether he was invested with the supreme power itself or acted only by commission under it, this is certain, that the integrity of his conduct is a pattern worthy the imitation, and was recorded doubtless that it might be imitated by those who should in after ages be honoured with the like employment, and fill the same high office as himself. "I put on righteousness, and it clothed me: my judgment was as a robe and a diadem", expressing the great love he had to justice, and the pleasure he took in exercising judgment; that what a robe and a diadem was usually to other men, that the doing justice and judgment was to him; the great object of his whole desire, the thing he principally placed his glory and delight in. For that we are thus to understand the metaphor in the text is plain from a like expression made use of by the royal prophet, who, speaking of the wicked, says, that he "clothed himself with cursing like a garment"; which expression in the verse immediately succeeding he explains, by telling us that his "delight was in cursing". So that what we are here to understand of Job is, that his greatest satisfaction and delight was to administer justice righteously; that his sense of true honor was not that which reflected from these external marks of dignity and state, but which sprang from those virtues of which those were but the outward signs—He put on righteousness as a garment, and clothed himself with judgment as with a robe and a diadem.

The things, then, which naturally offer themselves to our consideration from the words before us, are these three :—

First. The duties which this great example represents to us and which more immediately belong to magistrates, and those who are invested with public authority.

Secondly. How great a blessing every good magistrate must be to the state and community whereunto he belongs. And

Thirdly. The personal respect and reverence with which he ought to be treated upon that account.

The first then of those duties to which we are led by this great example, is that of doing justice and judgment with zeal and cheerfulness. Now justice is a virtue that not only in the common consideration of it is, as every other virtue is, honorable in itself, and much to be desired for its own sake; but it is a virtue so peculiarly necessary for human society, that it is scarce conceivable how any society can subsist without it; for the want of justice, if it destroys not the very foundations of society, at least it deprives us of all the advantages of it, and renders such political establishments at best but useless and undesirable things. A state of solitude would give more comfort and security than such a state, where the just claims of society are defeated by cruel and unrighteous men, and oppressions permitted with impunity; but where justice is, there the diligent and industrious prosper and the innocent dwell safely. And therefore the great Creator of mankind, who made them for a social life, has stamped upon their hearts this most necessary of all social virtues, and made it the indispensable law of their natures, that they should do to others as they would have others do to them. And was this law but universally and duly kept, it could not fail to promote the happiness, by its tendency to preserve the order of the world; it bindeth up every hand from doing violence, and every heart from forging deceit; and guards the common safety of mankind with the strict command, that we "render to all their due, custom to whom custom, honor to whom honor, fear to whom fear."

Nor let us be so deceived as to think that our own private interest is not equally concerned herein with that of the public: for the good of particular persons can in no society be distinguished from the general good, but is always and unavoidably included in it. So that if we wilfully connive at, if we suffer or neglect to correct abuses in the public, we do what in us lies to lessen our own security, and insensibly promote the ruin of our private interest and prosperity.

So much reason have we to esteem and to endeavour to secure the practice of this best of virtues, if we respect only the thing itself and the benefits thence resulting to ourselves, either singly considered or in society. But it is by the righteous and impartial exercise hereof that God also is most effectually glorified by us: for then only we can in any sense be said to promote the glory when we strive to imitate the excellencies of God; and justice being one of the principal of those moral excellencies which He has propounded to us as a pattern for our imitation, we do then in an eminent manner give Him the honor due unto His name when we study to be like Him in this perfection of His nature: when they particularly, who are His ministers for this very thing, that is, for the execution of justice, endeavour to resemble Him whose ministers they are, in being just even as He is just.

Another instance which Job here gives us of his own integrity, and wherein he has set us an example that we should follow his steps, is his forwardness to give relief and assistance to the injured and oppressed. "I was eyes unto the blind, and feet was I to the lame: I was a father to the poor, and the cause which I knew not I searched out." Every man, according to his place and power, is both in justice and charity obliged to use his best endeavours, and to lay hold on all opportunities, by all lawful means, of helping them to right that suffer wrong : of protecting the innocent from injuries, and securing them from the oppressions of " bloodthirsty and deceitful men." It is our duty every one to exert the utmost of his strength to deliver the oppressed, and it is extremely criminal to be " weary or faint in our minds" for fear of the oppressors, or "forbear to deliver those who are ready to be slain." That we may see more clearly then the necessity of this duty, and be animated to a cheerful and conscientious performance of it, there are various reasons that deserve our attention, but those which more especially demand it, and which, if we have any sense of religion left, will have their influence upon us, are the command and example of God Himself.

And first, we have God's positive and express command for this purpose. It is the general and fundamental law of our religion, the ground and basis of all moral virtues, that " thou shalt love thy neighbour as thyself." And how can we more effectually fulfil this second great commandment of the law, than by employing the power God has put into our hands, of whatever kind it be, for our neighbour's good ; for securing his person from violence, and his property from fraud and rapine ?

But, besides the command of God, we have His example also for the performance of this duty. This the Holy Psalmist has clearly set before us, to the end that we may be followers of Him herein, as dear children. " Now for the comfortless trouble's sake of the needy, and because of the deep sighing of the poor, I will up, saith the Lord, and will help everyone from him that swelleth against him, and will set them at rest." And if the great God of heaven and earth, He who " hath His dwelling so high," does yet " humble Himself to behold the simple that lie in dust," and to " lift up the poor out of the mire ; " it can be no disparagement sure to the greatest, to give attention to the welfare of their brethren, and to hearken to the complaints of their fellow subjects ; who by the influence of their high examples, and the weight of their authorities, are doing God and their country service ; and of whom in gratitude we therefore needs must own that they have justly merited the public thanks for the care and pains they have been taking for the public good.

The laws of God have made this duty of universal extent; all mankind are concerned in it; but they who are the governors of society, and are to act with the authority of magistrates for the support of it, are more especially obliged to this duty, to be followers of God herein ; because it has pleased Him to set a peculiar mark of honour upon them, in that He has called them by His Own name, " I have said," says He, by the mouth of the royal prophet, " that ye are Gods, and that ye are all the children of the Most High." And He said it doubtless to instruct them in their duty, and shew them the necessity they are under of imitating His conduct, Whose name they bear.

These magnificent characters, as they declare the source from whence all their power is derived, so do they imply the purposes for which it ought to be employed. Nothing less could be intended by such honorable appellations, than to point out the obligation they are under to provide for the prosperity of the world, and to endeavour, in compliance with the will of God, and the design of their own appointment, to render the situation of all persons as secure and comfortable as possible; that they may enjoy unmolested the fruits of their own industry, and "lead peaceable and quiet lives, in all godliness and honesty". This is the original end of government itself, and therefore ought to be the principal aim of those who are any way concerned in the administration of it. Whatever share they possess of the public authority was given them to employ for the public good. And when they thus fulfil the duties of their station, by an impartial and wise discharge of the high trust that is reposed in them; when with holy Job they can truly say, "I have put on righteousness, and it clothed me: my judgment is as a robe and a diadem"; then are they in the best and noblest sense the "ministers of God, and children of the Most High"; they do honor to their character, and are a public blessing to the community whereunto they belong.

This was the second thing I proposed to consider; and it is a thing that ought frequently and seriously to be considered, though it is so evident that it needs not to be proved. It ought, I say, as evident as it is, frequently to be considered, and sometimes to be inculcated upon us; because the blessings that are constant and familiar, and those which therefore we enjoy the most, such is our ingratitude, we are apt to think of and value least. And of this kind is the blessing of a well-established government; we who have the happiness of being under it, and reap the fruits of a regular administration of wisely enacted laws, can but with difficulty conceive how miserable the condition of mankind would be, were there no such laws to keep them within bounds, and are therefore generally less sensible than we ought to be, of the many great advantages resulting from them. But that we may form in some sort an idea of the wretched effects of such a want of government, the behaviour of some dissolute and abandoned persons which we have lately seen, and that too in a country where they could not but have acted under some awe of civil justice, may serve as a kind of specimen, to teach us what savage creatures they would be without it; what havock and devastation they would make upon the earth were they set wholly free from the restraint of laws, and left to follow the imaginations of their own evil hearts without hindrance or control.

And would we but sometimes consider what manifold inconvenience all societies must feel, where there is either no government at all, or, which is next to none, an ill-established or an ill-administered one; the consideration would certainly be useful, to give us a proper sense and relish of the blessings we ourselves enjoy under one of the best regulated governments in the world: a government adorned with all the advantages which human frailty will allow us to expect, and which the very meanest of its subjects enjoy in common with those who are in the highest stations. We are all in our proportion partakers of these benefits, and therefore all have reason to thank God, the bountiful Giver of them, and to pay with due submission what I proposed as the

Last thing to be considered, a proper regard and reverence to those by whom, as the instruments of His goodness, He confers these benefits upon us. Nature itself instructs us that they who discharge the difficult functions of a state with wisdom and integrity, should be highly esteemed and honored for their work's sake. Which natural instruction of undepraved reason we also find among the positive precepts of revealed religion ; for by the same authority that forbids us to speak evil of the rulers of the people, we are enjoined likewise to give honor to whom honor is due. This common and easy tribute then, which all men are capable of paying, they have a natural and just right to demand of all; a right founded upon the principles of reason, and ratified by religion : and therefore to defraud them of any part of so approved a claim is to transgress the bounds both of decency and duty.

There is nothing in the world is more generally agreed in than the necessity of government to obtain the ends of society. It was the desire of mutual preservation and defence, of protection against wrong and robbery, and the secure possession of their private properties, that was the first inducement to mankind to unite themselves together in distinct societies ; that they might sit every man in quietness under their own vine, and enjoy safely the fruits of their own labour. But these, as all other blessings and benefits, are the gifts of God ; and governors are the ministers appointed by Him, through whom He derives those blessings and benefits to the world ; so that the peace and prosperity of nations is owing principally, under God, to the wise care and conduct of their rulers, and the prudent administration of government therein. Without this, all those intolerable mischiefs must ensue, which men's unrestrained appetites and passions would produce, and which unavoidably break the bands, and are the sure destruction of all societies.

It is not to be expected that all the individuals of any community should universally agree as to the exact bounds and extent of civil power, any more than

it is, that all the different communities throughout the
world should pursue the same system, and frame their
governments upon the same plan : but without a due
regard and reverence paid to those persons who are
entrusted with the management of public affairs, and a
dutiful submission to their legal authority, the best
contrived constitutions in the world could not answer
the ends of their establishment, nor could any of the
purposes of life be effectually served by them.   But
farther,

Every high place of trust and power has its
burdens, as well as honors, that are inseparable
from it ; and the magistrate of justice, from the
very nature of his office, must have his share :
he cannot in the course of things but incur
great enmity and provoke all the outrage and
resentment of evil doers, if he be resolute in performing
faithfully the duty of his station, and endeavouring, as
that duty obliges him, " to break the jaws of the wicked,
and pluck the spoil out of his teeth".   One would think
then that a sense of gratitude should inspire every
generous mind with an esteem and reverence for those
who bear the weight of so important an employment as
the administration of public justice, and the execution
of the laws of a kingdom.   And it appears indeed to
have been the wisdom of all nations to treat their
characters with the most particular regard.   For from
hence, it is probable, arose the practice, now in universal
use, of appropriating to magistrates external marks of
splendour and distinction ; that by the distance
naturally created in the minds of the people by the
outward ensigns of dignity annexed to their office, the
reverence due to their persons might be properly preserved, and their authority thereby maintained and

upheld. But lest this should fail of its effect, and the principle of gratitude not have force sufficient to secure the practice of this duty, the Holy Scriptures have bound it upon us by all possible obligations.

There are no duties that our blessed Saviour in the institution of His laws had a greater regard to, than those which arise from civil society, and tend to make us useful members of the community to which we belong. Accordingly as He laid the best foundation for such a general practice of truth and justice as, if duly followed, would secure effectually the properties of private persons; so He was particularly careful to save the rights of princes, and recommended in the strongest terms that obedience which is due to those whom the laws have appointed rulers in every nation. And although, when the Jews maliciously accused Him of treason against the state, and impeached Him before Pilate as an enemy to Cæsar for declaring Himself a King, He does not deny that He was a King, because, as He tells, it was "for this end He was born, that He might bear witness to this truth;" yet to shew that He had no evil designs against the person of Cæsar, nor any intention of interfering either with his, or any human government whatsoever, He expressly asserts that "My kingdom is not of this world." And again, that the rulers of the world might have no reasonable grounds of prejudice, no enmity against Him or His religion, through any apprehension of danger from them to their respective governments, He enjoins it as an indispensable duty upon all His followers, to "render unto Cæsar the things that are Cæsar's," as well as "unto God the things that are God's." They, indeed, who are invested with the supreme authority, and act as God's immediate vicegerents in the world, are the

persons in respect of whom this injunction was
particularly given, but it may very fairly be extended
likewise, under due restrictions, to all that are com-
missioned under it and have any share of the authority
delegated to them.

Such then is the doctrine of the Christian religion, as
taught by the Great Author and Founder of it, Jesus
Christ Himself.   And His apostles, who followed Him
in the uniform practice of all those virtues by which
societies subsist, have both by their precept and
example taught us the same thing.   St. Paul in his
epistle to the Romans, speaking of a Christian's duty to
the civil magistrate, commands that "every soul be
subject to the higher powers"; and deduces our
obligation to this duty from these two considerations:
first, that it is the will of God—for "there is no power",
he tells us, "but of God".   The powers in being are
ordained of Him: it must therefore, as he then
concludes, be the indispensable duty of all subjects to
obey; because if they resist, they "resist the ordinance
of God".   The other consideration is taken from the
general design of government, which shews it to be our
interest, as well as duty, to be obedient subjects; that
"he is the minister of God to us for good"; and that
therefore in regard to ourselves we should submit to
his authority, "not only from wrath, but also for
conscience sake"; as being truly sensible of the
advantages of government, that it is the ordinance of
God, for the good of mankind.   As an explication of this
duty of subjection to the higher powers, and to teach us
the extent of our obedience to it, St. Peter requires our
submission, not only to the supreme magistrate
himself, but also to all, in their degree and proportion,
who are invested with public authority.   "Submit

yourselves", says he, "to every ordinance of man for the Lord's sake, whether it be to the king as supreme, or unto governors, as unto them that are sent by Him for the punishment of evil doers, and for the praise of them that do well".

Now these scriptures, as they instruct us in our behaviour towards the persons of magistrates, so do they teach us likewise the great expediency and usefulness of magistracy itself, and shew us the grounds and reasons of its institution. They inform us that magistrates were appointed to be the guardians of the public quiet, and had the sword of justice put into their hands for this very purpose, " to execute wrath upon him that doeth evil ". And it is a melancholy truth, which I can only publish and lament, that never was the vigilance and courage of the civil magistrate more necessary than in these evil days into which we are fallen ; when to say nothing of the private vices that abound amongst us, an almost general licentiousness is practised throughout the kingdom, against both the common reason and the common interest of mankind, and in defiance of all authority, whether sacred or civil.

This is the unavoidable consequence of that contempt of religion which is so prevalent in this degenerate age. Men have been so accustoming themselves to look with scorn upon everything relating to it, that scarce any appearance of the reverence due to the Supreme Being is preserved amongst us. They deride the very notion of a wise and good God, that made and governs all things, and in consequence treat the duty of attending upon His worship as at best but a matter of great indifference ·whether it be observed or not. How much the influence and example of some of high rank and condition in the world have contributed to the

propagation of these pernicious notions, will best be left
to their consideration, in whose power it is to stop it ;
but however that may be, this everybody sees : that the
contemptuous impiety has got to a prodigious height,
and has overspread, in an uncommon manner, all sorts
of people. And when this is the case, when the
subjects of any kingdom have thrown off all regard
to God, so as to be kept no longer within the
bounds of duty by the fear of Divine justice, what is
there left that can procure their obedience to earthly
rulers, or hinder them from " walking every one in the
evil imaginations of their own hearts", from doing evil,
and that continually ? Take away religion, and the
obligation which it lays upon us to obedience, and all
human authority must fall to the ground. This is so
apparently true, that it has been the constant practice
of the wisest politicians in all ages, to use their utmost
endeavours to preserve religion, as judging it to be the
only thing that could preserve them. And their
judgment was well grounded ; for when once religion
has lost its influence upon the minds of men, and they
are come to " have no fear of God before their eyes ",
what can prevent them, upon this supposition, from
endeavouring to get loose from the restraints of government, and, whenever they can do it safely, throwing off
their allegiance to those whom they have no mind
should be rulers over them ?

The right of princes must, in different nations, be as
different as the laws themselves are upon which they
are founded. But be they what they will, the claim
they have to them is of Divine original, and derived
ultimately from Him, who is the " Governor among the
nations ; who ruleth in the kingdom of men, and giveth
it to whomsoever He will ". As long, therefore, as

men retain in their minds such a sense of God as
disposes them to give Him His right, they will probably
not fail in giving Cæsar his. But whenever it happens
that the Divine authority is disregarded, and God
Himself and His laws neglected, it cannot be any
wonder that the command of men should be so lightly
esteemed. These loose and irreligious notions, then, we
may fairly fix upon as one principal cause of that
depravity of manners, which so thrives and spreads
amongst us; that having first by their influence been
divested of the fear of God, we are come at length to
have no regard for men. Presumptive are we and
self-willed, and like that profligate and abandoned
people described by the apostle, " we despise dominion,
and are not afraid to speak evil of dignities ". What
will be the issue of this growing evil, or where the end
of those things will be, God only knows, who is the
Disposer of all events. That some care should be taken
to stop its progress, a prudential concern for our own
safety, had we no other inducements, renders absolutely
necessary. But there are motives of a higher nature ;
the regard we have for our religion, laws, and liberties,
should excite us to it; as an effectual means to promote
the glory of God, and to secure the peace of the kingdom.
And happy it is for us, that we have some illustrious
instances of persons, who have concern enough for both,
to engage in their behalf : and to give us hopes, however, that by this their seasonable zeal in " doing
justice and judgment," they may be able, with the
blessing of Almighty God, if not to correct all the
abuses of these daring and outrageous people, at least
give a check to their insolence, and keep them within
modest bounds ; that those who will not be persuaded
by the mercy of an indulgent sovereign, to pay him

willingly that submission which the very design of government gives an undoubted right to, a just severity may restrain from such enormous practices, as bring disgrace and danger to government itself.

Let us then humbly request of God, that, as he has now begun to make us happy, by settling us in a state of peace and putting away all fear of danger from our enemies abroad, he would go on to the completion of it, by repressing our disorders at home. That so we, who are blessed with a wise and well constituted government, administered by a mild and most gracious prince, may testify our sense and worthiness of so great a blessing, by living peaceably and quietly under it. That to·the fervency of our prayers we may add our endeavours likewise to preserve an establishment, which is the only means, under God, of preserving us; and, in a word, which is the common dictate both of reason and religion, that all, who share in the benefits, may join in the duties of an obedient people.

SMUGGLING IN SUSSEX.

BY WILLIAM DURRANT COOPER, ESQ., F.S.A.

Reprinted from Vol. X. of the "Sussex Archæological Collections."

———————◆———————

THE system of smuggling in Sussex and the neighbouring counties on the sea-coast, dates from a period long prior to that in which heavy customs duties on imports encouraged, what is locally and technically called, "the free-trader."

The southern counties were first used for an illicit export trade in wool; and, till after the reign of Charles I., it was only during our wars with France, Holland and Spain, when the products of those countries were prohibited here, that there was an illicit import trade of any magnitude.

EXPORT SMUGGLING.

A few notes on the wool trade will best illustrate the origin of the illegal export of that article, of which Dryden in his "King Arthur," says:—

> Though Jason's fleece was famed of old,
> The British wool is growing gold,
> No mines can more of wealth supply.
> It keeps the peasant from the cold,
> And takes for kings the Tyrian dye.

In the reign of Edward I., among the articles of inquiry before the jurors on the hundred rolls, 1274, was the illegal exportation of wool ;* the Sussex return shows that it had been sent from Shoreham.† Soon after an export duty was imposed on English wool, of 20s. a bag (or 3l. of our money), increased to 40s. (or 6l.) in 1296 ; then lowered to half-a-mark a bag ; and, ultimately, the higher duty was again imposed. At this time the price of the English wool was 6d. a pound (or 1s. 6d. of our money), and many English merchants transported themselves with it.

Attempts to prohibit the exportation of wool were, however, made by Edward III. That monarch had offered great facilities to the Flemings to establish the woollen manufactures in this country ; in 1336 the mayors and bailiffs of Winchelsea, Chichester (and twelve other ports out of Sussex), were directed not to allow the export till the duty had been paid ;‡ and he had so far succeeded, that the cloth produced in the year 1337 was sufficient to enable him to prohibit the wear of any cloths made beyond seas, and to interdict the export of English wool, under the penalties which then attached to capital felonies. His anticipations, however, were not realised. The merchants of Middlebourg, and afterwards of Calais, had great facilities for evading the English law ; they clandestinely exported foreign cloths to England, and imported the wool smuggled out of this country.§ The law was so severe that it became use-

---

* Henry III. had been advised to permit the export to Holland and Brabant, at a duty of 5 marks to the sack ; and it was calculated that this duty, willingly paid, would yield 110,000 marks (£66,333 13s. 4d.), implying an export of 22,000 sacks, in six months. Blaauw's " Barons' War," Ap., p. 2.

† " Rot. Hun.," ii., pp. 203-209.

‡ Rymer's " Fœd." (1821), ii., p. 944.

§ In 1340 the greatest store of wool was conveyed by stealth. John Smith's " Memoirs of Wool," 2 vols., 8vo, 1747, vol. i., p. 80.

less ; the punishment of loss of life and limb was soon repealed. In 1341, Winchelsea, Chichester (and thirteen other ports not in Sussex), were named, from which wool might be exported, on payment of a duty of 50s. a sack ;* and licenses were granted for all who should give 40s. upon a pack of wool of 240 pounds, beyond the due custom of half-a-mark a pack. The next step taken by Edward was to regulate the price of wool ; and accordingly, in 1343, an Act was passed, fixing, for three years, the price of Kent, Sussex and Middlesex wool—the best wool being fixed at nine marks (or 8l. 3s. 6d. of our money), and marsh at 100s. (or 13l. 14s. 6d. of our money), showing the distinction between the two breeds of short and long woolled sheep in this country. Similar attempts at regulating the price were, from time to time, made by the Legislature. In 1353, they gave the King duty of 50s. a sack† on exported wool ; and by the same statute, Chichester was one of the ten towns in England appointed as staples for weighing the wool. Ten years later, the staple was established at Calais, and there was a prohibition on exportation elsewhere ; this so lowered the price of wool, that in 1390 the growers had three, four and five years' crop unsold ; and, in the next year liberty was given to export generally, on payment of a duty. In 1363, it was declared that all merchants and others, for their ease, might ship wools at Lewes, where the customers of Chichester were directed to take the customs.‡ (In 1394, John Burgess, of Lewes, was

---

* Rymer's " Fœd.," ii., p. 1158.

† A sack was to contain twenty-six stones of fourteen lbs. each, or 364 lbs.

‡ Prynne's " Records," 37 Edward III.

pardoned for being at the port called Kingston, having at Goring by night shipped wool which had not paid customs, on the ship of Lawrence Blake, an alien [Pat., 18 Ric. II.] and two years after Thomas Kitte and Richard Barnard took on horses by night four sacks of wool, which the said Thomas and Lawrence Hildere had sold to a foreigner and promised to deliver: and Robert Smith, of Offington, Henry Elay, William Kitte, John Mitchelgrove, William Hobbin, John Mot, of Worthing, William Otham and William Garrett, lay wait for them the same night in the highway at Worthing, near the sea, opposite the port of Kingston, and took them with their horses and the wool, and detained them, but they paid 8 marks and more to help their cause [Pat., 20 Ric. II.]. In 1368, Chichester was still among the places for the staple; but in 1402 (4th Hen. IV.), the Lewes Burgesses prayed* that wool might be again weighed, for home consumption and for shipment, at that town as well as at Chichester, because they were near the sea, and a great part of the wool was grown near there, and the town and neighbourhood were inhabited by many great merchants.

At this period licenses were freely granted for the export of wool to any part of the Continent, on payment of a heavy duty to the Crown. It was to evade this duty that the smuggling trade was carried on. When, in 1423,† it was enacted that no license should be granted to export the "slight," i.e., the short "wools of Southampton, Kent, Sussex and York," except to the staple at Calais, a still more direct encouragement was given to the men of the coast to evade the law; and, in

---

* "Rot. Parl.," iii., p. 497.
  Act 2 Henry VI., c. 4.

1436, wharves* were assigned for the shipping of wool, to avoid the damage done to the King by those who shipped their wools in divers secret places and creeks, "stealing and conveying the same, not customed, to divers parts beyond the seas, and not to Calais." The shippers were required to find sureties and to bring back from Calais certificates of unlading there.

The price of wool fell considerably; and, in 1454, it was not much more than two-thirds of its price 110 years previously; the wool-growers were alarmed, and their representatives in the Commons complained of the great "abundance of wools, as well by stealth as by license, uttered into the parts beyond the sea,"† and prayed that wool might not be sold under certain prices; Shropshire marsh wool was fixed at fourteen marks; Kent at 3l., instead of 100s.; Sussex at 50s.; and Hants at seven marks a sack; whilst in the next reign (of Edward IV.) it was enacted that no alien should export wool, and denizens only to Calais.

In 1547, under Edward VI., complaints were made as to the falling-off in the amount of duty due to the crown; the irregularity with which it was paid; and the mode in which the price was artificially raised by the merchants. An enquiry was directed into the rate of subsidy due to the King, and the weight and quality of the wool in England and Calais;‡ and a bill was introduced for regulating the buying by staplers and clothiers. In the year 1548, the act against regrating was continued.

About this time, it would seem that the woollen

---

* Act 15 Henry VI., c. 8.

† "Rot. Parl.," v., p. 274.

‡ Acts 5 and 6 Edward VI., c. 6.

manufacture existed both in the counties of Kent and Sussex.* In 1551, renewed attempts to improve the English manufacture were made. A body of Flemish weavers was settled at Glastonbury,† and supplied with wools ; and the Legislature passed a very stringent act for regulating the times of buying wool—so stringent, indeed, that several of its clauses had to be repealed in 1553. Queen Elizabeth also favoured still more the immigration of foreign weavers. Although licenses were granted for the export of wools on payment of duty, and in October, 1560, we have an account of wools shipped legally to Bruges, ‡ yet practically the merchants of the staple had obtained a monopoly of exportation.§

The loss of Calais, however, and consequently of the staple there, had most materially injured the English wool-grower and the merchants of the staple. The latter laid their complaints before Queen Elizabeth, in 1560, representing the injury they had sustained since the loss of Calais,‖ and obtained such redress as was within the power of the crown, namely, by license to export wool generally, on payment of export duty. A similar license had been granted to Lord Robert Dudley, which was renewed in 1562;¶ and in 1571 the act of Edward VI., putting restrictions on the home trade, was extended.

---

* MSS. State Paper, Lemon, pp. 4, 5. A weaver is among the victuallers of Rye, 1626, Dom., 44.

† Ibid., p. 37.

‡ Ibid., p. 161.

§ By the Act 27 Henry VIII., c. 15, they had acquired the sole right of buying wool in Sussex and twenty-seven other counties.

‖ MSS. State Paper, Domestic, Lemon, p. 168.

¶ Ibid., p. 199.

The Parliaments of Mary, Elizabeth and James granted the high duty of 1l. 13s. 6d. a sack on wool exported by natives, and double the amount by foreigners. It is noticeable that at this time short wools had become of still less value; and that the long Cotswold wool had come into the most favour.

These restrictions operated very prejudicially on the trade; and in 1572 the Company of Woolmen petitioned the Queen to take off the restraints imposed by the act of the preceding year and by Edward VI.;* and five years afterwards (1577) the scarcity and high price were so great as to give rise to grave complaints against the merchants of the staple from the clothiers of Wilts, Worcester, Gloucester and Essex † (then the principal seats of the woollen manufacture). In August of that year commissioners were appointed in sundry counties to have the special oversight for the restraint of the unlawful buying and engrossing wool; ‡ and towards the close of the reign of James I. (in 1621-24-26) bills were introduced prohibiting all exportation of wool.§

On April 17, 1630, Charles I. also published a proclamation against the export of wool, but still granted licenses. In 1647, in consequence of the high price, an ordinance passed wholly prohibiting the exportation of wool and Fuller's Earth.‖ Again, on November 18, 1656, a further proclamation was issued against the exportation; yet it was avowed, by an

---

* MSS. State Paper, Domestic, Lemon, p. 456.

† Ibid., p. 550.

‡ Ibid., p. 554.

§ It was prohibited, without license, by proclamation, July 20, 1622.

‖ Fuller's Earth was found at Nutley Common, in Sussex.

authority writing in that year,* that, though the
exportation was prohibited as almost a felony, there
was nothing more daily practised.   Nor was the loss,
said he, in this case all the injury; for when honest
men did " detect these caterpillars," and endeavoured
by due course of law to make stoppage thereof, and to
have the offenders punished, so many were the
evasions—such combination and interests in the officers
who ought to punish ; such favour had they in the
courts of justice, and in general, such were the
affronts and discouragements—that the dearest lover of
his country, or most interested in trade, dared not to
prevent that mischief which his eyes beheld to fall upon
his nation.

After the Restoration, in 1660, an act was passed
entirely prohibiting the export of wool; and in 1662,
the illicit export was made felony.   The severity of the
punishment had no effect in discouraging the active
spirits along the southern coast, and they readily risked
their necks for 12$d.$ a day.   Seven years after the last
enactment, it is stated that from Romney Marsh the
greatest part of the rough wool was exported, being put
on board French shallops by night, with ten or twenty
men well armed to guard it ; whilst in some other parts
of Sussex, Hants, and Essex, the same methods were
used, but not so conveniently.†   In 1671, Mr.W. Carter
declared that the misery of England was the great
quantity of wool stolen out of England.   Holland drew
from Ireland whole ship-loads of wool, besides what
came from England, being stolen out from the Kentish,
Essex, and Sussex coasts.   In the town of Calais alone,

---

* " The Golden Fleece," by W. S. Gent, 1656, p. 67.
† " England's Interest Asserted," 1669, p. 17.

there had been at least, within two years, brought in forty thousand packs of wool from the coasts of Kent and Sussex; for Romney Marsh men were not content only with the exportation of their own growth, but bought wool ten or twenty miles up the country, brought it down to the seaside, and shipped it off;* and all attempts at effective prosecution of the offenders were defeated.†

In 1677, the landowners endeavoured, without success, to obtain a direct sanction for a legitimate export trade; and " Reasons for a Limited Exportation " were published. Andrew Marvel, writing in this same year, describes the owners as a militia, that, in defiance of all authority, convey their wool to the shallops with such strength, that the officers dare not offend them.‡

After the revolution of 1688, the penalty of felony, imposed by the Act of Charles II., was thought too severe. Very few convictions had taken place under it; and, in 1698, a milder punishment was inflicted;§ whilst, in 1698, a direct blow was aimed at the Kent

---

* " England's Interest in Trade Asserted," by W. C., 1671.

† Joseph Trevers, in 1675, says (p. 40) :—" It is well known that smugglers are not of meanest persons in the places where they dwell, but have oftentimes great interest with the magistrates ; and, being purse-proud, do not value what they spend to ingratiate themselves with persons of authority, to distrust all such as discover their fraudulent dealings, or else by bribes to stop their mouths . . . The smugglers are not only well acquainted with some attorneys and clerks, but they make good interest with the under sheriffs in the counties where they drive their trade ; and these have strange tricks and delays in their returns, in which some of them will take part with the offenders, instead of executing the law against them."

‡ " Letter from a Younger Brother in Ireland to an Elder Brother in England." Published anonymously, 1677.

§ 7 and 8 William III., c. 28.

and Sussex men by an enactment which lasted till our
own day,* that no person living within fifteen miles
of the sea, in those counties, should buy any wool
before he entered into a bond, with sureties, that all the
wool he should buy should not be sold by him to any
persons within fifteen miles of the sea ; and growers of
wool within ten miles of the sea, in those counties, were
obliged, within three days of shearing, to account for
the number of fleeces, and where lodged.

All the care of the Legislature had been to no
purpose ; the coast men had set the law at defiance—
openly carrying their wool at shearing-time, on horses'
backs to the sea-shore, where French vessels were ready
to receive it—and attacking fiercely anyone who
ventured to interfere. Mr. W. Carter himself was
sharply attacked in 1688. Having procured the
necessary warrants, he repaired to Romney Marsh,
where he seized eight or ten men, who were carrying
the wool on the horses' backs to be shipped, and desired
the Mayor of Romney to commit them. The Mayor—
wishing, no doubt, to live a peaceful life among his
neighbours—admitted them to bail. Carter and his
assistants retired to Lydd, but that town was made too
hot to hold them—they were attacked at night ; adopt-
ing the advice of the Mayor's son, they next day,
December 13, came towards Rye. They were pursued
by some fifty armed horsemen till they got to Camber
Point ; so fast were they followed, that they could not
get their horses over Guilford Ferry ; but, luckily,
some ships' boats gave them assistance, so that the
riders got safe into the town, which had been "put into
much fear ;" and "had they not got into the boats,"

---

* 9 and 10 William III., c. 40, secs. 2 and 3.

says one of the witnesses, "Mr. Carter would have received some hurt, for many of the exporters were desperate fellows, not caring what mischief they did.*

The new law was not, at first, much more efficient. Mr. Henry Baker, the supervisor of these counties, writing on his tour from Hastings, on September 18, 1698, refers the customs department to some observations he had made in relation to the "owling"† and smuggling trades; and in his letter of April 25, 1699, he states that in a few weeks there would be shorn in Romney Marsh (besides the adjacent parts in the level) about 160,000 sheep, whose fleeces would amount to about three thousand packs of wool, "the greatest part whereof will be immediately sent off hot into France— it being so designed, and provisions, in a great measure, already made for that purpose."‡ All that the new law seems to have done at first was to send the wool grown by the Sussex and Kent men some fifteen miles up the country, to be thence recarried to the sea and shipped.

Under the new act, seventeen surveyors were appointed for nineteen counties; and 299 riding officers, whose salaries and expenses came to £20,000 a year. They seized only 457 packs of wool, got only 162 packs condemned, and had 504 packs rescued. In Kent, sixty-five packs were seized and eight only condemned; in Sussex, twenty-six were seized, and twelve condemned.§

The illicit exportation of wool was never stopped;

---

* "An abstract of the proceedings of W. Carter: being a plea to some objections urged against him," 1694.

† Wool smugglers were called "owlers."

‡ Treasury Papers: Customs. Rolls House.

§ Smith's "Memoirs of Wool," ii., p. 166.

and, in 1702, Mr. William Symonds, of Milton, near Gravesend, in his " New Year's Gift to the Parliament : or, England's Golden Fleece preserved, in Proposals humbly laid before the Present Parliament,"* makes twenty-five proposals to prevent the exportation of wool, which was illicitly carried on to a great extent ; and, by the first, he suggests six staples, or registry offices, at Ashford, Faversham, Maidstone, Tunbridge, Gravesend, and Dartford, for the prevention of clandestine export from these places.

In 1717, an act passed, directing that smugglers of wool, who should be in prison, and should not plead, might have judgment against them, and, if they did not pay the penalty, might be transported;† and yet, on May 19, 1720, it was necessary to issue a proclamation for enforcing the law.

In 1731, and in the five following years, the manufacturers petitioned for greater vigilance against the clandestine exportation of wool ; it being alleged that the great decay of the woollen manufactures was, beyond dispute, owing to the illegal exportation of wool, of which 150,000 packs were supposed to be shipped yearly ; and it was " feared that some gentlemen of no mean rank, whose estates bordered on the seacoast, were too much influenced by a near but false prospect of gain," to wish for the application of a remedy proposed, viz., the registration of all wool at shearing-time, and a complete system of certificates till it was manufactured ; " so that no smuggler or owler would venture to purchase it, by reason he would have no opportunity of sending it abroad in the dark."‡

---

* London, 4to, p. 45.
† 4 George I., c. 11.
‡ " The Golden Fleece," 1736.

In the preamble to the Act of 1739,* it is expressly avowed that, notwithstanding the penalties imposed for eighty years, the exportation of wool, unmanufactured, was "notoriously continued." The stringent law of 1698 had failed in its object, and when, in 1787 (in opposition to the demands of the Lincolnshire wool-growers for power to export their produce), the manufacturers brought in a bill to prevent the illicit exportation, because of the then increasing practice of smuggling British wool into France, and the inefficiency of the laws to prevent it; and when, as a remedy, it was proposed to extend the restrictions imposed upon Kent and Sussex to the entire kingdom, the opponents of the bill shrewdly asked :—" How it was the manu-facturers could act so absurdly, to demand an extension of laws relating to those two counties, when it was supposed that the greatest quantities of wool were smuggled from those parts ?"†

The habit of export smuggling, then, has been, for some hundreds of years at least, part of the system under which the middle and lower classes in Sussex have been trained. Large fortunes were made by it in East Sussex, and it came to an end only during the last war with France.

IMPORT SMUGGLING.

The wars with France, in the time of King William and Queen Anne, revived and increased greatly the custom of *import* smuggling, for which the existing *export* system, already well organised, gave every con-venience.

---

* 12 George II., c. 21.

† In 1770 only thirty-two pounds of wool were seized ; in 1780 there were 12,383 lbs. ; and in 1782 there were 13,916 lbs. seized.

It was in Romney Marsh that Hunt, in the year
1696, ran cargoes of Lyons silk and Valenciennes lace
sufficient to load thirty pack-horses; and, under cover
of these proceedings, kept a house of resort for men of
high consideration among the Jacobites—of "earls and
barons, knights and doctors of divinity"—and established a clandestine post to London, and frequent
communications, by means of privateers, with the
Court of St. Germains.*

The vigilance necessarily used during the next war,
to prevent these clandestine communications with the
enemy, will be best seen by the following account of
some persons, as well English as French,† seized by the
riding officers appointed for the guard of the coast of
Kent and Sussex, coming out of France; and of some
other particulars relating to correspondence, &c., on
those coasts, since her Majesty's declaration of war in
May, 1702, to December 20, 1703 :—

JULY 25, 1702.—Some French letters sent from a
    privateer, and others found in the beach near
    Seaford, all delivered to the Secretary Hedge's
    office.

OCT. 8.—Near Seaford, two persons seized and sent to
    the Secretary.   Mr. Pelham and J. Goldham.

JAN. 4, 1703.—At Newhaven, five Frenchmen and a
    boy taken.   Hawkins.

MAR. 5.—At Felpham, two French prisoners.   Parratt.

MAY 3.—A Frenchman, from Calais, with letters and
    papers, under Beachy Head in the night, sent for.
    Messenger Fowler.

MAY 6.—Three French prisoners at Pagham.

---

* See Lord Macaulay's " History of England," vol. iv., p. 650.
† Egerton MS., 929, p. 38.

MAY 27.—Five or six French prisoners more, near Shoreham. Clark.

Captain Toosloe sett on shore, by Cleavell, from Dieppe. Clark.

Shoreham : Three French prisoners more. Mose.

Three came on shore in long-boat, and made their escape through the country. Ogilvie.

OCT. 2.—Mr. Herne seized : brought up per messenger. Seaford.

DEC. 12.—Major Boucher, Captain Ogiliby and five more out of France, seized at Beachy Head, by express ; brought up by messengers.

Out of a small hoy, near Selsea, seized five Frenchmen ; committed to Chichester gaol, broke prison, and retaken by J. Field.

SEIZURES OF SILKS AND OTHER FRENCH GOODS, &C.—Convictions and compositions made and obtained by the said officers, within the time first above-menconed, amounting to about six thousand five hundred pounds—as per records in her Majesty's Court of Exchequer may appeare. 6,500l.

The public records of this period give us other evidence of the calling to which the smugglers betook themselves in time of war, viz., the conveyance of letters and correspondence to the enemy.* Thomas Owen, on January 3, 1703, reported the capture of William Snipp at Lydd, and John Burwash and George Fuller—described in Mr. Baker's letter of 6th of the same month as "part of the old gang of those who were 'owlers' in the late war"—as openly in communication

---

* A custom as early, at least, as the time of Elizabeth. See "Sussex Archæological Collections," vol. v., pp. 195, 196.

with French sloops which came to the coast, and hoped
that the law would take hold of their carrying correspondence with the sloops, "else there would be more
wool transported than there has been for many years;"
whilst Mr. Baker declared that "the practice, if
permitted, would very much encourage and contribute
to the exportation of wool, and also the running or
smuggling of French goods."*

This system of carrying on correspondence with
France, in time of war, lasted down to and through the
last war, during which the daily newspapers and correspondence were regularly carried to Buonaparte, by a
family then resident at Bexhill.

From the following report, made by Mr. Baker in
December, 1703, it appears that the new law had by
that time abated, though it had not quite stopped, the
"owling" trade along these coasts, but that import
smuggling still flourished:—

"May it please your Honours,†—In obedience to
your Honours, commanding me to consider how the
charge of the ryding-officers appointed for the guard
of the coasts of Kent and Sussex may, in some measure,
be reduced without prejudice to her Majestie's service,
in preventing the exporting of wool, &c., from these
coasts. Upon consideration thereof, and from observations I have made of the state of that and the
smuggling trade, as they have been carryed on since the
present warr, I have observed and do beleive that the
neck of the ' owling ' trade, as well as the spirit of the
' owlers,' is in a great measure broke, particularly in
Romney Marsh; where I have, in several of my late

* Treasury Papers : Customs.   Rolls House.
† Egerton MS. 929, fol. 40.

reports and papers laid before your Honours, observed unto you, that in the latter end of the last warr, and the beginning of the last peace, wool used to be shipped off from thence and from other parts of that county by great numbers of packes weekly, there are not now many visible signs of any quantities being transported. But for fine goods, as they call them (viz., silks, lace, &c.), I am well assured that trade goes on through both counties, though not in such vast quantities as have been formerly brought in—I mean in those days when (as a gentleman of estate in one of the counties has, within this twelve months, told me) he had been att once, besides at other times, at the loading of a wagon with silks, lace, &c., till six oxen could hardly move it out of the place : I doe not think that the trade is now so carried on as 'twas then. Therefore, upon consideration of the whole matter, since your Honours are of opinion that it is for her Majestie's service to lessen the charge, I humbly propose :—That whereas there are now, for the security of those coasts, fifty officers appointed from the Isle of Sheppy, in Kent, to Ensworth, in Hampshire, which is coastwise more than two hundred miles, att 60*li.* per annum, with an allowance to each of them of 30*li.* per annum for a servant and horse, to assist them upon their duty in the night, the whole amounting to about 4500*li.* per annum, including the old sallary of the port-officers, &c., my opinion, upon consideration as aforesaid, is, if your Honours shall approve thereof, that the said allowance of 30*li.* to each of them, for a servant and one horse as aforesaid, may be taken off, which will completely reduce one-third part of the whole, and leave it then at about 3000*li.* per annum ; and for some kind of supply in their nightly duty, instead of their servants, and that the course of that may not be broken, especially in Romney Marsh, where the mischief has most prevailed, I further propose that the dragoons now quartered in Kent, and, by her Majestie's order of the 11th August last, to be detached into severall parts of the Marsh, to assist the officers in the exportacon of wool, &c., as from time to time I shall direct (as per said order may appeare), may, if your Honours shall so please, be made useful in this service, pursuant to the Order in Councell by his late Majestie, bearing date the 23rd June, 1698, wherein it was ordered that, for the encouragement of the said souldiers and the landlords of the houses that quarter them there (being an allowance of twopence per diem to each dragoon upon such service, and to the officers in proportion, the whole not exceeding 200*li.* per annum, to be paid by me—which was for about two years constantly paid them myself), being revived, I can soe dispose those souldiers that the nightly duty of the officers shall not be interrupted, and every one of them shall always have one or more of them in the night upon duty ; I mean all those in the Marsh, that is from Folkestone inclusive to East Guldeford the same ; and this being soe ordered, your Honours do reduce the charge from what it now is full 1300*li.* per annum. The same use may be made of them upon the coast of Sussex (if it be thought for the service, as in my opinion it would very much be), as well in other respects as those afore-mentioned. To all this, if your Honours can obtain the guard of cruizers, as they are appointed by the 7th and 8th of the late King, for those coasts from the North Foreland to the Isle of Wight, and shall be pleased to remove your weak and superanuated officers, as soon as you can provide otherwise for them, and for the future resolve to admit none into the service; but that the officers (according to proper and apt instructions to be prepared for them) be kept to a strict and diligent discipline in the performance of their duties. These methods being taken, I am humbly of opinion both coasts may be ventured with a single guard, soe as aforesaid, during the warr, or for one year's tryall, &c.

"HEN. BAKER.

"December, 1703."

The new force was utterly inadequate to the suppression of the trade. In the next forty-five years the daring of the smugglers grew with the impunity with which they were enabled to act. Large gangs, of twenty, forty, fifty, and even one hundred, rode, armed with guns, bludgeons, and clubs, throughout the country, setting every one at defiance, and awing all the quiet inhabitants. They established warehouses and vaults in many districts, for the reception of their goods, and built large houses at Seacock's Heath, in Etchingham (built by the well-known smuggler, Arthur Gray, and called "Gray's Folly"), at Pix Hall and the Four Throws, Hawkhurst,* at Goudhurst, and elsewhere, with the profits of their trade.

We have in the treasury papers† many particulars of the daring and desperate acts of these companies or gangs of men in both parts of Sussex, during the first half of the last century, principally in the smuggling of tea.

In an engagement between the custom-house officers and upwards of sixty armed men, at Ferring, on June

---

* *Ex. inf.* Miss Ann Durrant, æt. 89, 1858.

† Notorious instances of riots and assaults in running tea and other goods.—Customs : Rolls House.

21st, 1720, William Gouldsmith, the custom-house officer, had his horse shot under him.*

In June, 1733, the officers of the customs at Newhaven attempted to seize ten horses laden with tea, at Cuckmere; but they were opposed by about thirty men, armed with pistols and blunderbusses, who fired on the officers, took them prisoners, and confined them whilst the goods were carried off.†

In August of the same year, the riding officers observed upwards of twenty smugglers at Greenhay, most of them on horseback, armed with clubs, and their horses laden with tea, which the officers endeavoured to seize, but the smugglers fell upon them, and with clubs knocked one of the officers off his horse, wounded him, and confined him for an hour, whilst the gang carried off the goods.

On December 6, 1735, some officers of Newhaven, assisted by dragoons, met with a large gang of smugglers, well armed, who surrounded the officers, and confined them for about an hour and a half. The smugglers were afterwards met by three other officers and six dragoons, whom the smugglers attacked, but the officers got the better, pursued them, and seized five smugglers, armed with pistols, swords, and cutlasses, and twelve horses.

In July, 1735, some of the officers of the port of Arundel watched on the coast, expecting goods to be run out of a smuggling vessel, but being discovered by upwards of twenty smugglers armed with pistols and blunderbusses, the officers were confined till two or three boatloads of goods had been landed and conveyed

---

* Letter of Francis Briggs, July 26, 1733.—Customs: Rolls House.

† Notorious instances, &c.—Ibid.

away on horses ; and in the same month, some other officers having received information that a parcel of brandy was to be run at Kingston, and going in pursuit of it, met with ten smugglers, one of whom presented a pistol in order to rescue the goods ; but the officers getting the better of the smugglers, seized the brandy and carried it to the custom-house.

In the natural course of events these affrays must end in bloodshed ; and in March, 1737, a fatal engagement took place at Bulverhithe, with one of the then numerous gangs of Sussex smugglers, an account of which is given in a letter, dated March 10, from a person writing under the assumed name of Goring, to the Commissioners of Customs :—*

" May it please (your) Honours,—It is not unknown to your Lordships of the late battle between the smuglers and officers at Bulverhide ; and in relation to that business, if your Honours please to advise in the newspapers, that this is expected off, I will send a list of the names of the persons that were at that business, and the places' names where they are usually and mostly resident. Catt† (Morten's man) fired first, Morten was the second that fired ; the soldiers fired and killed Collison,‡ wounded Pizon, who is since dead ; William Weston was wounded, but like to recover. Young Mr. Brown was not there, but his men and horses were ; from your Honours'

" Dutifull and Most faithfull servant,
" GORING."

---

* Treasury Papers.—Customs : Rolls House.

† The Family names will be familiar to many in our own day as very active, bold men.

‡ Another well-known name.

"There was no foreign persons at this business, but all were Sussex men, and may easily be spoke with.

"This (is) the seventh time Morten's people have workt this winter, and have not lost any thing but one half hundred (of tea) they gave to a dragoon and one officer they met with the first of this winter; and the Hoo company have lost no goods, although they constantly work, and at home too, since they lost the seven hundred-weight. When once the smugglers are drove from home they will soon be all taken. Note, that some say it was Gurr that fired first. You must well secure Cat, or else your Honours will soon lose the man; the best way will be to send for him up to London, for he knows the whole company, and hath been Morten's servant two years. There were several young chaps with the smugglers, whom, when taken, will soon discover the whole company. The number was twenty-six men. Mark's horse, Morten's, and Hoad's, were killed, and they lost not half their goods. They have sent for more goods, and twenty-nine horses set out from Groomsbridge this day, about four in the afternoon, and all the men well armed with long guns. . . . There are some smugglers worth a good sum of money, and they pay for taking. . . . The Hoo company might have been all ruined when they lost their goods; the officers and soldiers knew them all, but they were not prosecuted. . . Morten and Boura sold, last winter, someways, 3,000 lb. weight a week."

In fact, the smugglers overawed most of the riding officers, and bribed many others, so that the peaceable inhabitants of the villages were completely at the mercy of these lawless bands.

On June 13, 1744, the officers of the customs at Eastbourne, having intelligence of a gang of smugglers, went, with five dragoons mounted, to the seashore, near Pevensey; but one hundred smugglers rode up, and after disarming the officers, fired about forty shots at them, cut them with the swords in a dangerous manner, loaded the goods on above one hundred horses, and made towards London.*

In "Seasonable Advice to all Smugglers of French Cambricks and French Lawns, with a brief State from the Honourable Commissioners of His Majesty's Customs of Smuggling, in the year 1745,"† it is said that before the Committee of the House of Commons, which sat in 1745 to inquire into the causes of the most infamous practice of smuggling, it was in evidence:— " From Chichester it is represented that in January, 1745, nine smuggling cutters sailed from Rye, in that month, for Guernsey, in order to take in large quantities of goods, to be run on the coast ; and they had intelligence that one of the cutters had landed her cargo." The remedy suggested was the annexing the Isle of Man to the Crown of England, by purchase, and the employment of 2,060 sea officers and men, in sixty vessels, to be stationed on different parts of the coast.

The most formidable gang, however, that had hitherto existed, and that which luckily furnished the climax to these scenes of crime, was known throughout our own county and Kent as the " Hawkhurst Gang." In the year 1747‡ the smugglers in those parts were grown so numerous and so formidable by their daring and repeated attacks on the persons and properties of the inhabitants, and the cruelties exercised on some who

---

* " Gentleman's Mag.," vol. xiv., p. 334.

† King's " Pamphlets," Brit. Mus., Lond., 1751, p. 13.

‡ Dearn's " Weald of Kent," 8vo, Cranbrook, 1814, p. 100.

had opposed their extravagancies, that the people of
Goudhurst found themselves under the necessity either
of deserting their houses, and leaving their property
wholly at the mercy of these marauders, or of uniting
to oppose by force their lawless inroads.　The latter
alternative was at length embraced; a paper, expressive
of their abhorrence of the conduct of the smugglers, and
their determination to oppose them, was drawn up and
subscribed to by a considerable number of persons, who
assumed the appellation of "The Goudhurst Band of
Militia," at the head of whom was a young man of the
name of Sturt, a native of Goudhurst, who had recently
received his discharge from a regiment of foot, under
the command of General Harrison, and by whose
persuasions they had been principally induced to this
resolution.　Intelligence of this confederacy soon
reached the ears of the smugglers, who contrived to
waylay one of the militia, and, by means of torture and
confinement, extorted from him a full disclosure of the
plans and intentions of his colleagues.　After swearing
this man not to take up arms against them, they let
him go, desiring him to inform the confederates that
they (the smugglers) would, on a certain day named,
attack the town, murder every one therein, and burn it
to the ground.　Sturt, on receiving this information,
convened his little band, and, having pointed out the
danger of their situation without exertion and
unanimity, engaged them in immediate preparation
for the day of battle.　While some were sent in quest
of firearms, others were employed in casting balls,
making cartridges, and taking every means for
resistance and defence which time and opportunity
afforded.　At the time appointed, the smugglers,
headed by Thomas Kingsmill, made their appearance

before the entrenchments of the militia,* and after some horrid threats and imprecations by their leader, a general discharge of firearms was given by the smugglers, and returned immediately by the militia, by which one of the smugglers fell ; but it was not till two more had lost their lives, and many had been wounded, that they quitted the field of battle ; they were pursued by the militia and some of them taken and executed.†

Thomas Kingsmill escaped for a time, and became the leader of the desperate attack made in October, 1747, by thirty smugglers on the custom-house at Poole. This man was a native of Goudhurst, and had been a husbandman ; but, having joined the smugglers, he was distinguished and daring enough to become captain of the gang—an honour of which he was so proud that he sought every opportunity of exhibiting specimens of his courage, and putting himself foremost in every service of danger.

Perrin, another of the gang, was a native of Chichester, where he had served his time as a carpenter, and had successfully practised his trade, as a master, for some years, till a stroke of the palsy had deprived him of the use of his right hand ; he then became connected with the smugglers, and used to sail to France as purchaser of goods for them. In this capacity he, in September, 1747, bought a large quantity of brandy, tea and

---

* My great grandfather, Wm. Durrant, afterwards of Lamber-hurst and Boreham, M.D., was at that time resident with Mr. Hunt, a surgeon in the town ; and (like Mr. James, in his novel of " The Smuggler ") laid the scene of the attack at Goudhurst Church.

† " General " Sturt was for some time prior to his death master of the poorhouse of Cranbrook. See also " Gent. Mag." vol. iv., p. 679.

rum,* which was loaded on board a cutter (" The Three
Brothers "), with the view of running it on the coast of
Sussex ; but intelligence reached the revenue officers,
and Captain Johnson, of the revenue cutter at Poole, on
September 22, caught sight of the loaded cutter, took
her, and carried her and her cargo into Poole—Perrin
and the crew escaping in the boat.

On Sunday, Oct. 4, the whole body of smugglers
assembled in the Charlton Forest to consult on the
possibility of recovering the goods, when Perrin proposed
that they should go in a body, armed, and break open
the Poole Custom-house ; this was agreed to, and a
bond was signed to support each other. The next day
they met at Rowland's Castle, armed with swords and
firearms ; at the Forest of Bere, adjoining Horndean,
Kingsmill and the Hawkhurst gang met them ; they
concealed themselves in the wood till the evening of
the following day, and then proceeded to Poole, which
they reached at eleven at night. A report from two
who were sent to reconnoitre, stating that a sloop of
war lay opposite the quay, so that her guns could be
pointed against the door of the custom-house, led some
of the gang to falter; but Kingsmill and Fairall (a
native of Horsendown Green, Kent, of no business,
inured to smuggling from infancy, and remarkable for
his brutal courage†) addressed them, saying: " If you

---

* The tea was 41¾ cwt., packed in canvas and oilskin bags ;
and thirty-nine casks of spirits, slung with ropes, in order to be
loaded on horses.—" History," p. 132.

† He had been arrested and sent to London by James Butler,
Esq., near Lewes, but escaped and rejoined his companions. It
was proposed to burn down Mr. Butler's house ; but that not
meeting with general assent, Fairall, Kingsmill, and others of
the gang determined to waylay him, near his own park, and shoot
him ; but, by accident, he did not return home that night, and the
matter becoming known, a watch was kept, and the design laid
aside.—" History," p. 147.

will not do it, we will do it ourselves." Then a fresh report was made, that, owing to the ebb-tide, the sloop could not bring her guns to bear. Animated with this intelligence, they all rode to the sea coast; Perrin and another of the gang took care of the horses, whilst the main body went down to the custom-house, taking with them a boy they chanced to meet, to prevent his alarming the inhabitants. The door was forced open with hatchets and other instruments, the smuggled tea was carried off on the horses to Fordingbridge; the band, after having travelled all night, there stopped for a time, but continued their journey to Brook, where the tea booty was divided in the proportion of five bags of twenty-seven pounds each per man.

A reward was offered for their apprehension, but it was months before any were taken. A man named Diamond was captured, and lodged in Chichester gaol, when a portion of the gang committed murders in West Sussex to prevent evidence being given against their fellows. The victims were William Galley the elder, a custom-house officer at Southampton; and Daniel Chater, a shoemaker of Fordingbridge. The murderers were Benjamin Tapner, a native of Aldrington,* who had worked as a bricklayer; John Cobby, an illiterate son of a Sussex labourer; John Hammond, a labouring man, born at South Berstead; William Jackson and William Carter, natives of Hampshire; Richard Mills the elder, a native of Trotton, where he had been a horse-dealer, but, failing in business, had commenced smuggling, and become one of the most hardened of the gang; and Richard Mills the younger, who lived at

---

* Trial of Benjamin Tapner and others, at Chichester, January, 1749.

Stedham, and had been with his father in business. It seems that, on February 14, 1748, Galley and Chater were on their road to Major Battine's, at Stanstead, to have Chater's evidence taken, when they were induced to stop at the White Hart, at Rowland's Castle, the landlady of which, being afraid that they were going to hurt the smugglers, sent for Jackson and Carter, and communicated her suspicions to them; others of the gang came in, and Carter soon got from Chater the real business. The men were then made nearly drunk, and put to bed; from which they were awoken to be tied to one horse, with their legs under the belly, and to be whipped till they fell twice, with their heads under. They were then taken to a well in Lady Holt Park, where Galley was taken from the horse and threatened to be thrown into the well; this, however, the smugglers did not do, but, putting him again upon the horse, whipped him to death on the Downs, and then dug a hole and buried him. Chater was then chained in a turf-house, from which, after being maimed in his nose and eyes by a knife, he was taken in the dead of the night to Harris's Well, and Tapner, having fastened a noose round Chater's neck, bid him get over the pales of the well; they tied one end of the rope to the pales, and pushed him into the well; the rope, however, was short, and he, being some time without becoming strangled, they then untied him and threw him head-foremost into the well; and, to stop his groans, threw upon him the rails and gate-posts round the well, and large stones. Galley's body was found by Mr. Stone whilst hunting; and six miles off, in the well, the body of Chater. The murderers were tried at a special assize for smugglers, holden at Chichester, before three judges —Sir Michael Forster, Knight, Sir Thomas Birch,

Knight, and Mr. Baron Edward Clive—January 16, 1749. The sermon, which has been printed,* being preached by Sir William Ashburnham, then Dean, but afterwards Bishop of Chichester, from *Job* xxix., 14-16. The first three were convicted as principals, and the others as accessories before the fact to the murder of Chater ; and Jackson and Carter for the murder of Galley. Jackson died in prison the night he was condemned. The others were hung on January 18— the two Mills's not in chains ; but Carter was hung in chains, near Rackley ; Tapner, on Rook's Hill, near Chichester ; and Cobby and Hammond, on Selsey Isle, on the heath where they sometimes landed their smuggled goods, and where they could be seen a great distance east and west.

John Mills, another son of Richard Mills and one of the gang, who, with some of his associates saw the judges travelling over Hind Heath, on their way to the special assize at Chichester, and proposed to rob them;† but his companions refused to concur with him. Soon

---

* "A Full and Genuine History of the inhuman and unparalleled Murders of Mr. William Galley, a Custom-house Officer, and Mr. Daniel Chater, a shoemaker, by Fourteen Notorious Smugglers ; with the Trials and Execution of Seven of the Bloody Criminals, at Chichester." Written by a Gentleman of Chichester.   Fifth Edition, 8vo. London : W. Clowes, 20 Villiers Street, Strand. N.D.

† Ibid., p. 32. The judges set out from London on Friday, Jan. 13th, and arrived at the Duke of Richmond's house, at Godalming, that evening.   The next day they set out for Chichester, and were met by the Duke at Midhurst ; and he entertained them with a dinner at his "hunting house," near Charlton.   They reached the Bishop's Palace at Chichester, at five that evening. The report that they were guarded there and back by a party of horse is erroneous ; the judges, counsellors and principal officers were in six coaches, each drawn by six horses.

after his father's execution, he met with Richard Hawkins, put him on horseback and carried him to the Dog and Partridge on Slindon Common, where Mills and his companions accused him of having stolen two bags of tea; and on his denying it, flogged and kicked him to death, and then, carrying his body twelve miles, tied stones to it and sunk it in a pond in Parham Park. Mills was entrapped to the house of an outlawed smuggler named William Pring, at Beckenham, and there betrayed. He was tried and convicted at the assizes holden at East Grinstead, and there hung on Aug. 12, 1749, being conducted to the place of execution by a guard of soldiers, as a rescue was feared from the smugglers; and after execution, he was hung in chains on Slindon Common. Others of the gang were tried at the same assizes as highwaymen, and executed.

At length two of the smugglers, who had been evidence against the men hanged at Chichester, gave information as to the place of meeting of Kingsmill, Fairall, Perrin and Glover; they were arrested for the breaking open of the custom-house at Poole, tried at Newgate, and convicted,* Glover being recommended by the jury to the royal mercy. Fairall behaved most insolently on the trial, and threatened one of the witnesses; Glover exhibited penitence; but Kingsmill and Perrin insisted that they had not been guilty of any robbery, because they only took the goods that once belonged to them. Perrin's body was directed to be given to his friends, and he was lamenting the fate of his associates, when Fairall said: "We shall be hanging up in the sweet air, when you are rotting in your grave;" and the night before his execution,

---

* See p. 131 of the same work as referred to on previous page.

Fairall kept smoking with his friends till he was ordered by his keeper to go to his cell, when he exclaimed : "Why in such a hurry, cannot you let me stay a little longer with my friends ? I shall not be able to drink with them to-morrow night." Kingsmill was only twenty-eight and Fairall only twenty-five years of age, at the time of their trial.

Glover was pardoned; the other three were hung at Tyburn on April 26, 1749, and the body of Fairall was hung in chains on Horsendown Green, and Kingsmill's on Goudhurst Gore.

This most formidable gang was thus broken up ; but Horace Walpole's letter of August 5, 1752, and the diary of Walter Gale,* show that to Sussex men, the profits of the illicit trade were too great a temptation to allow it to be given up.

The habit of smuggling, wrecking† and privateering led to perpetration of many other crimes ; amongst others, to a revival of those acts of piracy which disgraced the Cinque Ports in the thirteenth century.‡

On Aug. 11, 1758, Nicholas Wingfield and Adams Hyde, of Hastings, masters of two privateer cutters, piratically boarded the Danish ship "Der Reisende Jacob," on board of which was the Marquis Pignatelli, Ambassador Extraordinary from his Catholic Majesty to the Court of Denmark; assaulting Jurgan Muller,

---

* "Sussex Archæological Collections," vol. iv., p. 185 ; vol. ix., p. 194.

† Congreve, in his Epilogue to "The Mourning Bride," alludes to this habit of the Sussex men. See also "A Descriptive Narrative of the Wreck of the Nympha Americana, near Beachy Head," Nov. 29th, 1747, with the tailpiece by Mr. J. H. Hurdis ; Lewes : Lee and Co., 1840.

‡ "History of Winchelsea," p. 18.

the master of the vessel, and stealing twenty casks of butter. The Lords of the Admiralty offered a reward of 500*l.* Nicholas Wingfield and Adams Hyde, with four others, having been betrayed by some of their accomplices, were arrested; and on Jan. 15, 1759, were brought under a strong guard of soldiers, and lodged in the Marshalsea. They were tried at the Admiralty sessions, March 9, 1759, when Nicholas Wingfield and Adams Hyde were found guilty; and on the 28th of the same month, were hung at Execution Dock. The four others were acquitted. The punishment did not operate as a sufficient warning to the Hastings men. For seven years a gang known as Ruxley's crew, most of whom lived at Hastings, boarded and robbed several of the ships coming up the Channel; and in particular in 1768, they boarded a Dutch homeward-bound hoy, called "The Three Sisters,"* Peter Bootes, commander, about two leagues from Beachy Head, and chopped the master down the back with an axe. In November, 1768, the Government sent a detachment of two hundred of the Inniskilling Dragoons to Hastings, to arrest the men, who had been betrayed by their bragging to one another how the Dutchman wriggled when they had cut him on the backbone; and a man-of-war and cutter lay off Hastings to receive the men.† The soldiers had strict orders not to allow

---

* The usual method was to go alongside, under the pretence of trading; they frequently mastered the crew, clapped them under the hatches, and then plundered, and afterwards scuttled the ship.—" Public Advertiser," Nov. 16, 1768.

† The man who had given information had arrested one of the gang, upon which the others swore they would murder the informant, unless their colleague was released.—" Public Advertiser."

their mission to be known; but the day after their arrival, the Mayor (who was supposed to have aided in the evidence) was assaulted in the town, because he would not tell what the soldiers came for; the soldiers were thereupon called out, and several arrests made of parties, who were conveyed to the Marshalsea. At the Admiralty sessions holden on Oct. 30, 1869, Thomas Phillips, elder and younger, William and George Phillips, Mark Chatfield, Robert Webb, Thomas and Samuel Ailsbury, James and Richard Hyde, William Geary, alias Justice, alias George Wood, Thomas Knight and William Wenham, were indicted for the piracy of " The Three Sisters," and capitally convicted; and of these Thomas Ailsbury, William Geary, William Wenham, and Richard Hyde were hung at Execution Dock, Nov. 27.

So great was the panic occasioned by these arrests, that a shop-keeper, reported to be worth £10,000, absconded on information of having bought goods of the smugglers.*

In 1779 it became necessary to pass another act against smuggling; and, in a pamphlet making the new law known,† it is stated that the practice of smuggling had made such rapid strides from the sea-coasts into the very heart of the country, pervading every city, town, and village, as to have brought universal distress on the fair dealer; that the greater part of the 3,867,500 gallons distilled annually at Schiedam, was to be smuggled into England; that a distillery had

---

* " Public Advertiser," Nov. 10, 1768.

† " Advice to the Unwary," 1780.   The well - known " Smugglers' Act " was passed in 1736 : it was modified in 1779 and 1784 ; and a review of all the statutes relating to the subject was made January 5, 1826.

lately been set up for making Geneva, for the same
purpose, at Dunkirk; that the French imported five or
six millions of pounds of tea, the greatest part of which
was to be smuggled here;* that the trade of Dunkirk
(where, and at Flushing, the Sussex smugglers, so late as
thirty years since, had regular resident agents) was mostly
carried on by smugglers, in vessels not only large, but so
well constructed for sailing, that seldom one of them was
captured; that in many places near the sea, the farmer
was unable to find hands to do his work, whilst great
numbers were employed in smuggling goods from one
part of the country to another; and that the smugglers
paid for what they bought in cash, or by the illicit
exportation of English wool, no other articles of any
consequence being carried abroad by them.

Although the illicit trade in the bulky article of wool
came to an end with the commencement of the war of
1793, yet the trade in tea, silks, tobacco, and spirits
continued; and, after the close of the war, was largely
carried on. By degrees, tea was not easily got, and
the duty on silks left little profit to the smuggler.
Spirits increased in value, by being some forty per
cent. over proof, and tobacco still, however, gave a
profitable return, and lives were freely risked.†

In such a society as the Sussex, it would be improper
to enter into any details which might involve the
characters of persons still alive; but I may glance
briefly at some of the encounters which have taken
place within my own time. The trial for murder, and

---

* When Pitt first lowered the tea-duty, it was averred that
the smuggler was so great a rival with the open trader, that the
tea-trade was then shared between them nearly equally.

† For epitaph in Patcham Churchyard on Daniel Scales, a
smuggler shot on Nov. 7, 1796, see p. 262 of this work.

conviction at Horsham, on March 28, 1821, of George
England, a preventive man, for shooting Joseph Swaine,
a fisherman of Hastings, in a scuffle, is in the recollection
of many fishermen still alive there. On Feb. 11th, in
the next year, three hundred smugglers went to Crow
Link, near Eastbourne, to land a cargo, but were
stopped by a signal from the sentinel; four nights
afterwards, they landed at Cliff Point, Seaford, three
hundred half-ankers, losing only sixty-three and a
horse. On the 13th, they attacked the sentinel at
Little Common with bats;* he, however, shot a
smuggler with his pistol; the boat made sail from the
land, and a coach-and-six, which was waiting at the
back of the beach, drove off empty to Pevensey. In
September, 1824, a run was attempted to Bexhill, when
seven smugglers, with one hundred tubs of spirits, were
taken; and one of the blockade-men, named Welch,
having jumped into the boat, the smugglers pulled off
with him, and his dead body was found on the sands in
the morning, with the head and face bruised and lacerated.
In May, 1856, a smuggling galley, chased by a guard-
boat, ran ashore near the mouth of Rye Harbour, and
opened fire on the guard. The blockade-men from
Camber watch-house came to the spot and seized one
of the smugglers, when a body of not less than two
hundred armed smugglers rushed from behind the sand-
hills, commenced a fire on the blockade, killing one and
wounding another, but were ultimately driven off with
the capture of their galley, carrying off, nevertheless,
their wounded. On another occasion, four or five
smugglers were killed whilst swimming the military
canal at Pett-horse Race, having missed the spot where

---

* Thick ash-poles, about six feet long.

it was fordable. On April 13, 1827, about twenty
smugglers went down to the eastward of Fairlight; a
struggle ensued; the smugglers wrested some muskets
from the blockade men, beat them with the butt-ends,
and ran one through with a bayonet; the smugglers at
length retreated, leaving one of their number dead;
another was found afterwards, having been apparently
dropped by the smugglers; a third, some distance on
the way to Icklesham, the body scarcely cold; the rest
of the wounded men were carried off by their companions; and I have been informed that one of the
party alone carried one of his fellows on his back, from
the scene of the conflict at Fairlight to his residence at
Udimore, a distance of six miles at least.

Another, and nearly the last of these bloodsheddings,
took place on Jan. 3, 1828, near Bexhill. A lugger
landed between that village and the little public-house
at Bo-peep; a party of smugglers, armed with bats,
rushed to the beach, landed the cargo, and made off
with it in carts, on horses, and on men's backs straight
to Sidley Green; here they were come up with by the
blockade, reinforced to about forty men; the armed
portion of the smugglers drew themselves up in a
regular line, and a desperate fight took place. The
smugglers fought with such determination and courage
that the blockade-men were repulsed, after many had been
severely bruised and the Quartermaster Collins killed.
In the first volley fired by the blockade, an old smuggler
named Smithurst was killed; his body was found the
next morning, with his bat still grasped in his hands,
the weapon being almost hacked in pieces by the
cutlasses and bayonets of the blockade-men. Here
again, as was their invariable habit, the smugglers
carried safely away all their wounded.

At the spring assizes at Horsham, in 1828, Spencer Whiteman of Udimore, Thomas Miller, Henry Miller, John Spray, Edward Shoesmith, William Bennett, John Ford and Stephen Stubberfield, were indicted for assembling armed on this night, for purposes of smuggling, and were removed for trial to the Old Bailey, where, on April 10, they all pleaded guilty ; as did Whiteman, Thomas Miller, Spray, Bennett and Ford, together with Thomas Maynard and Plumb, for a like offence on Jan. 23, 1828, at Eastbourne. Sentence of death was passed on all, but the punishment was commuted to transportation. They were, with three exceptions, young men under thirty years of age.

Other, but minor affrays took place on Jan. 3, 1831, two miles east of Hastings, when two of the smugglers, William Cruttenden and Joseph Harrold, were shot dead ; on Feb. 22, 1832, at Worthing, between two hundred and three hundred men there assembled, when one William Cowardson was shot dead, and several more were carried away wounded ; and on January 23, 1833, at Eastbourne, when the smugglers, having killed the chief boatman, George Pitt, formed two lines on each side till the cargo was run, and then left—not, however, without having several of their party wounded; but on no one of these occasions was any of the gang discovered. The last occasion on which a life was sacrificed was on April 1, 1838, when Thomas Monk, a poor fiddler of Winchelsea, was shot by the coast-guard, in an affray at Camber Castle.*

The Abbey ruins, the dismantled Castles,† the

---

* "Ex. inf." E. N. Dawes, Esq., Deputy Coroner.

† Addison's play of "The Drummer" was founded on the scheme of a French gardener, to conceal the doings of the smugglers at Hurstmonceux Castle.

" haunted " houses, were all used without interruption
by the smugglers, as depositories for their goods. I
have been present, in a house at Rye, when silks, for
sale, were mysteriously produced from their hiding-
places; and it was the custom of the farmers, in that
neighbourhood, to favour the smugglers so far as to
allow the gates in the fields to be left unlocked at
night; and to broach, without a scruple, the half-anker
of Schiedem, which was considerately left in some hay-
rick or outhouse, in acknowledgment of the farmer's
accommodating and kindred spirit.

*The following is taken from an interesting article, entitled,
"Extracts from the Journal of Walter Gale, school-
master at Mayfield" ("Sussex Archæological Collections," 1857, pp. 194-5).*

" '10th March.—Being disappointed of my Bourn
journey, I set out for Laughton after drinking a
quartern of gin, and came to Whitesmith's, where was a
hurley bolloo about Mr. Plummer's (now a custom-
house officer) having seized a horse loaded with three
anchors of brandy, which was carried off by him and
two soldiers, and afterwards stabled at Parish's; John
Willard and Wm. Bran being there, followed and
overtook them, and prevailed with them to go back.
Parish took the seized horse and put it into Martin's
stable.'

"Two years only before this occurred, a special commission, at the head of which that great judge, Sir Michael Forster, presided, had been sent to Chichester to try seven smugglers for the murder of two custom-house officers under circumstances of atrocity too horrible to be related. They were convicted, and, with the exception of one who died the night before the execution, they were all executed and hanged in chains in different parts of Sussex. A company of foot guards and a troop of horse attended to prevent all chances of rescue, so thoroughly were the feelings of great numbers of the people enlisted on the side of the smugglers. Seven more were tried and convicted at the following assizes at East Grinstead for the barbarous murder of a poor fellow named Hawkins (who was suspected of giving information against them, and who was literally flogged to death), and for highway robbery. Six of them were executed. Most of them belonged to the celebrated Hawkhurst gang, who were the terror of the counties of Kent and Sussex. Three more were tried at the Old Bailey for joining with sixty others in breaking open the custom-house at Poole, and taking away a quantity of tobacco which had been seized and deposited there. They were executed at Tyburn. The place called Whitesmith's was celebrated for its nest of smugglers long after this time. It has been stated, by a person who took the office of overseer of a neighbour-ing parish about forty years ago, that one of the outstanding debts of the previous year was due to —— of Whitesmith, a well-known smuggler, for "two gallons of gin to be drunk at the vestry"!

"There were places of deposit for the smuggled goods, most ingeniously contrived, in various parts of Sussex. Among others, it is said, was the manorial pound at

Falmer, under which there was a cavern dug, which could hold 100 tubs of spirits ; it was covered with planks, carefully strewed over with mould, and this remained undiscovered for years.

"In the churchyard at Patcham there is an inscription on a monument, now nearly illegible, to this effect :—

Sacred to the Memory .

OF DANIEL SCALES, WHO WAS UNFORTUNATELY SHOT ON THURSDAY EVENING, NOV. 7TH, 1796.

> Alas ! swift flew the fatal lead,
> Which pierced through the young man's head.
> He instant fell, resigned his breath,
> And closed his languid eyes in death.
> All you who do this stone draw near,
> Oh ! pray let fall the pitying tear.
> From this sad instance may we all
> Prepare to meet Jehovah's call.

"The real story of his death is this. Daniel Scales was a desperate smuggler, and one night he, with many more, was coming from Brighton, heavily laden, when the excise officers and soldiers fell in with them. The smugglers fled in all directions; a riding-officer, as they were called, met this man, and called upon him to surrender his booty, which he refused to do. The officer, to use the words of the editor's informant, a very respectable man and neighbour, who in early life was much engaged in such transactions, knew that 'he was too good a man for him, for they had tried it out before ; so he shot Daniel through the head.'"

Extract from " Newspaper Cuttings relating to Sussex," (*Sussex Archæological Collections,"* 1872, *pp.* 140, 141.)

"Smuggling was, as we have seen in many previous volumes of these " Collections," a great snare and a grievous curse to Sussex. The following is from the ' Daily Post ':—

"' London, September 19, 1721.

"' They write from Horsham, in Sussex, of the 13th instant, that Lieutenant Jekyll, of Brigadier-General Grove's Regiment, with a party of Grenadiers, near Burwish (40 miles from that place) — [something omitted]—the chief Ringleaders of the Owlers, nam'd Gib. Tompkin ; and pursuing one Jervis, another noted Owler,* with several of his accomplices, came up with them ; upon which Jervis fired his pistols, and retired with his men to a wood ; whereupon some of the Grenadiers were ordered to fire likewise, but the Smugglers being very well mounted, got off, and Lieutenant Jekyll continued to pursue them all that day and night, and the next morning surrounded a lane at Nutly, where he took Robt. Sergeant, Wm. Blackman, Wm. Kemward, and Thomas Highsted, with five Horses, and all their Ropes and Running Tackle,† which he carry'd with him, and the Men were committed to Horsham Gaol.' "

---

* " Owler," a smuggler. See Halliwell *in. voc.*

† To " run " meant, in Smuggler's phrase, to land a cargo of contraband goods, and this " running tackle " was part of the Smugglers' stock in trade.

KING, THORNE & STACE, PRINTERS, BRIGHTON.